P9-DDG-458

In the Arms of Grace

In the Arms of Grace
One Saved Child's Journey

LeChristine Hai

UniVoice International, LLC
First Edition

Copyright © 2003 by LeChristine Hai

Published by
UniVoice International, LLC
P.O. Box 420276
Atlanta, GA 30342
1-866-5-ORPHAN (1-866-567-7426)

All rights reserved. This book, or parts thereof, may not be
reproduced in any form by any means – electronic, mechanical,
photocopying, recording or any other – except for brief quotations
in printed reviews, without the prior written permission of the
publisher.

Twenty percent of the author's earnings, minus limited expenses
incurred in the preparation, production and support of this book,
will be donated to achild.org, a 501(c)3 nonprofit organization, as
her tithing toward the Peace Project.

Library of Congress Cataloging-in-Publication Data

LeChristine Hai
lechristine@lechristinehai.com
www.lechristinehai.com

orphans@achild.org
www.achild.org

In The Arms of Grace: One Saved Child's Journey
FIRST EDITION

Project Editor: Pat MacEnulty
Cover and book designed by Bella Graphic Design, Inc.
Author photograph by Kevin Ames

p. cm.

ISBN: 0-9708881-0-4
LCCN: 2001087991

Printed in the United States of America

This book is dedicated to the many angels

God has sent along the way

as I grow and gain understanding

about choices and the freedom

to live and feel the abundance of

grace, healing, forgiveness, hope,

faith, love and peace.

Every tear of cleansing my soul was given to:

Le Van Son, *in memory of my father;*

Dao Thi No, *my Vietnamese lost and found mother;*

Lauren Christine, *my beautiful daughter;*

Jason (Le Van Sang), *my brother;*

Le Thi Le Thu, *my Vietnamese sister;*

Mr. And Mrs. Ha Xuan Nguyen,
founders of the Cam Ranh City Orphanage, Vietnam;

achild.org, *a dream of a global vision of
healing and reconciliation between the
United States and Vietnam for the sake of the
neglected children of Vietnam and the
wounded hearts of Vietnam veterans of the world;*

my untold friends, *who still love me on my worst days*

...Your hearts know in silence the secrets of the days and the nights.

But your ears thirst for the sound of your heart's knowledge.
You would know in words that which you have always known in thought.
You would touch with your fingers the naked body of your dreams.

And it is well you should.
The hidden well-spring of your soul must needs rise and run
    murmuring to the sea;
And the treasure of your infinite depths would be revealed to your eyes.
But let there be no scales to weigh your unknown treasure;
And seek not the depths of your knowledge with staff and sounding line.
For self is a sea boundless and measureless.
Say not, "I have found the truth," but rather, "I have found a truth."
Say not, "I have found the path of the soul." Say rather, "I have met
    the soul walking upon my path."
For the soul walks upon all paths.
The soul walks not upon a line, neither does it grow like a reed.
The soul unfolds itself, like a lotus of countless petals.

By Kahlil Gibran
The Prophet

CONTENTS

ACKNOWLEDGMENTS

I respectfully thank the late Pastor Ha Xuan Nguyen. This book is written in memory of this man, our headmaster who dedicated his life to the Cam Ranh City Christian Orphanage in Vietnam and continued to be our father here in America until all the orphans had the opportunity to create lives for ourselves. To Mrs. Ha Nguyen, Mrs. Xuan and Mr. Tam Dao and the orphanage staff who supported Pastor Ha's vision with their strength and their trust in his vision and in God to bring 100 people to safety from Vietnam in April, 1975. I am blessed to have this opportunity to speak for all the orphans who share my gratitude.

I am also grateful to the church missionaries who sponsored us and clothed, fed and sheltered us in Vietnam and continued to take care of us when we arrived in America. I am grateful to the Buckner Children's Home, which took us in when we arrived in America, and to the adoptive families who gave us the precious gift of "family" and to all those who had the children's best interests in mind. All of you touched many lives with your generosity. You made it possible for us to live out our lives and to fulfill our own destinies.

Though war is a tragedy for everyone, I am grateful to the Vietnam veterans, especially the soldiers who helped build and support our orphanage. Some said we were enemies, yet I saw you as my giant friends with gum, candy and warm hugs just for us children. We all looked forward to receiving these gifts and kindnesses. After the rage of war, healing is necessary but we must go beyond that as well. I hope that we may all celebrate LIFE and let go of the many inner personal wars that we silently carry.

There have been so many angels along the way who have encouraged me to heal and to thrive beyond the circumstances of the Vietnam War and beyond my own personal wars. I am so grateful for the lessons and the insights that so many people have shared with me. This book would not exist without them.

Many levels of friendship have touched my life in various ways. My precious friends are my extended family. I am so privileged to have my "weather-all" old friends who will be in my life forever as I move through different stages of self expression. Thank you to my newfound friends with whom I have connected. I believe a handful of real lifetime friendships is a rare and precious gift that shines more brilliantly on the bad days than on the good days. I would like to personally recognize these friendships that have so brilliantly illuminated my cloudy days and that brighten my view of life: Ray & Myra Carson, Terry and Danelle Dietrich, Jim Eberle, Tom Hope, Haney and Carol Howell, Ed Knight, Dr. Ben Mathes, John Meluso Jr., James Price, Bob and Nhu Sada, Nancy Scalera, Sister Christine Troung My Hanh, and my two spiritual ministers, Don McLaughlin and Ken Snell, at North Atlanta Church of Christ.

Thank you to a very special man, Dr. George O. Waring, III, for sharing your tenderness, wisdom, support and love. Knowing you has expanded and enriched my sense of being a woman. Your ageless, boundless and free spirit connected with mine in so many ways. I am grateful to have the joy and excitement of our connection.

Thank you to John D. Ward and his family for believing in my vision and message by investing in the business of making a difference.

To my book designer, Donna Brown, for creative support and friendship. This project has given us a special friendship that went beyond business. I appreciate your keen sense of my vision and your understanding of my story, my style and my sometimes unreasonable design requests. You are a joy to work with. Thank you for beautifully helping me communicate to the world through your design talent.

To my editor, Pat MacEnulty, for honoring and respecting my unique voice and style of writing. Thank you for your professionalism, sensitivity and hard work. I appreciate your understanding of the gift of my writing and your support of me as I become a better communicator through my words.

Thank you to those who support my vision and join my belief in achild.org, a non-profit organization, established to promote healing and reconciliation by rebuilding Cam Ranh City Orphanage for the many children of Vietnam who still need our help today. This mission is an important part of my personal journey, and I believe deeply in this worthy cause. Whether it takes three years or thirty years to make it a reality, I know it will happen in God's time when the right people join together to nurture this seed.

Most of all, I would not be here without God's grace, love and protection. I am not an orphan but a blessed child of God.

Photo by Jim Eberle

Former U.S. Senator Max Cleland
and LeChristine Hai

In the Arms of Grace is a moving collection of stories from the life of an extraordinary woman, LeChristine Hai. With remarkable honesty, LeChristine Hai draws back the curtain to reveal the people and events that have shaped her life. A child of Vietnam, she endured the loss of her father and a heart wrenching separation from her mother. Eventually escaping the cruelties of war, she made the journey to a new life in the United States only to face the fresh personal challenge of adjusting to a strange new culture.

In this exploration of her personal challenges and her desire to find the lessons that life has to offer, she inspires us with the simple reflection that although "pain is a part of life... suffering is optional."

In LeChristine Hai's determination to look beyond the pain and grief, she provides us with an uplifting message of forgiveness and hope.

The theme of healing is common among the survivors of war. Each of us, in our own way, is a survivor of something. LeChristine Hai's touching memoir serves as a vivid reminder that the scars of war take many forms, but that with the help of family and friends, healing occurs.

A lady who knows more than most what it means to become "Strong at the Broken Places."

— Former United States Senator
MAX CLELAND

PROLOGUE

*T*his book is a collection of true stories from my life, brutal in honesty and raw in content. The names of people and places have been changed to turn attention away from the personalities involved and toward the universal lessons portrayed. My goal is to share the insights I've gained through my experiences. I have learned the importance of healing and thriving beyond adversity. My life has shown me that our experiences and our lessons make us who we are.

As we all know, "Pain is part of life but suffering is optional." I have personally learned the truth of these words. It is my wish that my story and the depiction of my experiences, thoughts and feelings will give you hope in your life, your journey. When we can step into our own vulnerability and push past the deafening roar of our fear, then we will reach our place of peace and safety. It was with this insight that I found the courage to share my book with you.

As a small child in Vietnam, I was placed by my mother in an orphanage in the hopes that I would survive the war. We never knew I would be taken to the other side of the world where I spent many desperate years hoping to reunite with my Vietnamese mother. But when my dream came true and I finally went back to Vietnam, I could no longer remember, understand or speak her language. Our translator at the time was very limited, and the verbal exchange was minimal.

Returning to America, I was emotionally choked from the experience, filled with thousands of feelings I hadn't been able to express. The foreign words I had to use to communicate with my mother in her native tongue felt like a gag. In the end, I was "incomplete" from the trip but I came home sensing that it was in our silence that my mother had slowly healed my heart and eased the pain of my abandonment. I came back to America comforted by having seen my mother again, ready to begin healing my own personal battles.

One day I sat down to write in my journal so that I would remember the incredible journey that took me to the other side of the world. The writing also provided an outlet for me to speak to my mom in English, my language, on paper. This book began as a journal for my Vietnamese mother. It contained my private thoughts…all the secrets that you would only confide to your own mother.

As I wrote, the flood gate of the pain I had carried for many years opened. My mother's spirit was there for me to release my secret hurts, and I began to heal. The more I let go of my past on paper, the closer I came to understanding my present life. It was a magical, fulfilling spiritual experience which allowed me to regain my sense of self and begin to be present in my life. As I released more and more matters of the heart, my future was created. From always being a survivor in the past, I transformed myself into someone who could thrive in the present.

After shedding thousands of tears and gaining profound insights into my life and into the human spirit, I left what I had written alone for a couple of years to continue my personal journey of healing. I stepped away from my busy schedule to get "complete" with a second trip to Vietnam. Then my life shifted. I began a new career path as a writer and speaker. This, too, was part of the journey. As I grew, I came to find the real me, the authentic me, and I decided to finish the book in its current form.

In the year 2000, the 25th Anniversary of the end of the Vietnam War, I began to make my journal into a book. I decided to tell my personal story not only to share with others the healing of one individual human spirit but also to help heal the wounds between my two countries. One of the visions that became clear with my decision to publish my story was to give back to other orphans by rebuilding my orphanage home in Cam Ranh City. This is my "Peace Project," my intention to make a difference in the world somehow.

My life brings together two different perspectives—that of a Vietnamese orphan and that of a successful American businesswoman. This book is my effort to promote the integration of Vietnam and the United States, to heal the fractured places in all of us, including veterans and civilians, communists and capitalists, traditional baby boomers and radical gen-Xers, adults and children alike. I encourage all of us to embrace our diversity and do away with divisions as we move forward toward a new world vision of balance. As we connect within ourselves and heal, then we outwardly become whole also.

President Bill Clinton shared some of our common history in his address to Hanoi University upon the historic signing of the Vietnam-American trade agreement:

"Two centuries ago, during the early days of the United States, we reached across the seas for partners in trade and one of the first nations we encountered was Vietnam. In fact, one of our founding fathers, Thomas Jefferson, tried to obtain rice seed from Vietnam to grow on his farm in Virginia 200 years ago. By the time

World War II arrived, the United States had become a significant consumer of exports from Vietnam. In 1945, at the moment of your country's birth, the words of Thomas Jefferson were chosen to be echoed in your own Declaration of Independence: "All men are created equal. The creator has given us certain inviolable rights—the right to life, the right to be free, the right to achieve happiness."

Almost 200 years ago, at the beginning of the relations between the United States and Vietnam, our two nations made many attempts to negotiate a treaty of commerce, sort of like the trade agreement that we signed today. But 200 years ago, they all failed, and no treaty was concluded. Listen to what one historian said about what happened 200 years ago, and think how many times it could have been said in the two centuries since. He said, "These efforts failed because two distant cultures were talking past each other, and the importance of each to the other was insufficient to overcome these barriers."

Let the days when we talk past each other be gone for good. Let us acknowledge our importance to one another. Let us continue to help each other heal the wounds of war, not by forgetting the bravery shown and the tragedy suffered by all sides, but by embracing the spirit of reconciliation and the courage to build better tomorrows for our children."

My journey to Vietnam to meet all our lost and found mothers offers a glimpse of the child who lies dormant in all our souls. This journey is universal.

My story is one of many about the wars of the soul and the battle for self-esteem. The Vietnam War was my introduction to life. I was born in that war, and I carried it with me for the rest of my life. After I came to America, I experienced another war, a war with no name. Most people wouldn't call it "war," because there was no killing or physical combat— no guns or grenades. Nevertheless, the destruction of life is the same. It is a more powerful war which slowly wounds the spirit and then kills the soul.

You see, while the adults fought a war with guns and knives, bombs and bullets, we children fought a different kind of war…a personal war with no name. The bullets that wounded me were abandonment, the loss of love, the loss of family. I was a lost child.

Imagine the pain if a bullet penetrated your flesh. When they rushed you to the hospital, the first thing they'd do is to remove the bullet. Well, I felt a bullet pierce my soul during the Vietnam War but there was no hospital to extract that bullet. I fought this personal war every day of my life for many years.

I share these experiences with you in my memoir as a child of God. God has granted me the freedom and the inner peace in my own journey to be able to give it to others like you. I pray that our daughters and sons never have to go through similar experiences. Some of you will face crises and storms in your life. When that happens, just know that you have God's grace to count on. We can learn from our experiences, and we can find God's purpose if we are willing to search for it. First, permit yourself to heal your wounds. Then allow yourself to move on to your next level in life. Claim the human and divine rights bestowed on us freely and abundantly by our Creator.

Remember, there will be calm after the storm and a rainbow after the rain in your journey. The importance lies in the transformation afterward.

LeChristine Hai

CHAPTER 1
Preparing for the Journey Home

The anticipation was overwhelming, physically and emotionally, the night before we left on our journey for Vietnam. There weren't enough tasks around the house to keep my mind and nervous energy occupied. I came into the bedroom and watched Michael gathering his belongings to put in his travel bag as I sat on the bed staring at my neatly organized bag in the corner of the room. I was ready to leave at any moment.

It had been 25 years since I'd left Vietnam, and I was finally returning to my homeland. Three of us—my boyfriend Michael, my brother Jason and I—were journeying together to Communist Vietnam, returning to the past. I only had faded memories of my childhood in the orphanage. I could still see that little barefoot village girl running to greet the American GIs to get her share of gum. I was still waiting for the return of a mother's love. I needed to find many answers to the questions I left behind.

"Where are you, Christi?" Michael asked.

"Oh, I'm sorry, honey," I said, breaking free from my thoughts.

"I'm so glad you decided to be in the same room with me," he teased and smiled. Then he asked, "When does Jason's flight arrive?"

"His flight from Dallas was delayed. He said not to worry about picking him up. He can catch a taxi." I paused. "The waiting is killing me."

Michael sat next to me and hugged me. I felt his weight on the bed as his arms held me.

"I know it's hard, honey. Just hang in there. We'll leave soon." He searched my eyes tenderly. "How was it saying goodbye to Lauren tonight? Does she understand where you're going?"

I thought about my daughter's smiling face and the nervousness in my stomach began to ebb slightly.

"Spending some extra time with her tonight before the trip was just what I needed," I said with a sigh. Earlier I had picked up Lauren at her father's home in Dunwoody, a suburb of Atlanta, and taken her to get May's famous Vietnamese "Pho" soup. She busily played with chopsticks and spoons on the table while I tried to explain to her that I would be gone for a while.

"Lauren, do you know where Mommy is going?" I asked her.

"Nope," she answered.

"Well, Mommy is going to meet Grandma in Vietnam on this trip," I reported. "Can you say 'Vietnam?'"

"Vietnam, Vietnam!" she happily shouted with pride, playing the chopsticks like drumsticks.

"Okay. Shhhh! Inside voice, please," I said and waved my hand to soften her voice. I took the chopsticks out of her hands and then I hugged her tightly. Her strong little arms circled my neck.

Since the age of two, she has had to live with our divorce. Living in two separate homes and with two closets of clothing has given her a different world from other children. She will never know what it is like to be in the same house with her parents again. I am so sad for the adult decisions that affect our children. Her world is already a blending of two cultures. She lives one lifestyle with her all-American Southern father and another with a mom who was born on the other side of the world in the midst of war.

"Grandma is going to be excited to see your pictures," I said. "When you get two years older, you can go with Mommy to see Grandma."

"Can we have my birthday party when you get back?" she asked.

"Is it your birthday already?" I asked, teasingly.

She nodded and said, "I'm going to be four years old, Mommy."

"I know you are, and we will have a great big birthday party for you and your friends," I said. "And maybe we'll have a pony, too. Would you like that?"

She shrieked in joy, picked up the chopsticks once again and began beating them against the stack of porcelain spoons.

It is so hard not to live with her anymore, but I had to give my only daughter a family and the stability I couldn't provide. It was the price I was willing to pay. The value of staying in one place with her father was greater than any joint custody laws or my own needs. I knew what it was like to be torn from my family, from my home. I couldn't do that to my own daughter. She will have the security of the only home she has ever known, the stability that my ex-husband and his family can give, and she will always have my love. But I must put together the pieces of my own life and my own past if I am ever going to be whole and complete as a woman and as a mother.

Michael rubbed my back gently as I ruminated about my daughter's life.

"We had a great time. I promised her a cowgirl birthday party on her next birthday," I told him. "Do you know where I can rent a pony?"

Michael laughed.

"What a lucky kid she is," he said, smiling.

I knew that he was right. Lauren's childhood is so much better than mine was. But still I am so sad for her.

"I know it has to be hard for her. I wish I could make her life ideal but it didn't work out that way," I said and took a long deep breath. "Did Joe and I ruin things for her, Michael?" I asked with a heavy heart.

"Don't torture yourself this way. Life is complicated. Things happen for the right reason. You will have her back again, sweetie."

Michael stroked my hair as I put my arms around his waist. My right ear pressed on his chest as I listened to his heartbeats. I noticed the isolated sound of every beat, and his breathing surrounded me like a lullaby.

Michael and I had been dating for the past six months. It took me a year and a half after the divorce before I could risk getting into another relationship. I still wasn't ready for the commitment of another marriage. I wanted to be loved without the demands of a serious relationship as I sorted out my current life.

Michael was my strength and my friend. He could sense the longing my spirit endured as I faced the only thing standing in the way of meeting my mother—time. I watched the clock hands slowly inch their way toward our moment of departure.

The doorbell rang.

"That must be Jason," Michael said.

When I opened the door, Jason stood there with his suitcases. For a moment, I just stared at this grown man—so different from the frightened little boy who had left Vietnam in a frail boat.

"Are you ready to go home?" he asked.

"I've been ready for years," I answered.

My journey into my past and future

CHAPTER 2
Flight into the Past

The moan of the jet engines shifted as I stared out the small window, taking my first look at the homeland we left so long ago. The foreign landscape carried my mind back to my childhood, a childhood erased by the need to survive. Somewhere below waited my mother, who on this day I would meet for the first time as an adult.

My brother sat beside me, lost in his own thoughts. Our separate experiences gave Jason and me different journeys from each other. We still had not found a strong tie between us. We lived our busy lives separately and rarely stayed in touch. Yet we had a common past and a common desire to return to our beginnings in Vietnam. Within us, Vietnam was very familiar, even though we had become strangers to it. Now we needed to rediscover our home and embrace it as adults.

Twenty-five years ago, Jason and I had left part of ourselves, the little girl and the little boy, in Vietnam. We each took on the identity given to us upon our arrival in America. Christi became my persona and Jason became his. Inside we also kept our childhood histories and names. Our past was something we could never forget.

A middle-class family in Texas adopted my brother and me. I tried to adjust and become just another American girl. My adoptive family gave me a new identity to replace my Vietnamese name, Le Thi Hai. Christi became my persona, yet she also possessed memories of a childhood I wanted to forget. I lived in a fantasy, choosing to remember tales of my own invention. I tried to excuse my differences as those of an Asian in America. I played my part perfectly as an American. But I was Vietnamese, too. Both histories left their scars and confusions in me.

As I came nearer to our forgotten homeland with my blond-haired, blue-eyed American boyfriend, I wondered where I stood between these cultures. We represented diversity—the true nature of the American concept of the melting pot. Unfortunately, my brother and I were that lost generation in both cultures. We were the result of the American-Vietnam war. We could not shake off our past, no matter how hard we tried.

I was being called to discover my life. I wanted more than the vicious cycle of empty routines and so I sought for purpose and meaning beyond my successes in living the "American Dream." My calendar was full, but my life was empty. My many turbulent relationships often failed with the men in my life. I felt empty and disconnected from the love I deserved.

In America, we practically grew up on our own. Television, movies and magazines were part of the environment that shaped me. The players in Hollywood, New York and Paris provided role models for me to emulate. With the emphasis on appearance, I felt that a beautiful self-image was part of being a success. I had learned to succeed in that atmosphere. I justified expenditures on fine clothes, expensive make-up and manicures as part of my persona. Making my appearance impeccable was as important as learning my perfect English.

I worked so hard to change my accent to sound American. In phone conversations, I sounded like any other American, yet my Asian ancestry became evident when people met me. With my long jet-black hair, flat nose, slanted brown eyes, and petite size, I always stood apart from my American peers. I always disliked being different, and my need to fit in was all-encompassing. Being 'exotic,' as some of my American friends sweetly suggested, was still being different.

My persona was my only protection as I tried to offset my pain and loneliness. I always looked like a million bucks but never felt good enough inside to wash off my unworthiness. My choices always seemed second best. I constantly moved to new ground in my relationships and careers. My changes made it so I would not have to feel.

My beauty and 'exotic' appearance has been a blessing yet a curse in my life. Too often, my beauty is all people see, but my soul is what I wanted people to see and value more than my exterior appearance. I struggled to find a mate who could see me clearly. Yet, true love proved elusive.

No matter how well I adapted to my environment, I was still a barefoot village girl. My heart bridged two continents. I yearned to go back to Vietnam, to go home. I held the faded memory of a mother. I remembered her only in my dreams. Her pleasant, gentle face always smiled. Many times I remembered her morning routine of pulling back her long black hair, folding it in half and pinning it into a full bun that sat perfectly on her head. With her hair pulled back, her high cheekbones and deep-set eyes were accentuated, an image forever imprinted on my mind. I have carried this image of her in all my secret dreams. Would this imaginary figure ever hold and hug me?

The loss of my first love, my father, brought wrenching memories and derailed later relationships in my life. Was I the only one in the world seeking to mask my pain with love? Was I alone and naïve in seeking love? Would I always feel alone? This journey home held the keys to my future. My peace awaited me. Some people say we must "confront" our past, but I wanted to "carefront" my past in order to know more about myself.

The anxiety took me back to the little girl who still waited for her mother to show up at the orphanage. It was difficult for me to remember my childhood without feeling pain. I pretended for so long that I did not have a childhood.

I still waited for the brave prince to show up at the orphanage and take me away into the sunset. I once thought I had found my prince, but it didn't work out. I pretended for so long that I didn't have that dark childhood, and yet my past was intertwined with my present life and I couldn't forget it. Having it all was not what I expected. An ideal image of a family, becoming a mother with a beautiful Amerasian daughter, a successful career and status only brought destruction and resulted in a grueling divorce. My divorce brought such disappointment in my life. How could I escape the hollowness of that dream? Were all marriages the same? Would life ever be truly fulfilling?

We waited for those last few hours to enter into Vietnam. The politicians allowed no American airlines to go directly to Vietnam, so we caught another airplane. The pressure lessened a bit once we were on our way, yet there was a constant, treacherous drag in my head, and I wanted to speed up the time and the long flight to get there.

"I feel like we are in this time machine from the future to rediscover our past," I commented to Jason. "How do we explain this to our American friends? Though we lived there as children, we never knew it the way many Americans remember it."

"I know," he nodded.

"I only remember Vietnam vaguely and painfully from behind the walls of our orphanage home," I said to Michael. "We left when I was 10 and Jason was 12."

Jason had become a handsome, shy and successful young bachelor from Dallas. I knew he had his questions and hopes for this trip, too. I could only hope that he would find what he was looking for in our home country and perhaps, for the first time, share himself with his family and me. He disguised his sad life with his silence. But many times we understood each other without words.

I held tightly against my heart a photo album in which I had collected pictures of my mother and me. The photos put me adrift in my own memories. I thought about my earlier years. Previously I pushed that memory deep into the abyss of my mind. Now I allowed them to surface.

Our headmaster told us we were the children of a sweet, loving family. My mother was charming. Her natural beauty and her love for fashion set her apart from the other women in her farming village. I grew up knowing I had received the best of my mother's looks and my father's tenderness. I was the cute, personable daughter my mother took pleasure in spoiling. Those qualities became my most useful assets as I fought for my survival.

As a child, I used my cuteness and charm to win more gum and candies from my American soldiers. I loved dancing for the Americans. That love brought me affection, and the same dance gained me an American family the first day I arrived in the United States. I used my cuteness and bubbly personality well into my adult life. My 'fun' persona enhanced my 4'11" stature. It also brought Michael into my life.

Michael looked out the window of the jet at the tiny world below us.

"They say the beauty of your native country is like paradise and that the mountains are breathtaking," he said, turning to look into my eyes. "But the war brings back bad memories for a lot of Americans."

I nodded.

"Jason and I were like any other children reading about a war that became a part of American history," I said. "We knew what we knew about this country as part of our history, while we learned and understood a little of our own country's history through American schoolbooks. We were too young to understand the political agenda that caused the war. But we knew it changed the lives of thousands of children, including my brother and me. "

Throughout history, Vietnam has presented many different views and perspectives to both natives and visitors. We were natives, yet we were also her visitors, as we tried to put together all the pieces of our lives. Our lives began in Vietnam. Could we now be reborn?

The plane tilted with the turbulence and startled me from my thoughts. I pulled the blanket tight around me when I felt myself shivering. I did not know if the chill was from the air conditioner on the jet or from the unknown that awaited me on the ground. Michael checked and double-checked his camcorder and his Nikon camera. His methodical way of making sure everything worked was the way he calmed his nerves. He was almost six feet tall, and his years of hard work and baseball gave him a fine physique. I looked at his handsome face and smiled with satisfaction, knowing that to the Vietnamese mind, he would fit the mold of the perfect American boy. Willing to take the risk of this adventure, he was the catalyst for me to be on this airplane.

The chilled air on the plane reminded me of the many times I had searched for encouraging words from God as I began to break down my barriers and heal my wounds. In His steady way, He gave me the courage to go toward further discovery. On this day, it became clear. I had been searching to belong. Could someone or something define my identity? Who was I? A Vietnamese girl raised in the American culture, now situated between two nations. The airplane became the capsule between our present lives as Americans and our Vietnamese ancestry waiting below. Jason and I were Americans, yet we did not look American. We were Vietnamese, yet we could not speak our first language. Language would be a barrier, but we were determined to bridge the language barrier and let our motherland heal our pain.

The pilot's voice came over the speaker to tell us we would be landing soon. His voice was another step closer to a new reality. I moved with anticipation to a window seat across the aisle to find another view of Vietnam from up above. Excitement and anxiety filled me, like a country kid's first bus ride to New York City. I watched other people slowly gather their belongings to prepare for the landing. A great mix of people was on the airplane. College students spoke French and dressed for an adventure. They were ready to hike across a foreign land they had heard so much about in school. Older Vietnamese family members traveling with their children and grandchildren appeared ready to revisit their homeland. A newer generation, well dressed, showing their prosperity, got ready to remember their past; businessmen with their briefcases at hand sat still, not stirring about the plane, as though the route had become part of their normal business travel. These people made a wonderful tapestry as rich as Vietnam itself. I wondered if their reasons to be here were as important and astounding as ours.

And then there were the three of us, sitting in various seats to catch a better glimpse of Vietnam. I felt my stomach tighten and sink as the plane lowered its wing flaps. My nerves grew taut and my anxiety grew. Rumbling noises began in the pit of my stomach. My pulse raced with the lowering of the landing gear and the thrust of the reversing jets as we touched ground. I took a deep breath as Michael held my hand tightly. We mentally prepared ourselves for the ultimate meeting. I wondered if I would have made this journey without Michael's love and support. I doubted it.

Jason picked up his things and joined us as we began to exit the plane onto the tarmac of Ho Chi Minh City, formerly known as Saigon. He nervously asked, "Are you ready?"

"Yes," I answered, my hands sweating as I grasped my carry-on bags.

"Don't worry about me, " Michael said. "Just do what you feel like. This is your moment." He put the camera around his shoulder and smiled. "Your mom is right around the corner!"

I leaned over and kissed Michael.

"I love you for being here."

We hugged each other tenderly and with understanding. Soon we would be out of sync with each other. My own thoughts occupied me from that point on.

Dear Mom,

I have waited so long for this moment to express my feelings and to open my heart to you.

I have carried an emptiness and loneliness with me since I was a small child. My heart's only wish was for love. I needed shelter and protection from fear. I wished for the love only a mother gives. Why was that absent? Did I do something wrong? I missed the bond only a mother and daughter can share.

I wandered through life, missing a crucial piece of my life. I have always felt alone and lost. I fought to be so strong without you beside me, yet inside I was always that little girl you left behind. I never stopped crying for you all these years.

Your greatest gift of love gave me a chance in life. But without your guidance, that very gift created such confusion in my heart and mind. I wish I had understood the gift then so that I could have blossomed into a greater soul than what I am.

Although distance and time separated us, I never felt disconnected from you spiritually. Your spirit in me never died because I always carried a pain in my heart and a loneliness in my soul for you.

Share with me now the gifts that only a Mother can give. Your hugs. Your smiles. Your tears. Your laughter. Your time and memories with me.

I have traveled far from my home to yours to meet you again. We are strangers, yet we are not. I still need you to be that torch of light that brought me into this world. My heart has ached for so long!

This is my moment with you, Mom, a chance to find a part of my soul that was left behind. This is the end and the beginning of my long search for home. I hope to find it in your heart.

Mom, I pray you will accept my gift. The only thing that truly belongs to me, my heart, is yours.

I missed you, Mom. I love you, Mom.

Your daughter,
Le Thi Hai

My lost and found mother
Dao Thi Ro

CHAPTER 3
My Mother

My body tingled and my eyes glazed over as I prepared to enter another dimension of history. Jason looked anxious and sober.

"I know how you feel," I said, squeezing his hand as we began to exit. We instantly felt the new climate. The steam and heat engulfed our bodies as we exited the plane onto the tarmac of Tan Son Nhat International Airport , Ho Chi Minh City.

As we stood in line waiting for customs, I felt like a snake coiling in and out of acid water. The anticipation was filled with a constant sense of fear, knowing we had arrived in a country from which we had fled with our lives 25 years ago.

"What are they looking for?" I whispered to Michael as I watched the customs agents rifling through suitcases. "Will they interrogate us?"

He laughed and whispered, "You've been watching too much TV."

"I was advised by those who have traveled here before to tip them $5 or more inside your passport so they won't give us a hard time," I whispered. I squeezed both their arms and glanced slyly to watch the other visitors doing just that. We all reached in our pockets to get our $5 for our passports.

"Just to be safe," Michael said.

"There are no rules here except their rules," I said.

The custom check-in procedure put me in my high intensity survival mode. I was too distracted to realize we were approaching the exit door. Michael grabbed my arm to slow me down and said, "Stop. Take a deep breath and relax a bit. We're about to walk out."

Flustered from jamming all the rolls of film back into my backpack, I avoided looking up at the exit door. Thirty feet away, an army of people leaned against a long iron gate. They pressed against each other and looked for their own relatives. Events moved in slow motion as my mind became overloaded with millions of thoughts. I stood there, physically and emotionally frozen. I could not move. Michael handed me my bag.

"Will I find them?" I thought as my adrenaline increased and I began to move again. I marched out beyond the door.

Just outside stood my mom. I recognized her instantly. She was directly in my view, strategically positioned at the gate. She began to fade away for a moment as my eyes become unfocused and glazed with tears. I blinked to refocus. I saw the dreamy image of the woman who had lived in my thoughts. My body instinctively moved toward her as my mind wandered back to my many dreams of her standing, waiting for me with open arms, waiting for me as I ran toward her as a child.

Suddenly, a voice called out my name loudly as I woke from the spell. My mother was in front of the crowd, pressed against the gate, crying out, waving a handkerchief and wiping her tears. I went straight to her as she called my Vietnamese name, "Hai, Hai." I instinctively surged forward. How strange and wonderful to hear that name again, I thought.

As I approached the fence, my mother touched my face and grasped my hands through the bars. Her hands felt rough from years of hard work, yet tender against my flesh. She cupped my face with her hands and then squeezed my hands. We could not let each other go. She stroked my face and hair frantically. Tears ran down her face. I cried as I watched her. My heart felt so heavy. Her heartbeat pounded against my chest. Her tears blended with mine.

Michael came up from behind me. He helped me with my bags as I frantically hung onto my mother between the bars. She called out my Vietnamese name again and again.

Michael supported me through the crowd. My mother was stunned that her lost son and daughter were finally standing in front of her, touching her. I was overwhelmed by my tears and the indescribable feelings of finally seeing this tiny woman I'd dreamed of so many times. She was still that beautiful woman from my dreams, though in real life she was shorter and had short, wavy hair that proved her adaptation to modern times.

In my first moments with my mother, I found part of my soul in her eyes. I had loved this woman painfully for years. Now our tears communicated our feelings. Our tears were beyond any language barriers. Our feelings eloquently communicated what our words could not.

Despite 25 years, we connected immediately as only mother and daughter can. I only wished time would stop its course so we could enjoy our moment longer. But we had to let go of one another as the crowd surged around the gate and pushed both of us along.

Our letting go was inch by inch. We both feared that we would once again be lost to each other. The constant calling of my Vietnamese name from the back of the crowd assured me that this reality was not going to fade away. I wiped my tears. The crowd pushed us involuntarily, both of us feeling pain and happiness.

Suddenly, I noticed my sister Le. She hung on Jason's arm from behind the fence. Both were ahead of me. In her, I saw a mirror reflection of myself. She had a smaller figure and such beautiful, long black hair. She tearfully hung onto my brother as I approached her. She was the sister I had heard of—now a grown woman—a sister I had never known or even seen.

My only memories of her existence were in my mother's large belly when I traveled to the orphanage. Stunned, I again saw my reflection in her as we hugged each other. As I held her, I felt a natural protectiveness for my delicate sister. I experienced being an older sister for the first time.

A voice yelled out 'Ms. Hai' in the midst of the crowd. All our eyes located the voice from the back of the crowd. A thin, forty-ish man jumped up and down. He pointed his finger toward the right, to the end of an iron gate. We realized we had to let go. I walked around as my mother's hands still hung onto me. Then we all ran toward the end of the entrance barrier to be with our newfound family.

Finally free of barriers, we walked through the main entrance. My mother and sister hung onto us as we exchanged long, meaningful touches. My mother again looked us over to make sure we were real. Her face was filled with sheer delight and amazement. Smiling and crying at the same time, I watched her looking at us. She hugged me and kissed my cheek; her nose nudged against my face and sniffed me to inhale the aroma of her child, a Vietnamese way of kissing.

As we left the airport crowd and walked toward the van, the interpreter's voice repeated excitedly and impatiently, "We go to van, we go to van."

I realized I had been so lost in my own moment, I had forgotten to introduce Michael. I staggered and stopped, fully embarrassed, and waved to Michael to come out from behind his camera.

"Mom, my special friend in America," I said as he walked toward us. It was a moment I will cherish forever.

"Hello," they said, giving him hugs.

"I am very happy to meet you," Michael greeted them. I was glad to share this moment with him. He was fascinated.

The interpreter translated while Michael and my family looked at each other, smiling. Michael overshadowed everyone with his height, while for the first time in 25 years, Jason and I fit naturally into our Vietnamese surroundings.

I finally knew I had a real family again. The sound of "Mother" from my own lips gave me a sense of completeness. We took a moment as we hugged and cried. We could not speak, yet there was no need to interpret these thoughts and feelings.

I began to sort out our party. There was our mother, our sister and our stepfather, along with my mother's second son and the driver, who was walking ahead. The interpreter shook Michael's hand and showed his excitement over meeting an American. He tried to impress us with his broken English.

"My name is Doan," he repeated many times to make sure he was included. "I speak number one English. Do that for beaucoup GIs!" He had already jumped in front of Michael's camera many times to get into the family photos. His overbearing excitement woke me from the magic spell cast by my family. His nasal, high-pitched voice speaking English and his barrage of comments distracted me. Clothing two sizes too large covered his frail body and made him look even thinner. While I was focused on trying to understand what my mother and sister were saying as they spoke to us, our interpreter seemed more interested in impressing Michael with his English.

"Wait! Wait! What are they saying? Tell me what they are saying!" I asked again since the interpreter was too busy admiring Michael.

"Oh, oh, okay," he said and stopped and tried to translate again. He crossed his arms and put his finger on his cheek. He studied the situation while my mother talked at some length. I watched, anticipating all she was saying. Finally, he looked up.

"Ah… ah, your mother is very happy to see you. Her heart is not good waiting for you," he said, gesturing toward his heart with his hands to make certain we understood. I was relieved to understand something she had said. However, I knew there was so much more. Inside the van, I put my arms around my mother and held her tighter, to let her know I was happy, too.

I said to the translator, "Tell her how happy we are…."

"Yes, yes," he said, so anxious to interpret that he started to translate before I had finished. He only created more confusion with his incomplete sentences. He bounced around, trying to get into every conversation.

Our luggage filled the back of the van as we shed our backpacks. We stood by the door, waiting for everyone to settle down. Michael stood there in a stupor from the situation and the weather. Sweat soaked his shirt. All three of us tried to adjust to the climate and hoped to get some air in the van. But we experienced more culture shock: the van had no air conditioning.

Many conversations filled the van. We asked so many questions.

*The moment we've been waiting for...
joy, tears, and unforgettable*

Our family together at last!

Unfortunately, our translator answered few of them. He pursued his own conversation with us in English. Doan continued repeating simple information and telling us his story.

"I had many American GI friends... like you many years ago," he said with a big smile. He was fascinated to be with an American, and his attention increasingly focused on Michael.

Meanwhile, we quickly agreed to try to listen to his words together so maybe we could understand more. When he asked me how he was doing, I said "Good, good, but slow down. I don't understand at all—slow down for me. Okay?"

He nodded his head vigorously.

"Yes, yes," he said, then pointed to something outside the van and explained it at great length to impress Michael. This frantic behavior earned Doan the name "Energizer." Like the bunny, he just kept on going.

The excitement and the heat made the moment even more intense. Vietnam overwhelmed us. It was so hot! My mother took a hand towel from her large red floral bag and handed it to me to wipe my sweat. We sat very close to one another, holding hands, and tried to hide our amazement.

CHAPTER 4
A Mother's Cry

My attention and concentration focused inside the van and on the pieces of conversation I so desperately wanted to hear. We drove through Saigon, South Vietnam's Capital city, renamed Ho Chi Minh City in 1975 after the war ended. We drove for a long time before I could turn my attention to my surroundings. A huge number of bicycles and motorcycles pressed dangerously close to the van. The heat and smog suffocated us.

As if squeezed into a tight shoe, we crammed our bodies and our American perceptions into the massive chaos of this city. In Vietnam, there is no system or order to the traffic. In America, we have lanes. In Vietnam, they have courage. So many cars, vans, trucks and motorcycles, of all sizes and much older models, compete for a road with no yellow lines. Accidents were waiting to happen. The horns were their only communication, and we heard that if you sound the horn before an accident, you are not at fault. The way people traveled amazed us. The heat, smog and the strong odor of overheated engines, so much a part of this culture, shocked our senses. Many motorcyclists adapted by wearing mouth gauze. Outside, storefronts sold their goods oblivious to any obstacles.

All I wanted to do at this point was take a fresh breath of cold air. I needed to escape the claustrophobic surroundings. The heat rose, becoming unbearable, and I had trouble breathing. I pulled my denim shirt away from my wet skin, but it clung to me like Velcro.

The van stopped, and our conversation continued while my mother's husband left the van. He came back with three bottles of distilled water for us, which we gratefully downed.

"We check in hotel now," the translator announced as we waited for the driver and Mom's new husband to return to the steamy van.

"We stay here tonight. Go home tomorrow to Lam Doung. Not good to travel at night. Long drive," he explained during our wait. The driver came back to get our passports and visas to check us in. I wondered why we had to sit inside the van. My Vietnamese family showed no discomfort. They were accustomed to the heat while Michael, Jason and I sweated furiously. My mother poured water on the small hand towel and handed it to me. I passed the cloth to Jason and Michael.

"We go to restaurant—eat. Good," Doan said. Finally, we got out of the hot van. We took all of our baggage with us into the restaurant, as Doan had suggested. I could sense my family's discomfort in the city. Their eyes and actions showed caution and no desire for adventure. We could have left the van for air long ago, but my family was too uncomfortable in these surroundings, so we had suffered inside the stifling van.

We tucked our bags under the long table where we sat. They ordered the food as we drank more distilled water. We became new "bottle babies." The waitress brought glasses, and the three of us from America chanted "no ice" almost in unison. She brought hot beers for the men and cokes for the women. We sent my warm coke back. I sighed with relief when our waitress exchanged them for cold cokes. Michael and Jason accepted their hot beers. Mom continued passing the wet, cold cloth, a common custom to fight the heat in Vietnam. We took it gratefully, refreshing our sweaty and sticky hands and face. In the large room with the slowly rotating ceiling fan, we tried to eat and take advantage of the space and air.

A group of people at a large table next to us were curious about our reunion. They watched us and noticed the American guy at the table. We felt more American than ever. We knew nothing about these people, and yet we were undeniably part of them. Some stopped by the table to chat with us. They shook Michael's hands with welcome greetings, ready to see Americans come back into this poverty-stricken country. Jason and I heard them repeatedly refer to us as "Viet Kieu," which we learned was the name native Vietnamese gave to Vietnamese who live overseas and return to Vietnam.

I was at a loss for words. The overbearing interpreter continued with his constant chattering. His excitement to speak English hindered him from helping us understand the whole conversation. He interpreted many long conversations with only a few broken English words. I doubted his ability to understand English. After all these years, I wanted to say a great deal to my mom. Now, I was empty of words, and I had no energy left to fight the interpreter, who continued to try to show off his ability to speak English and meet his own agenda.

I blocked out his voice. I was in awe, finally being with my mother and sister Le Thu. We sat holding hands. Touch was our only truly shared form of communication. The food came, and Mother took some fish and put it in my bowl. She signaled me to eat. I appreciated the caring welcome and the motherly gesture, but I could not take a bite. Instead, I sat and absorbed the overwhelming experience. I struggled not to show my irritation with the interpreter and his careless treatment of only parts of the conversation. He seemed to make up the rest.

My frustration grew as I watched my mother and sister try to eat when we so much wanted to talk. I sat there, weighed down with mixed feelings of happiness and sadness. The language barrier and the hot sticky air burdened me.

"Michael, I don't think he understands everything to translate," I said quietly. "It's going to be a long 17 days."

Jason agreed as he sat quietly across the table, tolerating Doan over his beer. The dinner conversation was short. We used only small words. My mother refused food and tenderly held my hand.

We absorbed each other's presence as best we could. Mother finally spoke, and he translated.

"Two months waiting for your visit since letter. She lose weight, no good, head hurt and her heart ache like today. She very happy today to see you," he said.

I could only gesture to her, "me too," as I squeezed her hands gently.

"After we eat, we go to room. Now talk no more but we talk tonight. Yes? In room?" he asked.

All I could think was, oh no. I had looked forward to checking into the hotel for some privacy and a good, cold shower. We grabbed the luggage from under the table and walked into the street. It had rained while we ate. The rain continued to fall.

Anxious to get to the hotel, I rushed out into the rain ahead of the group to cross the street toward the neon light of a hotel. The others followed as I walked into the lobby. Michael followed close behind me. Much to our surprise, the hotel had very nice décor. It had a marble floor and fresh flowers on a coffee table with a couple of contemporary chairs beside. An Asian lady sat in the lobby, obviously a tourist, dressed in modern clothes. I turned around and realized that only Michael and I were in the lobby. The others were outside while the valet held the door, either waiting for them to enter or for us to exit.

The driver walked in the other direction, gesturing that our hotel was next door. We went outside and walked toward an old, decrepit hotel. We entered the small lobby and jammed into the elevator. The elevator shut down briefly as if to remind us of its age before crawling upward. We watched the concrete wall, waiting for it to stop on the fourth floor. The three of us and my mom and Doan checked out the room.

"Very nice, very nice," Doan said, gesturing at the old room with the tall ceiling. Two twin beds on wood frames stood against the wall opposite two dark chairs. The walls, crudely painted in yellow with a baby blue border near the ceiling, hurt our eyes and horrified our American sensibilities. A light bulb dangled from its wire through a ceiling hole.

Imagine our joy when we saw an air conditioning unit in the

window and a small refrigerator nearby. Imagine our disappointment when we found neither worked. Fortunately, the problem was only a circuit breaker, which could easily be fixed. We turned on the light. As I checked out the dirty, old-tiled bathroom, Michael admired the two hand-carved wooden chairs and the wall mirror in between.

Doan took his seat in one of the chairs and placed Mom in the other, preparing for his role as an interpreter. Michael, Jason and I faced them, sitting on the beds. My jet lag and my years of pent-up emotion exhausted me. I shuddered at the prospect of talking all night, especially through our frustrating translator.

Beaming at Michael, Doan said, "We talk now."

I looked at Michael and Jason and then back at my mom. We all sat there quietly, gazing at each other. Torn between exhaustion and the impoliteness of limiting our conversation tonight, I did not know how to begin or what to say. I felt it was my duty to say something first. "It has been an overwhelming day. I am lost for words. I cannot talk now. Can we talk tomorrow?"

Anxiety came over me. I felt my voice losing its strength. I felt desperate to be alone. I needed to sort out all my mixed feelings. My frustration choked me, and my solar plexus tightened. Not enough air filled up my lungs. I could not breathe. A dizzy spell came over my body. I needed to separate from the others for a while to pull myself together. My mother sat there patiently, having waited for more than 25 years to speak to my brother and me, only to hear that I was overwhelmed. Mom did not understand my request. She thought that I did not want to fatigue her. She began talking. Her words tumbled fast.

"I looked for you after the war. I went back to the Cam Ranh City orphanage looking for you." Her voice sounded desperate, a mother's cry to her baby. She wanted to make sure I understood. She did not abandon us. She had waited all these years to explain. We sensed the plea in her voice, a plea which needed no translation.

"I went to the orphanage. I only found rotting children's bodies. The smell was unbearable. I turned over each child. I looked at each of them, afraid one of them was you or your brother. My heart ached with each child, knowing it was someone's child. I felt guilty that I thanked God that the dead child was not you. The people in Cam Ranh City told me they saw the whole orphanage leave a week before the Viet Cong came. I was relieved to hear that there was a chance you were still alive."

Her face looked sad as she waited for me to hear the translation.

I sat there numb. I looked at her small frame, both feet tucked under her in the chair, sitting Vietnamese style as I listened to her story. She continued to spill out her feelings. She told me of waiting for this moment. The length and the uncertainty during the wait, she barely endured. She continued. She wanted to release all her guilt and pain. She wished for a release of years in moments. I understood her need.

"Soon after that I heard there was an airplane crash with children on board. I cried, thinking my children were dead now. Before, I had some hope. That news killed every thought I had that you both were still alive."

She hid any impatience with the slow translation. She needed to speak. Nothing stood in her way.

"Three years later, I received an envelope with your pictures with no explanation, no letter, from America. For 20 years, I wrote many letters to anyone Vietnamese in the United States. I tried to find you. No one could find you. Some said you died. I did not believe that and continued writing my letters to Canada and America."

My heart sank deeper, and my lungs hurt from the lack of oxygen. I could not breathe. My brain struggled to absorb the new information. My mother had missed me as much as I had missed her.

"Why didn't I hear from you until now?" she asked.

How could I explain my life in America? How could I describe survival in America? How could I explain how disconnected I was from everything Vietnamese? How could I explain my war of the last 25 years? How could I tell her that I was isolated even from my brother, her son? How could I tell her that our isolation was our only survival tool? How could I tell her the pain I endured?

"We were the first children to be adopted," I explained. "We were separated from the other Vietnamese. We went home with an American family. The family got a divorce after three years. We lived many, many places. No one knew where to find us." I heard my voice slowly dissolving into tears. I felt a choking in my heart and lungs and a desire for release.

After the translation, I stood up holding my weak stomach and said, "I'm sorry. We have to talk tomorrow."

"Please don't cry. You be happy today. Happy day," the translator said.

They stood up to leave. My mother wiped her tears and hugged me. The others turned to leave. Michael stood up with me. He was there to support me. I felt too weak to stand on my own. Everyone understood the tears between a mother and daughter. We remained quiet. The solemn visit ended with a touch and a tear.

Finally all the others flowed out of our room, leaving Michael and me alone. Michael closed the door behind them, and I sat on the bed, sorting out my excruciating experience.

"Are you okay?" Michael asked, holding me. I hung onto him and cried.

"Do you think my mother and the others understand the reason I couldn't talk tonight?" I asked.

"I think so. It's just as overwhelming for them, I'm sure," he assured me.

"I'm part of her, yet I am a world apart." My thoughts boiled to the surface. "We're strangers, yet we're not. I reach for all those familiar things of my past, and they're gone. I forgot my childhood. I feel so odd. After all these years, I finally meet the woman in my dreams and guess what I do? I cry and want to be with my boyfriend!"

"Is she the way you remembered?" he asked.

I gave myself a moment to think while I combed my hair.

"She is smaller than what I remember as a child. I guess we all grew some, huh?" I smiled. "There is so much I want to tell her and ask her. I just want to be with her, yet I can't understand her and she can't understand me." Again, the frustration stirred in me.

"She's beautiful, and so is your sister," Michael commented. "You two look so much alike, especially when I look at the two of you from the side. Your sister Le is like your twin."

"I know. It is weird," I said, voicing my thoughts from my first glance of my sister at the airport. "Looking at her, a thought occurred to me about all of us. I could have been her, the one who stayed behind in Vietnam. We are so different from each other now, yet we have the same heritage."

Michael and I cuddled into bed. The others did not hear the muffled sounds of my tears, only slightly audible over the motor-scooter traffic. The tears, like the traffic, lasted all night. We were in a different world, vaguely familiar and terrifying at the same time.

CHAPTER 5
The Village Attack

I t is natural that tears come frequently in my life. Tears come quickly in many Vietnamese families. Our family history started in the small farming village of Nong Son near Da Nang. How many times had I dreamt of hearing about our family? How many times had I put fragments of dreams and memories together to have a past?

When we met again, my mother began to share our history with us.

Firstborn is an important role in our culture, and my older brother, Le Van Sang, filled that role. His birth was two years before mine. My given name was Le Thi Hai. My mother confirmed that my birth was in a year of the dragon, and that she felt it a good omen.

My mother remembered when French soldiers came to Nong Son and burned and bombed her village when she was a little girl. War seemed always around her life. She wondered if it would ever end. So often with war, death is the inevitable result, and my grandfather died when my mother was only two months in her own mother's womb.

Grandma suffered while she carried my mother inside her. The French put her in jail. They had no known, clear reason. Her other two children survived by themselves, while she was in jail. Uncle Hai tended after buffalo and oxen while his sister, Cuc, gathered rice in paddies and picked vegetables for a living. When the French released Grandmother, she came home. Seriously sick, she desperately hung on to the life of her unborn child. Both of them were in jeopardy. The family did not have a blanket or even a mat for her to sleep on.

Her two children went deep in the forest to find leaves for a medication for her sickness. Slowly, she regained her strength as her children nursed her back to health. My mother, Dao Thi No, was born in 1937. From then on, all of the children helped keep the fatherless family alive. My grandmother was a weaver. They depended on a tiny plot of land for the vegetables they did not have the money to buy. The landlord even took that from them. My Uncle Hai tended the landlord's buffalo for a little food. My Aunt Cuc scavenged the rice paddies for any fallen grains. They were landless peasants, clinging to life in the midst of enormous change.

My mother, the youngest child, stayed home with my grandmother to learn her trade. She would also go into Da Nang, dodging the bullets to reach the marketplace where she sold Grandmother's weaving.

My father came from the same village. He grew up in poverty and lost his mother at the age of five. His father remarried. My father's stepfamily ignored him. I sadly learned that this is an accepted custom in the Vietnamese culture. When the parents are no longer together, and one parent remarries, the new family can reject the children. The new family often abandoned the unwanted children. My grandfather's new wife chose to follow this custom and sent my father out into the street. How could those children survive? My heart grew sad hearing about my father and his ordeal.

As early as a boy can walk, my father worked for his keep. He could only watch while other children passed by him on their way to the local school. Desperately wanting to go himself, he worked to earn money for his education. He fed and tended to the water buffalo and oxen for the people around the village and went to school to learn as much as he could. He wanted an education. He committed to become something in life. His desire to learn was great as he struggled to overcome the simplest obstacle. He used dried banana leaves as his notepaper and bamboo splits for his pen. My father, not a farmer like many in his rural village, eventually became a teacher instead.

After he and my mother married, he studied and received his license and went to work as a car driver. This was an important job and gave him more income. The war had provided him with a great job to support his family. As our family grew, he needed the money. Their lives were better now.

Mother remembered the year of my birth, a year of disaster in Nong Son. Storms and floods swarmed over the land.

"One morning the typhoon came and killed many people and animals. It forced our family to take refuge on the high floor of the Catholic Church. We didn't have food for three days. I chewed raw rice and fed you the gruel from my own mouth. My milk dried up from the hunger and thirst. I could not nurse you. I felt you might die like some of the other babies that were crying just the day before. I fought hard to keep you alive," she said.

As she continued relating our story, I realized that my family and many other Vietnamese had shown acceptance and determination rather than resignation and sadness. American settlers, immigrants from all over, also developed this strength during their many trials. Unfortunately, the Vietnamese culture had come to regard suffering as part of life. We did not have to travel to gain our strength; the suffering and the opportunities to gain strength came to us. However, along with the suffering, the love of family and children remained strong.

My brother, Sang, is the oldest and the firstborn. Mom allowed him to make his own discoveries with little supervision. He became my protector when Mom was not around. I hung onto Sang. He carried my weight, and we were in constant contact. I began to remember more of my own past.

1968

I only knew chaos, confusion and excitement, growing up in Vietnam. Big, scary noises crowded my world. At night, red flames and explosions lit the dark sky from afar. They lasted a few minutes. They disappeared, only to reappear minutes later. I fell asleep with the lullaby of continual hustling and bustling around the village. But I always felt safe with my mom's arms around me as I slept.

I often heard that Mom overfed me to make up for my beginning. People told her she spoiled me. She prided herself on giving her children plenty of food. She wanted us to become healthy and strong. We knew she went hungry so we could have more.

Our family happiness ended after an unusually joyful New Year's holiday of Tet in 1968. This Tet holiday was the famous Tet offensive that I read about in my history books in high school. The turning point in the war for the Americans became a nightmare in the villages.

Once the Americans stopped the communists in the cities, the army came into village after village to find and kill all their feared enemies. One day, the usual commotion came closer to our village than ever before. People everywhere gathered their belongings. I cried for my mom. She was nowhere in sight. I had stayed home that day while she worked in the fields. My grandmother grabbed Sang and me by the hands and ran. We did not know where we were running, we just ran. Everyone just ran. The thundering noises grew louder and louder. The world collapsed on us.

My grandmother picked me up and carried me on her waist. She held Sang's hand tightly and ran toward the field. I reached out for my mom. She ran toward us. She took me from my grandmother and put me in her basket. She put Sang in another basket. Then she lifted us up on her shoulder with a long bamboo yoke bar. It held both baskets, me in the front of her and Sang in the back one. She ran faster that way. My grandmother scurried behind her.

We were in a crossfire. Bullets flew at us. People died in front of our eyes. Chaos reigned. We ran for our lives to escape the invasion and the giant green trucks with many men on them. My mother stopped and yelled at my grandmother. She was far behind.

"Quick! Run and hide. They are too near to me. They can't see you. Hurry, hurry! Run the other way!" My mother took both of us from our baskets. We ran with her to hide. Her grip on my hands hurt as the

*Another time, another place far, far, away...
yet so near in our own hearts*

Our Family Portrait

truck full of soldiers came toward us. We could not hide from them.

They gathered the other women and men along with us in a group and made us walk toward the village. Nearby the entrance, we stepped over the bodies of people who had futilely attempted to leave. At least our father was safe. His job kept him driving in Da Nang.

The soldiers lined the women and men together in a straight line with guns pointed toward their heads. The villagers screamed and pleaded for their freedom. A gun went off. A woman fell to the ground. Her death silenced the rest.

My mother still hung onto both our hands. She held us tightly by her sides as we lined up. We stood at the end of the line. We all knelt down. We grabbed our knees to make ourselves small like a ball. Maybe we would be too small to see or maybe we could roll away. The guns continued to fire. My mother's hands gripped ours. Our hearts leapt at the sound of each shot as they got closer and closer.

"I am no harm to you. Please, please... I must raise my children. I have lost everything except my children," my mother blurted out. She pled to the soldiers. " They need me. I beg you! Have pity on me. I'm just a farm girl."

I never saw so many tears running down my mother's face before. I began to cry with her as she held me close to her chest in the shadow of a man in green. Sang and I both cried, hanging onto our mother's side, listening to the gunfire and explosions.

"The enemies go that way," she lied. She pointed toward the opposite direction from most of the people's escape route. "We are friends." Her words somehow saved our lives. They got what they wanted. They left us alive among the 175 who died that day. The confusing thing about this war was that even the natives could not distinguish who were the enemies. We did not care as long as we still had our family alive. My mother would do anything to save our skins.

Later, Mother brought us back to the village. Dead bodies littered the streets. It took days to take care of the dead. The stench overwhelmed us as our family tried to find a way among all the dead ghosts in the village. I still remember the blank stares and the smell. I remember how hard our father hugged me when he returned. I do not know who cried more when we reunited, Mom or Dad.

Our respite from the war did not last for very long. Soon the bombs came back, their fire smashing and tearing the village into a devastated war front with their powerful machines. The airplanes came. We ran again.

The force of the bombs and napalm closed in on us. We felt the flames. The burning torched everything in its way. The haunting smell of burning flesh gagged us. Destruction and death laid its path with waves of bullets. Mothers and children cried for each other. This endless nightmare forever imprinted our young eyes and ears.

The strike of the giant monsters took its toll in human lives. Bodies laid in our path as my mother desperately tried to escape. How could anyone ever forget such devastation? I remembered this ride. To my bewildered eyes, I again rode in the basket. It twirled around from the bouncing of my mother's shoulders. I saw Sang in the back, and I saw a panorama of death all around. My grandmother stayed close by as we continued our run for safety. This time our father was with us, desperately trying to protect us.

My mother screamed to Father, "Come on! Come on! Are you okay?"

"Yes, yes!" he called back. He ran toward us with fury. His muscular build and his strong, short legs calmed our fears. Just then, an explosion lifted his body in its fury and carelessly returned his broken pieces to the earth.

My mother shrieked his name, "Son! Son!" as if to try to freeze the moment we saw our father's life taken. My father's death stunned the whole family. In shock, we looked at his mutilated body lying along the path.

Mother paused. She yearned to be close to him and pick up the pieces, but her motherly duty pushed her on. Panic-stricken as she cried for her husband, she ran to save our lives and escape the open battlefield. As she ran for shelter, she looked back at her husband. Bewildered, Sang and I cried out from our baskets, "Papa, Papa!" All our senses screamed with shock. How could such a thing happen?

Away from the danger zone, my mother finally stopped and sobbed in despair for her husband. Only a few hours before, we had eaten together. Only a few minutes before, Father gave me a loving pat on my head. Only seconds before, his smile filled my heart.

Our father was a very handsome man at 30. His stocky build carried large burdens. Our village considered his round, good-looking face to be a good sign. He had a "trusting face." A quiet man, he spoke when there was an important message to get across. In his silent way, he was a tough and passionate man.

Now he was gone, and my mother could not even claim his body.

We lost everything. My mother and grandmother begged strangers for our shelter and for food. We had nothing. We lost our safety, our past, and all of our papers and identification in the ashes of our village home. It was a strange and desperate time for everyone. People clung tightly to their families and became suspicious of everyone else. The war turned neighbors against each other.

Without our farm, we were now condemned to poverty. Disheartened by lost, uncaring and suspicious people, my mother continued her journey toward Da Nang, the nearest city. She had been told to flee to the fringes of cities and towns to survive. It was safer than the remote villages in the countryside. She needed shelter for our weary bodies, but no one would take us in without papers. We could not prove to suspicious people that we were not Viet Cong. Everyone feared each other. A thousand times, the Green Monsters took their revenge. They repeated the history of Nong Son village as if their exterminations could never wipe out their suspicions.

Some 60,000 American soldiers died in Vietnam, and some 600,000 Vietnamese. How many family farms and rice fields were bombed? How many of the dead were fathers? How many of those 600,000 dead were children? How many sons and daughters were sacrificed in this war?

We walked through many fields and hard clay from unharvested lands. After receiving many rejections, my mother approached a

A face of a father I never knew

Le Van Son

1937 - 1968

grass-mud home. These people had a roof and food. In the yard, they dried rice and cleaned vegetables for dinner.

She begged them to let us rest at their home. The two young children and two women permitted us to stay outside in the front area of their home to rest. It became our first fugitive home. We thanked our hosts for the help they gave our family. Later they gave us some rice and silently we ate. We tried to forget reality, but it was impossible.

"When will this war ever end? Will I live to see peace again?" my grandmother asked. "What has happened to this country? The people are so shameful. We do not trust each other any longer. They suspect women and children. Huh!"

We made our next home beside a sidewalk in Da Nang. The city was so different from our countryside home. Neon lights blazed from big buildings, and children ran around everywhere. Their parents were nowhere to be seen. Pretty young girls in high heels locked arms with soldiers in uniforms. It was all part of the landscape.

We were now homeless people on the streets of the city. My mother spread out a bamboo mat for us to lie on. The long journey and the lack of food and water made us weak. We barely had enough food to keep us alive. We never ate enough to be full. Famished, we sometimes fainted from hunger. My mother became frantic. Seeing her children lying still, she feared death would take us away from her as well.

Unable to cook the rice, my grandmother and mother were forced to take the little bit of rice left from the basket and chew it into mush. They took it from their mouths and hand-fed our still bodies. My grandmother fed Sang while Mother held me in her arms and fed me. As we slept on the wood bamboo mat, Mother gently touched us and promised that she would always take care of us.

"You are all I have left, my children. I will see to it that you have a full life. I will try to be both father and mother to you, I promise." She curled up close to us as she finally laid down to rest. As she closed her eyes, tears poured down her face for her dead husband. She faced an unknown future. She faced a life as a woman without a husband, and her children had no father.

We were one of the many families who were victims of the war. The war brought pain, loss and devastation into our lives. Without our papers, we lost our identities and anything permanent to claim for our own. The world seemed smothered with deception and distrust. Vietnamese policemen and American interrogators selected random people for questioning. We were homeless in a country on shaky ground.

My mother soon went to prison because they suspected her to be Viet Cong. She had no papers to prove otherwise. She spent three months in prison for the crime of not being able to prove who she was. Our grandmother took care of us while they took our mother away.

The hours were long, and the suffering was great in prison for her. They treated her as a criminal and assaulted her mind and body. Had she not suffered enough? They beat her for information she could not give. Her body soon gave out. She became ill from more than just the effects of the pain. She discovered in prison that she was pregnant. Just before his death, my father had given to my mother his last seed. She now had the added burden of carrying another child. When she was no longer able to endure the pain, they finally released her.

Life became very hard. Mother supported us in every way she could. She farmed fields for other families. That work brought some rice to bring home. She became increasingly tired. The sun and the bending hurt her back and her body so much more than before.

She was a young woman. She tried many other jobs as well. She helped carry wood bundles across the river or delivered concrete and building materials to construction sites to earn money for her family. Each day when she came home, she was weaker and weaker. Her physical pain was only part of her pain. She felt the growing agony of her last moments alone with my father.

No longer able to continue her physically demanding jobs, she stopped them. Her body grew weaker from the lack of nutrition for herself and now for this baby. Sang and I were as content and adjusted with this borrowed time as children could be. We understood that our father was never going to be with us again. At least, we always had our mom around to hang on to. Mom soon moved to Dalat to work as a maid and prepare for the birth of her unborn child. Sang and I played during the day as other children walked back and forth from the local school. Since we had no papers or proof that we were not the enemy, the schools forbade us to attend. We spent our days carefree with our mom and grandmother. Mom taught me songs. She hummed them with me until I knew the words. My mother was my teacher.

Mother knew that she needed to do something to save her children. She could no longer protect Sang and me without her papers or provide school for us, and she could not tend to us and to her unborn child in such poverty. Then she heard of a minister who provided shelter for children of the war. Would he be able to save her children?

CHAPTER 6
The Orphanage

a knock on the door startled us. Michael jumped up, slipped on his jeans in an instant, and opened the door. It was the driver, trying to communicate with us. "We'll leave tomorrow for home at 6 a.m." We were relieved that everyone was settling down for the night.

Exhausted from the trip, the heat and the lack of food, Michael grabbed a granola bar from our survival kit to settle his stomach and handed me one. We slept or at least tried. I tossed and turned. I listened to every motorcycle passing by, to the chattering and the beating of wooden sticks outside in the hallway. A fear of being in the country we escaped from 25 years ago surfaced. I was alert and on guard. I stayed awake all night, tightly hanging on to Michael's side. I woke up and wrote down my fears and my feelings in my journal. I paced the room, anxious to find answers from this journey. Michael kept me company and encouraged me to try to sleep.

The morning could not come fast enough. When it did, we loaded up the van and began our trip to my mother's village. As we left the city to go into the Vietnamese countryside and watched the changing landscape, I was haunted by old ghosts. The people worked hard in the field. Everyone hustled in the many markets we passed. I sat against the window with my mom in the middle and my sister Le on the other side. We held each other's hands as if our lives depended upon it.

The quietness of the long trip placed me in a trance. The repetitious pattern of the van's horn put me adrift among the images of women in cone hats working in the fields. Their labor supported their families and livelihood. My mother's image transcended onto that field. I still can sense the bond of closeness I felt as a child in my mother's shadow in those fields. I remembered being that small child always clinging to my mother's side. How much harder was work in the fields when your child hung from your back?

1968 - 1969

My mother only knew hard work. I ran behind her as she left for the fields. She waved for me to go back home. I usually stopped until she continued her walk. Slowly, I continued to follow her again. Many times, she spanked me to make me go home. Other times, she allowed me to be with her or wrapped me on her back as she worked. Or sometimes she placed me on her chest when her back was tired. I enjoyed just being there, close to her. I often fell asleep in a small bed she made for me in the field.

For all these years, I have held onto that closeness. My dreamy image of this beautiful woman with her long black hair transfixed my mind and heart. I see her bending down over a large metal bowl of hot water scented with dried beans as she created an herbal formula for her silky hair. Sometimes she gave me sticky rice in a ball. I loved her sticky rice with sesame seeds. It tasted delicious!

One day Mom took us with her to the market. I was happy to be with her all day again. She often packed up her things and disappeared until nighttime. We went to the market that day to pick up some food. She stopped to talk to neighbors, and then we continued to travel.

"Where are we going, Mama?" I asked.

"On a trip," she casually answered.

Sang, always quiet, said nothing. I was more talkative, sometimes even singing for my mom and others. Sang and I hung onto her, filled with excitement. Would she play with us today? She brought us desserts to eat along the way. We boarded a bus with many others and their belongings of vegetables, meat, live animals and supplies. The aroma, familiar to us from the market, filled the air. However, this market moved!

We huddled together on one seat. People and their belongings stuffed the bus. My mom sat me on her lap, and I felt her large, pregnant belly against me. Sang leaned against the window. He felt sick on this rocking, bouncing bus. So Mom kept a plastic bag out for him so he could throw up. I enjoyed all the excitement and the bouncing in her lap. I waited to see what would come next.

The bus made many stops, yet we stayed on. The trip was far too long to hold my attention. Sang and I fell asleep as the day grew darker and darker. We had not stopped or returned home. I did not know when we actually stopped that night, but finally we were no longer moving. As usual, we curled up tightly asleep with Mom, Sang on one side of her and me on the other. I only woke to snuggle closer to her. I fell back to sleep until morning. We woke up, sister and brother, curled up together without our mom. Perhaps she was preparing breakfast somewhere.

Once awake, we saw many unfamiliar things. Where was our home? This was not our home. Big tractors pushed dirt around. Big metal arms lifted people and bricks into the air. Concrete and bricks were stacked all over. Men in green uniforms walked and ran everywhere. They were giants. I had never seen such white skin on such big people. These people in hard hats with hair on their arms and skin were strange to our eyes. Rows of houses filled the area, very different from the shacks of our village. Finally, we found a large metal gate. I did not know if it was to keep us in or our mom out. Sang, silent and more aware of what was going on, took my hand. We walked around the area. It was so big, and we were so small. It seemed monstrous to be lost inside it.

I cried for Mom. Sang held my hand. He pulled me along. We both looked for her. Instead we found a man and woman with a small child and a few older and younger kids. They ate breakfast, and we were hungry. They waved for us to come to the table. We hesitated, still looking for our mom. I cried and called out, "Mama!" Sang looked everywhere for her. There was no sign of her. Devastation crept over our hearts.

Some people sent us to a house and to a table to eat. Other children were there, yet no adults ate. An older girl waved me to the table with four other children already sitting at the table. I glanced over to see another child my size at the end of the bench. I sat next to her. I watched the others while eating our bowl of rice in silence. We ate hungrily. We ate fast to get our share of breakfast.

After breakfast, they all went outside as though they knew all about this place. We followed them out. One of the older boys pointed toward those strange men and said, "Those are the American GIs. Bet you haven't seen them before, huh?"

Sang and I were amazed and wide-eyed to see men with white skin who were giants, working and walking around the area. Afraid, yet curious, we wandered around. Sang took my hand again, not forgetting to look for Mom. We walked around and around looking for any woman that might be her. Sang saw the front metal gate and ran toward it, leaving me behind crying. I watched Sang run toward the gate that seemed too far away for me to catch up. He disappeared at the front of the gate. Slowly he reappeared, standing on top of a big rock beside the gate. He blocked the sun from his eyes with his hand and looked beyond to see if Mom was out there.

An older girl took my hand and led me away. I walked hesitantly. I kept turning back toward the gate, keeping my eyes affixed on my brother. The bigger girl showed me how to clean up, and we went toward the kitchen. An older white-haired woman ran the kitchen. She reminded me of my grandmother. I felt sad remembering my grandma and not being able to find my mom.

They sat me down by a bowl of "rau muong," a Vietnamese green vegetable. An older girl showed me how to break it into sections. I sat and broke each stem. I felt lost. Was my mom lost, too? When would she be back?

Maybe she went to the market as always and would be back tonight.

I continued to learn new tasks to do in the kitchen. During that first day, I helped prepare lunch. I glanced toward the gate, hoping to see Mom walking back with Sang to get me. I only saw Sang's head. He stood and looked for her all day.

For the next few days, we stayed occupied doing numerous chores around the kitchen. Young and old, we did our parts. Sang still stood on that rock and waited for Mom to come back.

During free time, I walked around and played with rocks along the yard. I waited for her return, too. I stopped crying for her as much after the first two days. The other two older girls had teased me for being a baby. The luxury of childhood with my mom was no longer a reality in this new home. They gave us responsibility in the orphanage. The chores made us grow up fast. There was no time for affection. We were older somehow, and they expected us to be adult-children and to carry on with our duties.

I sang my old favorite songs to myself. It comforted me. Mom often let me sing for her as I played with the rocks along the paved street. Now, I sang to fill the loneliness. Sometimes, I sang because I missed my mom.

One day I suddenly stopped my singing, as a big shadow fell over me. The shadow frightened me. I looked up and saw one of the American soldiers. His size and his strangeness scared me. He sat down and handed me a piece of gum. Even sitting down, his size was intimidating. I reluctantly took the gum. What was this?

He took another piece of gum from his pocket. He showed me how to unwrap it and chew it. As he chewed his gum, he held his throat to let me know not to swallow it. I did what he did and found it a very tasty treat. For the first time, I smiled. He played with me a bit and talked to me in a strange language. I did not understand. He took my hand, and we walked a bit. Then he carried me in his arms since I was very small, and it was difficult to keep up with his giant steps. We visited with other soldiers in uniform.

My giant friend and I walked toward the office building. I saw the headmaster and his wife go there often. He carried me in. I saw Mr. Ha, the headmaster. He always wore a white shirt and tie and looked very nice. He was the authority figure in my new home.

One moment in time; a hug, a smile,
a loving affection can imprint a
heart for a lifetime

In the arms of Soldier Grace, 1969

Farming people in my village wore very different clothes, and his glasses were something I had never seen before.

Mr. Ha stood up from his desk to greet the soldier. He shook his hand and then he smiled at me. As they talked, Mr. Ha nodded and looked at me. I stood beside the American soldier and held his hand. Mr. Ha said to me, "This is Airman Grace, and he likes you very much, and he wants to help you while you are here."

So I asked, "Will he take me home to my mom?"

"She is home, far away. She will visit you and your brother often." Mr. Ha looked at Airman Grace. "This soldier saw you playing and singing out there. Why don't you sing for him?" Then he gestured for me to sing "Frère Jacques" in Vietnamese, a song that all little girls know how to sing and dance to.

I looked up at the soldier and smiled. He smiled back at me. I felt very special and wanted his attention and affection. Mr. Ha told me that I was very lucky that he wanted to help us. I did not understand the conversation, but I understood that I should sing my favorite song and dance. I always felt comfortable singing and dancing in front of my family and relatives. It made me feel more at home to do it now. My new soldier friend sat on the desktop while Mr. Ha stood by. He instructed me to continue singing. Others stopped by to watch and listen.

After I was done, I realized other Americans, women soldiers, too, watched. They clapped when I was done. The women soldiers held the other children in their arms. Mr. Ha instructed us to sing and dance for the new arrivals. We all sang and giggled together. Some Americans came over and patted our heads. Other green giants came to play a bit. Soon Airman Grace carried me toward the playground that the soldiers had just finished building for the children. All the other children came running to play on the slides and swings, too. As we left the office, I saw Mr. and Mrs. Ha talking. I sat high on Airman Grace's shoulders. They looked toward us.

It was then I knew that this was my new home. I could no longer be with my mother. At four years old, I was now alone to make new friends. The separation from my mother left me with the deepest pain of solitude. That pain was always with me. A new sense of loneliness set in. Would the ache of waiting ever go away? Would she come back to visit? Did she not want me? I developed a special attachment to these friendly Americans who gave us attention and became our new sources of love and a sense of belonging.

I was the youngest among the other children in the early days of the Cam Ranh City Christian Orphanage. The memory of my mother always haunted me. I was no longer the child that my mom and grandmother would baby and spoil. The affection I received as a reward for my singing and dancing would come from others, if at all. Always a part of me still looked toward the gate. I hoped to get a glimpse of my mother coming to take me home.

Our home in Vietnam, 1969-1975
Cam Ranh City Christian Orphanage

CHAPTER 7
My Wartime Family

t was only as an adult that I learned the vague details of the founding of the orphanage where I had lived as a child. Jason and I were discussing our upcoming trip to see the old buildings. We wondered if they still stood. My mother looked sad as I told her of the death in 1998 of Mr. Ha, the man who became our father figure.

To the children of the orphanage, Mr. Ha was our "abba." He had a slender frame and stood only 5'4". He looked youthful, yet he also seemed very wise behind his wide blacked-framed glasses. He had a great spirit. We respected and looked up to him. He forever imprinted our minds with the memory of a gentle and powerful man.

Mr. Ha represented the second generation of Christian ministers in his family. After he graduated from Saigon college, he was assigned to a church in Dalat, the former imperial city 180 miles north of Saigon. There, the weather was cool and the landscape coveted by visitors. There were many resorts for wealthy families. It was in Dalat, where he came up with the idea of founding an orphanage in Cam Ranh City. The idea soon outgrew the local church's ability to support it without the help of the nearby American Air Force base. But the United States government avoided local projects and so the church was discouraged and the orphanage project abandoned.

However, the young spirit and heart of this new graduate saw things differently and made it a part of his faith and call from God to build the orphanage. Mr. Ha fought the odds without any government help and instead relied on goodwill and his strong faith in God to help him. He moved his young family, then consisting of his young son and wife, to Cam Ranh Bay and started down his path in 1968.

The Cam Ranh City government granted him seven acres of undesirable land against a mountainside. The land was still wild and undeveloped with rocks and steep banks. Every day, he intensified his campaign for support from the neighbors in Cam Ranh Bay and from our allies at the Air Force base, the American soldiers. His distinctive gifts of persuasion for a good cause won him support from many individual soldiers. The contributions had to come from individuals willing to help without any government involvement. Slowly, the soldiers and neighbors helped level the rugged land. This undeveloped, unwanted piece of land soon became the Cam Ranh City Christian Orphanage. The sign painted on the metal over the gate proudly announced its opening.

An organized and well-bred man, Mr. Ha worked diligently around the orphanage. To those of us who were children of the war, Mr. Ha appeared as our guardian angel. His wonderful magic protected us from the war. Like the solid concrete walls and metal gate he had built around us, his love protected us. As a businessperson, he solicited funds in Saigon to help "his children." Soon he enlisted an American missionary and his family to assist us. Rev. Walter A. Routh, Jr. was the first contact from an organization in the United States.

Mr. Ha, as our father figure, always provided the finances. Those generous donations he obtained provided food and clothing to his children. He had a great ability to sell and convey his faith. Donations covered the expenses of the orphanage. Constantly he worked and found enough to take in more children.

*It started with a vision,
a cause that created
futures for many orphans*

Mr. Ha's charisma brought in the friendly faces of American soldiers. With their huge hearts, they helped him build a better place for his children as we grew in numbers. Desperate families and children arrived as the news began to spread of this sanctuary for children. With the orphanage built, more and more children came for refuge.

1969 - 1974

My first childhood boyfriend was a little boy named Luah. We often climbed onto the lounge chair in the evenings and fell asleep together. Other kids teased us when they found us innocently curled up together the next morning. They separated the boys from the girls at a later point and took my brother, my only connection to my family, away from me. I lived with other girls in a dorm full of bunk beds up the hill. Far away on the opposite hill, the boys slept.

I only saw my brother Sang at mealtimes. Even so, we never talked, and he became increasingly withdrawn. Silent even among the boys, he fought and set himself apart. He was the youngest boy and the smallest, but he would also get into more fights with boys twice his size and win.

The boys had the responsibility of growing the crops, feeding the animals, and boiling the well water on the bottom of the hill where they lived. The girls lived closer to the main part of the orphanage. We had classrooms, bathing houses and a staircase leading down toward the kitchen. Those stairs connected to the mess hall where everyone ate. American supplies and support built all the buildings in our new home. All the women and girls were responsible for cooking the meals and, of course, cleaning up.

We washed our own clothes and ourselves. They gave us two outfits of clothing and a pair of shoes each year. They told us to take care of them. It was the hardest rule for me to follow. I was not used to shoes in the country. We never had to wear them before, so I never paid attention to them at all and lost many pairs.

Every time they caught me barefooted, they asked "Hai, where are your shoes today?" I would shrug and answer, "I don't know."

My wartime family album...

That answer was unacceptable. They walked me straight to the disciplinary office for a smack on my bottom. Sang and I often met in that office for our various punishments. While my crime was losing my shoes, his crime was usually for fighting or skipping school. As we grew, the disciplinary instruments grew from a ruler to a branch to electric wires. It became more painful each time we took our lessons.

As Sang became more rambunctious with his fights, our paths only crossed in the disciplinary office. He was always silent, no matter the circumstances. I chose to become the free-spirited one. As I grew older, I would get sent to the office to be disciplined for not doing chores, not studying, skipping school or breaking the rules.

Our dorm's big sister would also discipline us for various things. The most famous and painful punishment we endured was horrible. We had to bring rock chips and pieces from the side road and place them on the floor. Then, we would have to kneel down on the rocks for a long period. I was fiercely stubborn and never showed an interest in day-to-day chores. I did not like to do some of the tasks that the other girls so diligently followed, delegated by our big sister. I tolerated school. It also was a bore to me, and I often skipped my classes. I never learned my ABCs. The staff knew my interest was in singing and dancing for the Americans and not in schoolwork. They concluded I was a troublemaker and lazy in my schoolwork. I tended to maintain the last spot in the class and defied school rules. Nevertheless, I was always readily available whenever there was a school play or a singing event. I always managed to remember every word to every song while I forgot everything I learned in classes.

Soon I became the "chosen" little girl to sing and dance for the American troops when any officials came to visit the orphanage. My dance was my way to get the love and attention that I so desperately missed from my mom and my grandmother. Our new American friends gave us candy, gum and rides on their shoulders, showering us with attention and affection. I tagged along with them rather than doing my chores or paying attention to where I last left my shoes.

I purposely sought to be noticed when my American friends were near. I learned early that my personality would allow me to be bold. I became a part of the dance program when they discovered that our abilities to sing and dance touched the hearts of the soldiers. I sang hymns well and acted and played roles such as the bride in our famous Vietnamese wedding play or Mary in the Birth of Christ.

We visited the American base every Christmas to greet and thank our generous friends. Mr. Ha brought the children with him and put together a program for our supporters. We would sing and dance for our audience, followed by Mr. Ha's speech of gratitude and an update on the progress of the orphanage. We enjoyed our visits to the American base and admired the many young soldiers. These loving men and women became a part of our lives.

I developed and used my love for singing and dancing. I knew little about schoolwork but I felt important because of my part in helping Mr. Ha with what he enjoyed most—entertaining. The orphanage became our home, and Mr. and Mrs. Ha became a symbol of our missing parents.

I thrived on the special attention from the adults, but it also created jealousy among my peers. It was special for me to come into the Has' living quarters. They had two small children, and I helped babysit from time to time.

"The milk bottle is in the refrigerator, Hai," Mrs. Ha would call out when she wanted me to help. The icebox and the cleanliness of their surroundings fascinated me. Mrs. Ha was gentle and kind in my eyes, while I feared her sister-in-law, Mrs. Xuan, because she was our disciplinarian.

When I left their quarters, other girls began to attack me with hateful words. "You think you are special, don't you?" one of the girls commented resentfully.

"Just because you dance and sing doesn't mean you are better than us," another one chimed in.

"You can't even do your math," they laughed and teased.

"So what," I screamed back. "Are you jealous?" I egged them on, pressing my luck. My bravery matched any boy's.

Once one of the girls reached out and scratched my face. I held my hand over the wound while my temper boiled up. Fearing nothing I lunged at the three girls. I clawed their hands and scratched the girl who scratched my face. The other girls ganged up on me and a rowdy fight took place. Trying to escape, I ran back behind the quarters I had just left. Breathing heavily and holding onto the scratches on my face, I showed Mrs. Ha the blood. She followed me to break up the fight.

"You girls stop fighting and get back to your chores! Now!" she yelled.

"Are you okay, Hai?" She examined my bruised cheek. I nodded and showed no tears or fears. We stopped fighting and carried on with our duties.

The other girls left me alone to do the vegetables while they gathered around to break the peas for dinner. My fighting with the other girls soon became the most common reason for my disciplinary visits to Mrs. Xuan. I knew the whippings were never as painful as my feelings of isolation. My pain from the other girls' dislike of me was much more intense. I turned to my new American friends but discovered the friendships were only temporary. Quickly, they left. We never saw most of them again.

Life was also filled with going to Mr. Ha's office to do my part as an orphan. We wrote letters to the Americans. We sat at a table with a piece of paper and pen in his office and wrote thank you letters to donors. I never saw them and never remembered them since they all looked like the other giants to me.

When a letter arrived addressed to me in a card form, Mr. Ha showed it to me. I remembered a card with a picture of a beautiful glittering palace. Wow, I thought, my sponsor is a king who lives in a palace in a faraway land called America.

The Americans gave us supplies of canned goods. We stored them in a warehouse close by the main area of the orphanage against a hill. Many times I snuck in at night through a very small hole, looking for treats and open cans of food. We never got enough food to stop our hunger. My favorite was a white can with a picture of a cow in a sunflower. It contained thick cream. I pulled the tab open and dipped my fingers into the can. I got a gob of condensed milk into my mouth. The treat was rare and worth the risk of trouble.

The older woman in the kitchen reminded me so much of my grandmother. Sometimes she gave me a piece of bread or bits of leftover food. She gave it to me to hide and I ate it later. I learned how to survive and never forgot those lessons.

On a bright sunny day, I walked down the hill to see some of the boys busy doing their various chores. Something flew above me quick, and I looked up. A moment later a bird fell to the ground.

"I got one," Sang yelled happily, sitting on one of the branches with his slingshot. "Hai, go get it, would you?" he called down from the tall tree branch as he loaded up for his next victim. There were a couple of boys up in the trees at various spots, aiming at whatever they could find. The surviving birds flew away to escape.

"Shuutt - shuutt..." was the sound made by the rocks from the boys' various slingshots as they headed toward their quarry. Small birds and lizards dropped to the ground. The boys jumped from the trees and claimed their prizes. I ran happily to fetch the bird lying on the ground for my brother, and I would stop to watch the other birds drop from the limbs. Happily, I joined their hunt. I picked up the first bird Sang killed and walked toward the crowd. He picked up another dead bird under the tree.

They gathered around to clean the birds. They plucked their feathers and washed whatever was left. We stuck a stick in the middle of the body and held it over a large fire. The constant fire cooked food for the pigs and for other chores. Now it cooked for us.

The boys bragged among themselves about the hunt. Sang cooked his bird quietly and allowed me to cook the bird I picked up. Whenever I managed to get down there, or find an excuse to wash my clothes by the well, I would get to eat the day's catch. I ate birds, lizards and the other small creatures in the field. I did not mind doing chores when I could join the boys. I went to the well to wash or get water and grabbed a chance to get some extra food. We sat and ate our treat. We gently blew on the meat as we cooled down the hotness of its juices.

The others found some sweet potatoes left behind from the picking field, or corn on the cob. They buried them under the hot coals to cook. We continued to look busy when the bigger brothers and sisters checked our progress.

I still have fond memories of an oldest boy named Thuc. He was not an orphan, yet he helped around the orphanage. He got me extra food when I was there. Thuc was kind to me. He was like my older brother. I felt safe with him. I admired him and enjoyed his presence.

One day, all the orphan children ran outside the metal gate with the older kids. We ran out without permission, not knowing the reason for the commotion. We ran toward the intersection near town, close to the orphanage. We stopped along the side of the paved street where I saw two bloody bodies deformed with twisted broken limbs. It was evident that a large truck had run over them and their motorcycle. It had drug their bodies and left the two young boys, Thuc and Thien, unrecognizable. I stood there, motionless. Cold ran through my veins as I saw my guardian angel's body mutilated on the street. My heart sunk quietly for them. I covered my face, reminded of my father's death. Death again snapped my attachment to another person.

My eyes were transfixed on the blood when I saw Mr. Ha. He rode in a jeep headed toward the incident. He stood up to see over the crowd of children and bystanders. He took off his white shirt as the wind blew it away from his body like wings. Then he jumped off the jeep in his undershirt and ran over to cover the bloody bodies with his white cloth. He moved the two children's bodies with his fatherly strength. Covered with blood, he stood in the midst of the other wide-eyed children.

"Children, return to the orphanage," he demanded. My feet stuck to the spot as someone grabbed my hands to lead me back.

It was a very sad day for our orphan family when we said goodbye to them. We buried them behind the boys' dorm. I have seen those twisted, bloody bodies in all my dreams since that day. Another protector of mine was gone. Because I was the smallest and his favorite, Thuc gave me more help. I received more attention from him. I loved his kindness and his lessons in survival skills.

The food disappeared quickly during mealtimes. I never learned to eat fast like many others during mealtimes. Thuc taught me how to hide my food under my rice so I could get more pork or chicken to eat for my share. He told me to hold my bowl closely to me and reach to get a slice of meat—to quickly bury it on the bottom of the bowl and pretend you ate it. This way I could get more meat in my bowl while there was meat left. I could then eat later without eating so fast or missing my share. What was I going to do without his special treats and the teaching he often offered me?

During the holiday of Tet, people were happy and tense at the same time. They feared another uprising and more killings. We were sad and happy all at once. It was a festive time, filled with special food we never ate during the rest of the year. My favorite treat was sticky rice with sweet beans wrapped in banana leaves. We boiled sticks of them in hot water until they were cooked. Then we unwrapped the strings that tied the leaves around the rice. We used the leaves to slide the sticky rice on the plates and ate it with fish sauce.

For breakfast, we fried the slices in oil and ate them during the holidays. They allowed us many desserts during the holidays. We had two holidays, Tet and the Christmas holidays. We celebrated Christmas because of the missionary teaching. Many American soldiers played Santa and hung stockings of candies by our bunk beds on Christmas Eve while we were asleep.

One Christmas morning I woke up, expecting my stocking to be beside my bed, just as the others had hung theirs. Mine was not there. It crushed me. It was missing, and the other girls laughed at me and gaily ate their treats. I tried to act as if I did not need any candies and went about my normal tasks.

I looked forward to the day's special play. I always enjoyed being Mary in the play "The Birth of Jesus Christ." We often met for prayers and Sunday school in the orphanage, and I normally sang solos of church hymns in Vietnamese.

The sad time mixed with the celebration always brought confusion to my pain. It was during this time that they permitted many children to go home to visit their relatives. Most children still had at least one parent. Some were all alone. Many children suffered. The orphanage was a chance for families to offer a better life for their children during the chaos of the war. There was a sense of safety and protection from the dangers and hunger. While the adults fought with guns and knives, the children's enemies were

East meets West in many ways that influenced our adult lives and traditions

lack of family, food and a hopeful future. At the orphanage we could at least get food and an education. The greatest gift many parents could give to their children was to send them to an orphanage.

I missed my mother the most during the holidays. It was when all my pain for the year surfaced. The orphanage was usually empty as children left to visit their village. I usually was away doing my entertainment, and always anxious to get back to see if my mom had come to take me home. When she did not come, I stuffed my memories and heartaches away.

During the holidays, I would go with the Has to an event at the American base. The soldiers gave us a season's celebration for the orphanage officials including the children. I usually sang a hymn in front of the group as our Christmas gift for their generosity.

Preoccupied with my thoughts of wanting to go home to visit Mom, I sang reluctantly. Mr. Ha nudged me in front of the crowd to sing. I held the hymn book as if it weighed down my body and soul. I sang with sadness and disliked being there. It was one of the few times I did not enjoy entertaining. Anxiously, I returned to the orphanage to wait for Mom.

This year she came, and I was not there! She and Sang left a few days before I came back. It was rainy and stormy during the holidays that year. The orphanage was empty of the normal children's laughter and festive activities. I sat under a tin roof shed, looking toward the metal gate, wishing she had waited for me.

"What about me, Mom?"

I didn't understand why she had left. My mind filled with sadness and pain as if my heart was being torn apart. Sedated by the pounding rain against the tin roof, I peered for hours up the long path toward the gate entrance.

I finally gave up hope. No one ever came, and I walked up the hill in the rain toward my dorm room. I shivered, and I shivered, not from the soaked clothes but from the bitterness I felt in my heart. I entered the dorm, filled with empty bunk beds lined up to the other end. I stopped at the window, still looking for a sign as the rain continued to fall. I took my wet clothes off, and I heard a buzzing noise up on the sky. A small plane passed and played with my emotions. Would someone ever love me and come for me?

I stood by the window, soaked in my tears. As I began to shiver from the piercing coldness, I walked toward my bunk bed. I put on dry clothes and coiled up into the fetal position. In the empty, dark dorm hall, I cried to myself and fell asleep to the sound of the raindrops against the tin roof.

My little sister was born in 1969, and my grandmother named her "Le Thu," which means "autumn tears." Mother shed many tears during that year. My mother's final visit came in 1972. She let us know she had remarried, which allowed her and my sister Le shelter and papers. Sang and I went home to visit their new extended family and disliked the sense of superiority among the stepfather's five older children toward my mom and tiny sister. They did not accept us in their new family. So Sang and I returned to our orphanage home to stay and remain orphans. Mother assured us that she was working diligently toward having her own family together again.

War was part of my life, a life immersed with angry thunders.

Sang, Age 6

Hai, Age 4

CHAPTER 8
The War's End

I held back my tears and turned to my mom, who was now leaning back comfortably on the seat of the van. She shifted to make room for my hugs. I moved closer to her right side and away from the window that brought me back to my childhood. She held me, putting her left arm around me. I felt understood without exchanging a word.

Le lay across her lap and suffered from carsickness. Mom's other hand stroked her head to ease her nausea. Le had thrown up ever since we left Saigon. Her body looked weak from her hard life. I felt so much stronger and healthier than my younger sister. I sympathized with her in her sickness. She reminded me of our gruesome experience during our escape from Vietnam.

1975

The Vietnam War drew to its end, and America slowly withdrew its forces as the Communists closed in to take over South Vietnam.

Mr. Ha traveled to Saigon more frequently to keep abreast of the intensifying war. His sister Xuan and Mrs. Ha helped run the orphanage, for protecting us had became more complex. Viet Cong activities were evident, and the fighting moved closer and closer to our mountainside and our orphanage.

Once again, the terrible flares of fire against the dark sky thundered into our lives. Frequently, we saw dead bodies on the mountainside near the orphanage in the mornings after the fighting. The boys and girls played around the dead bodies, and we considered them part of our world. One time Sang took a stick and poked it into the bullet hole in a body's chest.

Our American friends slowly dwindled away as their country pulled out of our war. We no longer could enjoy our R & R time. Sadness set in amongst us. The smiles and gum were gone.

As the changes occurred, Mr. Ha planned for an escape. It was in the air around our home. He prepared his wife and sister for the move. He tried to get permission for all of us to leave with Saigon government approval. They turned him down. Continuing to track the war from Saigon, he went to the Social Welfare Division. They granted us permission to leave Cam Ranh Bay, as the Viet Cong were moving closer to the city.

When the Communists overran the Highlands early in the spring, he sent word to his sister to prepare to depart. We sensed something as our routines during the day changed. Now we met in the theater for morning, afternoon and evening prayers. They prepared us to leave and instructed us to keep our individual bag of rice and nametag on hand at all times. We were trained to line up like soldiers, ready to flee at any moment.

Fear mixed with childish fantasies of adventure as we took part in the preparations. Each day, as the unknown departure day approached, we played war and tested our escape skills. In our childish war games, we raced against one another. We each had our bag of rice and nametags in hand to see if we could escape the enemy with our speed. Other times, we had small children on our backs as we ran toward the finish line. We practiced our escape from the sounds of war that enveloped our once peaceful sanctuary. We prayed for peace, but we practiced survival.

Mr. Ha stayed in Saigon. He borrowed money from friends and relatives and used all his family savings to finance the escape of his children in Cam Ranh Bay. Mrs. Xuan gathered all of us on a Monday morning in March, and we boarded two buses for the trip toward Saigon. The staff counted heads to make sure we were all on the journey. We waved goodbye to the staff and the older orphans who had decided to stay behind.

The excitement built as we bounced on our seats. We looked forward to this new adventure, but at the same time fear and sadness welled within us as we left the only home many of us had ever known. The last glimpse of the long metal gate caused a tear in many. Exposed to the chaos and busy traffic on the streets, we ventured away from our safety to uncertainty.

People jammed the highway in every form of transportation: buses, army trucks, cars, taxis, bicycles and wagons pulled by oxen. Thousands of people on foot carried all the belongings they owned. Children ran along with their parents. The streets overflowed with panicked people running toward whatever destination they felt offered safety.

The bus stopped abruptly on the side of the road when nearby gunfire broke out. The other bus followed. Terrified by the gunfire and the profusion of refugees in the streets, we sat quietly. We were afraid to know what was going on. The shots forced us off the buses. As we hid along the ditches on the side of the road for safety until the firing stopped, we heard a cry from our bus. It was the smallest child, hidden under the seat during the gunfight. One of the older boys ran from the ditch and got her from the van. We watched and prayed for their safety. Finally, the gunfire stopped.

We reached our next destination, Phan Thiet, where we stayed with a missionary for rest and help. The pastor had already left the location. Mr. Ha met us there, but he faced a major dilemma. We could not continue along the highway. The radio announced that the Viet Cong controlled the highway, and they had stopped all travel. He then plotted a course along the river to Rung La, a jungle route that took us closer to the coast. The price the three boatmen demanded to take us across the river was extremely high. With little funds, Mr. Ha started to plan another route.

Meanwhile, the radio announced that the road might be clear once again. The owner of the boat finally took what Mr. Ha could afford to pay, once he heard this news. The children and staff were on the first two boats with the vans on the third. Then we heard that the radio was again mistaken about the highway. The boats were nearly swamped as more people headed back to the landing. The boats fought a strong wind as we struggled to cross the river. We all watched in horror as the boat carrying the vans rocked with soldiers, deserters from the war, fighting one another. They turned one of the vans on its side. Finally aware of the danger, they stopped fighting long enough to make it across the rough water, and our vans remained intact.

We continued on the three boats overnight. Tired and weary from the non-stop journey, we reached land at Rach Gai, 60 miles from Saigon along the southern tip of Vietnam. A roadblock outside of Saigon prevented anyone from entering. We stayed together while Mr. Ha disappeared to find another form of escape.

The last minute of evacuation was chaotic on that hot, humid day. Thousands of people pushed and shoved each other, hanging on to their family and their worldly possessions, ready to flee.

Our new surroundings confused and bewildered us. They had trained us to line up like soldiers. On our right shoulder, we had our emergency bag of rice, and on our left shoulder, they pinned our name on us: "Le Thi Hai belongs to Cam Ranh City Orphanage." We were prepared to flee, ready to go at any moment.

By then we had reached the coastline at a missionary compound. They helped feed and clothe us after our long journey. Mr. Ha returned and announced he had purchased a boat for seven million dong.

He emptied every penny he had in his pockets for an old, unwanted, ragged boat left on the shore. "Here, that's all I got." He came back to the monastery where all the children stayed and gave instructions to the big boys.

"You, you, and you come with me. We have a boat to mend," he said.

With all the manpower available, the bigger boys and the staff left during the day to patch the holes and rebuild the decrepit boat for our journey. They built two platforms with used, discarded plywood inside this small 30-foot x 10-foot long boat.

We raced against time as the war moved closer to its end. We sensed the end in the restlessness and hopelessness of some of the local people. Some hid around their homes, others panicked, while the rest, resigned, just slowed down their tempo and returned to their normal routines.

We attended church for the last time in Vietnam that Sunday as we prepared to leave on Monday morning. A few days later, all the children lined up as practiced. One by one, we marched onto the boat. They tucked us underneath and packed us like sardines, like soldiers. Fleeing for our freedom, we crammed in against each other, lying down, as tightly as possible.

Each child packed under the boat deck filled two layers of bodies. With no room to move, it was our only hope for safety.

The equivalent size of the boat we all crammed in to escape on April 30, 1975

CHAPTER 9

Escape to America

On April 30, 1975, 100 orphans and staff escaped, literally 15 minutes before the Communists seized Saigon. Our faith was in God and Mr. Ha. He took us to our unknown destination. Mr. Ha convinced the police that he wanted to take the children to the safety of the next island to avoid the war. They instructed us not to move because they feared that the boat would rock, as it carried 100 people into the South China Sea. A patrol boat guarded our boat a short time, but soon the patrol boat returned to land when the radio announced Saigon's surrender.

While the commotion raged on land, we continued our journey into the open sea. Mr. Ha had no charts or compass, only a textbook map to guide our journey. He and his brother-in-law, Tam, steered the boat in the direction they thought went toward Thailand in the hope of signaling American ships. We were not alone. Thousands of boats and ships of all different sizes and conditions were filled with people and belongings hanging onto any available space. They floated in the big sea as far as the eye could see.

We continued our exhausting journey among the chaos of other boats on the sea for the next five days and nights. The trip was long and grueling. The water tossed us back and forth and made us vomit and urinate on each other. The sickness, the suffocating gasoline and fumes from the engine, the sour odor of vomit and urine and the crying became unbearable. We had no way to escape, no room to budge from this dark dungeon.

Bam! Bam! Bam! Another boat plunged into us, poking a hole on the side. Water began to seep in. We screamed! We climbed on top and over each other to escape the water.

"Shut up, everyone! Stay still. Don't move!" A harsh, panicked voice called down from the top.

An older boy shouted, "All of you who are not sick and can move around, grab any cups or cans. Bail the water out. Plug the hole! Plug the hole! We've been hit! We've been hit! We've been hit!" I wiggled on my stomach to the corner while others tried to sit up. Others crawled on top of those who could not move from seasickness to get to the water.

They stuffed the hole with anything that was available to us. We used rags, paper, anything! We chewed the rice and used the gruel to paste around the hole along with the black oil from the engine. We had to slow the water from seeping in. To this day, I can't explain how we managed to stay alive.

Our heavy cargo of children, most of them constantly sick, overloaded the boat. Covered with each other's vomit and waste, our boat trapped us in a dungeon that *might* take us to safety and freedom.

The sour vomit, the whining of sick children, the engine smoke and the fumes of the gasoline lingered in the air, smothered us and kept us weak. Lined up like sardines, like soldiers on lower levels, we propped each other up. We leaned against each other and against the hull of the boat. There was not enough room to stir around for better positions. The constant pounding of the waves endlessly tortured our bodies.

Hunger was another demon, fighting for our attention. Our groaning stomachs cried for food, but the moving sea took it away. We lacked everything a body needs—water, food, sunshine, fresh air and warmth. Our rations ran out quickly, and we went the last several days of our journey without food. Exhausted and damp, we were smelly and cramped and weak.

As we waited for rescue, we prayed thousands of times, "Dear God, please rescue us soon." Our prayers became our sedative, our hope, and our meditation. Prayer removed us from the reality of the sea and placed us into God's hands.

We desperately flagged any boat we saw for help. None stopped. A ship from Taiwan, the "Taching," stopped for a moment, then continued on. Some 30 minutes later, the same ship returned to give us help. Its powerful engines pulled our slow, weary boat at the end of a long rope, and we feared the water that poured in. Before, our boat had only inched along. The journey would have taken twice as long if that ship had not returned to answer our pleas. But its powerful engines nearly swamped us as it pulled our little boat through the evening. We feared the tugging and the speed would tear our boat apart. When they towed us into the safety of international waters near Singapore, we let the tow rope go.

We stayed afloat in international waters and waited for permission to land. Would anyone recognize our cries for help? Finally, the police came and searched our boat. Mr. Ha went with them aboard their powerboat. He explained our dilemma. We had no papers, and he pleaded with them to send a message to a Baptist missionary in Singapore who had long ago promised to help.

We were all silent during this interrogation. Mr. Ha talked to them and took a piece of paper from the pocket of his dirty, torn remnant of a white shirt and wrote: "Please find Pastor Jim Gayle for us. We are the Cam Ranh Bay Christian Orphanage. I have 100 children and staff here on your waters. Please help us! God Bless You. Mr. Ha Nguyen, Pastor." Then he gave the message to the police.

We floated on the sea without much food or water for many more days while we waited to see if someone would answer our cries for help. There was a lot of movement up on the deck. Only a few older children and adults were allowed to be up there. I sat on top of another girl, out of desperation to ease my sickness.

A loud crash again jolted us. It shook the whole boat. The moaning of the children turned to panic. From the corner of the bow of the boat, the salt water began to flow in slowly from the hole. It was like being on the bottom of wet soil in your own grave.

We all stood up as much as we could or crawled away from the leak. The bigger boys from upstairs came running down with pails and rags to stop the opening and seal it again.

"We've been hit again! We've been hit again," a boy cried out to all of us.

"Stay where you are. Don't move around too much," another one shouted. "Don't bounce the boat or the water will seep in more."

Some of us had to go up on the top deck of the boat to make room for the repair. I jumped onto the deck, and felt the sun and the sea breeze penetrate my weak body. Like a laser beam, the sun cut through my body as if it were a paper wall. Energized with a bit of sunshine on my body, I felt alive again. I had not felt the sun for weeks.

I heard a commotion between our boat and a large ship full of people. They yelled at us, "Get out of the way! Get out of the way!" They signaled with their arms and bodies that our tiny boat was in their path. Its powerful engines and monstrous appearance cut its own path past us, damaging our little vessel.

Mr. Ha signaled to them, calling out, "Wait, you need to help us. Your ship crippled our boat."

Another hit would be our final blow. He turned to warn Mr. Tam, a member of Mr. Ha's family, a pilot for South Vietnam who had come to help the orphans escape. But the giant boat ignored us and continued on its way. Our faith and prayers intensified as we cried out for God to help us.

Early one morning, the boat seemed to be bouncing more aggressively on its side, as if to wake us up. There was an even bigger ship, cutting deep into the water, marking its path with waves that echoed in the open sea. A low, deep sea call sounded as they headed toward our boat.

Afraid that the second encounter would finish us all, we waved our bodies and arms and shouted, "We're here, we're here!" in hopes of catching the attention of this steel monster and getting it to stop. The big giant monster eased up beside our boat. It appeared to be a whole city floating on water, which came to us with such ease. The only word I recognized on its side was "Singapore."

All the children and staff now on deck greeted the visitors. We lined up as we usually did to put some order into the system. Mr. Ha then unrolled his sleeves and brushed his stained hands across his head to create a better impression. Smiling, he greeted these new friends with hope in his heart.

Mr. Ha came back and told the adult staff, "Get the children ready to board." We breathed sighs of relief, happiness shined in our eyes and smiles rose within us. We stood there another minute while Mr. Ha gave thanks to God for bringing us to safety. We left our decrepit boat in small groups. We allowed the smallest and the sickest children to go ahead in the smaller shuttle boat. It swiftly moved back to the giant ship. Another boat took the second load, until all of us had departed from our faithful, worn boat, which had successfully reached its destination. During our transport to the big ship, our tattered boat took on water and sank further and further into the sea. As we climbed up the giant's side to reach the deck, I saw our boat slowly sink into the abyss.

The rescue ship was massive. We stared at the many different devices on its decks and walked toward the meeting area. Walking immediately became a pleasure after our cramped quarters. The people gave us blankets to warm our bodies, and loaves of bread to pass among ourselves.

We sat on the deck, afraid to move as they passed out food. We tore the bread apart and ate heartily to kill the long pain of hunger. The bread's aroma smelled divine. It tasted so good and rich. I had never tasted anything like this before. And we never had bread wrapped up before. Some of us tried to eat that, too, until they told us it was plastic and took it out of our mouths.

Soon after, we lined up as we did in the orphanage, the younger ones at the very front, the next line with the taller ones, and the adults in the back. Then we sang a couple of hymns to our new friends as our meager way of thanking them.

We all were amazed at this steel city floating on the water. With time, we adjusted to the new environment. What was this place and where were we going? Mr. and Mrs. Ha left us to be with people elsewhere on the ship. We waited and realized we were on our way to somewhere.

As evening approached, the sea brought peacefulness. We seemed to creep along, yet we were moving ten times faster than before. The feeling of the sea breeze on our face refreshed us. A sudden commotion began among our group, and we frantically headed toward the side of the ship. The rich, simple food from our friends gave us stomach aches. We did the thing we learned so well on our little boat. We went to the bathroom over the side of the ship, our cheeks hanging to the wind. What did our new friends think? They probably had a good laugh—and someone had an unpleasant cleaning experience.

As we approached land, they gave us clean clothes to change into. I took the red pants and white shirt they handed me and changed. Delighted, I rubbed my hands all over the new outfit. This brought me new comfort and made me feel pretty. I enjoyed this feeling, especially in my favorite color, red.

CHAPTER 10
At Home in a Foreign Land

The 200-mile trip from Saigon to Mother's home in Ky Do in Lam Doung province took us all day. We stopped to rest and eat, and eat and rest. Street vendors swamped our van, sticking their food through the windows, trying to get us to buy. Fresh fruits, such as pineapple on a stick with a condiment of hot pepper crushed in salt and sugar, and local snacks of homemade fried bananas and rice cakes filled our mouths as we tried the plentiful varieties. Many of the tastes brought back long suppressed memories from my childhood.

Two Viet Kieu dressed as Westerners and an American on the van got the attention of the local people. Michael's blond hair and light skin were quickly and easily spotted by the people, and they gathered around to see him. It was rare at this time that an American would come this far into the countryside.

"American, American," they chanted as they waved and smiled.

They gathered around to see the Americans with money to spend. It was in the "air" that we were Westerners, with a foreign traveler in the van. Jason and I looked healthier and different from the natives. It was if they knew that our compassion would be to their benefit.

"So, how does it feel to be a minority for a change, honey?" I teased.

"I guess I better camouflage myself with some sun while I'm here," Michael said, taking all the attention in fun.

Jason seemed more at ease now on the trip, easily accepting Mother's affection and attentions. He joined in the ribbing.

"Here, you might as well sign an autograph, so you'll know how it feels to be a star." Jason handed Michael a wrapper and teased him with a grin. Seldom had I seen such a grin on Jason's face. I caught a glimpse of another side of my handsome brother. Our mom said he looked just like our father, and we learned the word "dep trai" means handsome. He was going through his own journey quietly, yet as he talked more, his personality began to appear.

Jason became more affectionate and protective toward our sister Le. She switched seats and leaned on his muscular frame and soaked up his brotherly love. A rare side of my brother emerged. I began to see an enormous heart and tenderness in him. I imagined the ghost of our father in Jason's smile. I no longer saw his trademark empty face, the one that showed no signs of feeling. For the first time, my brother seemed to feel at home. Michael soaked in the uncomplicated openness of the simple life while Jason and I found our roots and experienced the security of being home.

For the first time too, I felt comfortable openly expressing affection by holding hands and giving simple hugs. During those moments I thought of Lauren. I hoped my prayers would compensate for the tough decisions I had made during my divorce. The past two years made me realize that I didn't have a family to call when I needed help. I had nowhere to turn to talk about my pain and sadness.

Now, I looked at my own immediate family and felt filled with love for my daughter. I understood that to love her meant giving her stability even if I wasn't the one who could provide it. I knew that people in America might criticize me for my decision to allow my daughter to live with her father instead of with me, but I did so, knowing what was best in the long term for her. I had lived a life of terrible instability, but my mother had sacrificed for me and done what she could just to keep Jason and me alive. I understood a mother's sacrifice, and I felt at peace with my decision to let my daughter live with her father, but that didn't make it any less painful.

Thinking about my child halfway across the world, my eyes began to water. "Mommy has a family to offer you, after all," I wanted to tell her. This was where I needed to come to heal. Vietnam comforted me. The simple Vietnamese family environment and the distance from American society's judgment brought me a sense of acceptance. As an orphan, I often yearned for the simple, basic needs. Now, as a woman, I still had needs to fulfill. I still needed love.

The others in the van drifted off to sleep. I was preoccupied and absorbed in the new adventure. The air grew cooler as we drove higher up into the mountains toward my mother's home. I sat next to the window and felt the fresh, cool country air rushing across my face. The exotic, untouched beauty of this undeveloped country was breathtaking.

Rice paddies with thin, green blades swung in the wind. Banana trees weighed down with fruit dotted the roadside. The local people worked along the roadside. Children in their school clothes held hands as they walked or pedaled the family bicycle. Teen girls in their white *ao dai* looked like angels with their gown tails floating in the wind. They rode to and from school as visions of womanly youth. The white, elegant uniforms signified so much more than their approach to womanhood. The images offered beautiful glimpses of their innocence. The freshness of the open breezes danced with them and teased and captured young men's glimpses.

The innocence and slow pace of the land and its people brought us a sense of harmony and peace. We rediscovered Vietnam for the first time in our adult lives. The picturesque landscape transfixed us, and all three of us were silent in our own thoughts. The sights and smells resurrected my past and created a sense of familiarity. The ghost of my former self, Hai, the barefoot village girl, rose within me. I saw her new yet old path again.

I struggled with my two selves. It seemed like another life when we were here before. I had returned as my current self in this time

His silence was broken. Jason's healing begins at home with mom and sister Le

machine, a time machine that once carried us into another world when we left the giant ship. The giant ship that rescued us in Singapore surfaced in my mind as I remembered our journey toward America.

1975

We waited on an island amid coconut and palm trees, surrounded by tables and benches near the water of Singapore. Finally, a bus took us to another place where we would stay for the evening. The sight of men in uniforms walking around the base comforted us. It was a safe sight seeing soldiers in uniform from our perspective as children. The uniform represented strength, safety and solidness. Uniforms were a welcome sight for me.

Once again, we were on borrowed ground. We accepted it graciously. They lined us up to eat in the mess hall with the American soldiers. There were other people from other places too. A handsome soldier with blond hair and blue eyes came by and handed me an apple. When we left to go to another place, he took me in his arms. Other soldiers carried the other children to a big, square building. I sat on my new friend's lap. The light turned dark, and a moving picture captivated our attention. It was a black and white picture moving on a flat screen. Fascinated, we showed our excitement by jumping up and down. We pointed out our discovery to our friendly soldier giants.

After our excitement, I slowly wound down and fell asleep in my friend's lap. He carried me to another building, and I hung on to him ever so tightly. Even though I was considered an adult at nine, I enjoyed this special attention, this love that would soon leave. He patted me on my back as I rested on his shoulder and neck in my dreamy stage of sleepiness. That special soldier's cologne imprinted a feeling of protectiveness and strength with its scent. I still crave that safety he represented for me after the grueling escape, and men who exemplify that strength still enamor me.

I clung to the apple he gave me, but the next morning I found someone had stolen that apple while I slept.

My affection for my new soldier grew even stronger when he stopped by to say goodbye. He unboxed a case with a beautiful turquoise necklace and earrings to match and gave it to me. The other kids stood around to see. He put the necklace on me, positioned it, and smiled. He said things I did not understand. I knew our quick attachment was special, as if he meant these gifts for someone in his life that was no longer around to enjoy them. He handed me the case that contained the earrings. I carried it with me as we continued our journey.

We lined up to be counted and recounted to make sure no one got lost or was missing. We prepared to depart to another place. Where were we going? Would we ever feel at home?

We moved from one surprise to the next. Overwhelmed and delighted, we boarded a huge ship with wings. Unlike any of the airplanes we saw flying overhead during the war, this one had sleek lines. We all sat in rows in seats that swallowed our size. We could not sit still and looked around the plane. We peeped out the windows to see new perspectives. The start of the flight pulled our stomachs up a bit and the overpowering roar vacuumed our ears closed until it slowly balanced its thrust.

Quietness then took over the air on the plane. I remembered the friend who gave me my necklace and earrings. I wanted to look at my new earrings again. I looked forward to getting my ears pierced in order to wear my new gift.

They were gone! I looked everywhere near me, afraid to leave my buckled seat. I looked around at the others. I suspected one of the jealous girls took my prize. Many of the older girls disapproved that I got more attention than others did. After all, they considered us a part of the older group. Only the baby group deserved special attention, they felt. They scrutinized and criticized my "immaturity." I closed my eyes, put my hands protectively on the necklace with its pretty, blue turquoise stone. I fell asleep to the humming of the aircraft.

After we had been on the plane for eight or nine hours, we landed near some big buildings and joined other giant birds with large, rigid wings. Then we took yet another bus to our unknown destination. I stared out at the roadside and saw an abundance of beautiful tulips with a full array of colors in large areas between the large paved streets. The flowers separated the traffic. We never had seen such beautiful flowers. We drove along the street where they grew systematically all along the middle. The cleanliness and the flow of what seemed to be thousands of cars on the other side of the street introduced us to a new world.

We were in Switzerland. The beds of tulips made Geneva as beautiful as I imagined heaven would be. In awe of the beautiful landscape, the massive glass and concrete buildings, the big cars and the crispness of everything, we thought perhaps we were in heaven.

Soon, we stopped and entered one of the tall, glass buildings to spend the night. My imagination would have never dreamt of this kind of luxury. We got into a lighted box, which took us to the higher level from the ground floor. Each room had its own bed, bathroom and picture box. Fascinated with the moving picture box, we gathered around in one room to watch whatever it would show us. We understood not even one word, but who cared!

While the others watched TV, I snuck back to the lit elevators. I kept riding it up and down, up and down, again and again, just enjoying my own adventure and excitedly pushing every button on the panel. Wow! I thought. This is heaven! I died and went to heaven! I giggled with delight.

We spent two days in Switzerland and then continued on another airplane. With our many trips and destinations, the journey seemed endless and full of surprises and amazements. We did not ask too many questions. We just enjoyed the experience and trusted in God, Mr. Ha and the staff. We lined up and had head counts every time we took another trip.

This flight took us into the United States and New York City. New York and America was the biggest amazement of all. Before we landed, we pointed out the window toward a giant statue of a woman carrying a torch. We entered the place where my American soldier friends lived! The welcoming party greeted us after the landing. Many people cheered and TV crews and photographers took our photos as we walked down the steps. We felt like celebrities. The lights, the cameras, the excitement jumbled our already overloaded minds.

New York was our first sight of America—the land of giant buildings and flying metal birds. We did not stay in New York but changed planes. We flew to Arkansas. We lived in Fort Chaffee, a refugee camp where we met other Vietnamese refugees. We lined up for meals each day, not knowing how long we would be there. Our lives became unpredictable as we learned to adjust and adapt to whatever people gave us. We all helped the staff and took care of the younger children. We also took care of ourselves. We were very self-sufficient and even the youngest ones tended to themselves. For ten days, we waited to hear of our fate. Many families and children waited much longer for sponsors and papers.

From Fort Chaffee, we drove to Houston, Texas, to stay at a "Touch" ranch. The ranch belonged to a church member on the way to our next destination. During the bus trip, we stopped for lunch. We experienced our first American cafeteria. Amazing! We never saw so much food as we lined up in front of the serving lines. Each steam tray had multiple selections. The beautiful colors of the food made me dance with delight as my excitement and hunger built.

They allowed us to pick out what we wanted. I pointed to the prettiest colors until my tray was full. I pushed my tray with excitement and looked forward to fulfilling my lifelong fantasy—feeling full.

I lifted the large tray and tightly balanced it against my stomach. I possessively claimed the tray. I struggled to balance it. Determined to hang onto my new treats, I clasped it to my chest. An older woman took the tray from me! "No, it's mine," I yelled in Vietnamese, while she frantically tried to signal that she was putting it down near the others.

When I realized she was trying to help me, I became quite embarrassed. I sat on my seat and ate happily and heartily. I decided I liked America very much. But we all agreed that the food was bland compared to the spicy food we knew. As we boarded the bus again, I eyed an apple on the counter. A lady in an apron saw my desire to have one and held it out to me. I grabbed it from her as we began to load up.

CHAPTER 11
New Arrivals

 commotion stopped our van, waking me from my reflections and returning me to the present. My stepfather and Doan, our interpreter, signaled us to get out of the van. A sign written in English ahead surprised me. It said, "Restricted Area." We left the van at a restricted area outside our mother's village. A narrow wooden bridge greeted people on foot with their bicycles and motorcycles or loaded down with their farm products. Other vehicles also stopped, and people began to unload their belongings. Everyone took their goods and began on foot over this bridge. As we carried our bags across the damaged bridge, the interpreter explained its condition was due to a "typhoon, come only last week. No good." He shook his head.

We walked part of the way to the village and then entered a small beat-up cab. We loaded it with our luggage and ground our way up the hill. I noticed the sharply defined social status of women here. I could not help it. I naturally showed our American freedom as I swung out of the doorless side of the vehicle. Hanging onto its side, I took pictures of the men walking behind. My mom and sister showed their concern at my apparent bold action. I came back to our country as a tough, independent, adventurous woman. I sensed the differences between my American way and my shy and more reserved sister and mom.

The welcoming party overwhelmed us. Children and neighbors ran toward us. They gawked at us as we headed toward Mother's home. We walked into an entrance, which divided the bushes that outlined and fenced their home. Mom's house was beautiful. It was a concrete structure that looked like a commercial building. A dark, granite pattern enhanced its appearance. I had a preconceived notion of grass-mud huts. It was a surprise to us all. Pleased, we saw she owned one of the better homes in the village. I felt relieved. Perhaps her life had improved from what I remembered during the war. This country was still so poor. The five other children ran out of the house. Jason and I met our extended family at last.

All the neighbors trailed behind us. Her home multiplied with people as we entered her front door. The attention that was focused on us in front of my mother's home took me back to our own welcome in the United States.

1975

In July we arrived by bus with our same red and white outfits the people in Singapore had given us a few months before. The bus drove along a winding road into a flat area far out in the country. We reached an older, white house with a large barn in the back. It appeared peaceful with lots of care ready for us. The camera crew and people gathered around the bus as the orphans from Vietnam approached the ranch. Many people recorded our first step on the soil of our temporary home on that day in July 1975. Slowly, we got off the bus and stared back at the many strangers looking for our reactions.

As I stepped down, I hung onto the door side to reach the bottom step and noticed tables lined up with food and drinks to welcome us on that hot summer day in Houston. A Baptist church sponsored our orphanage in the United States, and the volunteers and members welcomed us.

I noticed an exceptionally tall man standing in the crowd with a woman in front of him. She held his hand and pointed toward me. Our eyes met. He smiled. Then they both waved at me.

The open air with grass and trees thrilled us. The land was so flat, and it seemed to go on forever. Coming from the hilly Vietnamese countryside, this landscape looked like another planet. They showed the girls their sleeping areas in the front house. They filled each of the bedrooms in the ranch with beds, positioning the beds closely to each other to get as many in the house as possible.

They stationed the boys in the back of the house, and they had converted a barn into a dorm hall with more beds. Our new home reminded us of our orphanage in Vietnam with separate facilities for the boys and girls. Volunteers handed clothes to us and helped us become comfortable.

After just a few minutes, we settled in and one of the older girls called me to come outside to see Mr. Ha. I saw the same tall man and his wife, alone with Mr. Ha, waiting to talk to me. We sat on the porch swing on the front porch while they talked over something I did not understand. Then the man and his wife introduced themselves to me and indicated with gestures that they liked me very much. Mr. Ha translated that these people wanted to get to know me better.

"They look to adopt children for their own," Mr. Ha said. Up to this point, I had not thought much about adoption, but each of us in our orphanage longed to have a home.

The man had dark, deep-set eyes set off by strong, high cheekbones and a finely sculpted nose. The mustache framed his smile and made him seem trustworthy. His 6-foot-7-inch frame towered over everyone else. He looked a little out of place. As big as the American soldiers had seemed to me, this man towered over everything. His dark hair with graying sideburns added a distinguished air and framed his strong, masculine face. I later found out he was part American Indian.

The woman handed me a stuffed animal and gave me a timid smile. Her very feminine features, set off by her perfectly styled brunette hair, showed she was a prim and proper lady. She stood 5-foot-3-inches tall. Alongside her husband, she seemed even shorter. This portrait pleased me, and I kept this snapshot in my mind as the image of the perfect American couple.

Mr. Ha introduced them as Jacqueline and Craig Willis. Mr. Willis took me in his lap while they continued to talk to Mr. Ha. Though I was older, my physical stature was comparable to an American six year old, and I sat in his lap, quite comfortably.

I only understood Mr. Ha when I heard my brother Sang's name mentioned. For the rest of the day, I was their chosen one. We spent the day playing and taking photos with both of my new friends. Later, they located Sang and told him to join us. After they left, Mr. Ha told us that Mr. and Mrs. Willis were interested in adopting us. They came back the next week and spent more time with us.

So soon, I thought. Again, I felt so special. I heard the other girls close by. They started teasing me. "Hai has a mommy and daddy," they called out in Vietnamese. They giggled as they stood around to listen in on the conversation. By this time, Mr. Ha had explained to us, "You are very lucky to have a family who wants to be your parents. They don't have any children of their own and want you two to live with them."

It was as if fate had already planned my life in America. Destiny seemed in control and in place from the day I was born. By this time, the whole orphanage referred to Mr. and Mrs. Willis as our new parents.

During our days at the ranch, we practiced and learned English, said prayers and reveled in the freedom to play out in the field. For the first time in our lives, we played without the worry of the angry thunders finding us. This wonderful journey continued opening new delights to my young eyes and mind. We knew this home was temporary. They planned to move us to a more permanent children's home in Dallas, but in the meantime we played, learned and waited for word from the orphanage in Dallas.

The Willises came to visit us as they promised, often. They brought gifts such as skin lotion and toys. Somebody called out as they approached, "Your mom and dad are here." How strange and wonderful it was to hear those words. Mrs. Willis opened the bottle of a large body cream jar, put it on her hands, and then put it all over my arms and legs. She shook her head and let me know my skin was dry and cracking.

The other girls giggled and teased me. My new mom pampered me. Mr. Willis spent a lot of time with Sang and talked to Mr. Ha outside in the yard. I liked my new woman friend. She babied me and did nice things for me. I attached myself to her side as my new mom. Mr. Willis frightened me because of his massive size. This giant scared me, and I avoided him.

After a few weeks of freedom and attention on the ranch, they transferred our orphanage to Dallas. They accepted us as part of the Buckner Children's Home. A camera crew and newspaper followed us to our final destination. Again, people greeted us at our new home. Our whole group stayed in one of the many colonial buildings in this home called "Pires" dormitory at the Buckner.

My new mommy and daddy came to visit me every weekend, even in Dallas. Soon, they said, we would go home with them. They constantly assured us of their interest through their letters and promised we would be a family soon.

On those weekends, we did American family things. We visited the Six Flags amusement park, took family pictures, and ate in fast food restaurants. We discovered our favorite dish, spicy chicken at Popeye's. Sang and I often asked politely for "spider chicken," in our mistaken English. They always laughed and granted our request.

"Spider chicken" was our first American food that had a familiar taste of Vietnamese spiciness. They encouraged us to drink milk but it was foreign to our systems. Milk upset our stomachs, and they did not understand why we so often went to the restroom. Soon they realized that our systems were lactose intolerant. Our bodies needed different amino acids to digest dairy products.

We stayed the weekend with our new parents whenever they would drive to Dallas from their Houston home. Our visits took place in hotels as we learned about each other. They gave us new clothes and shoes. We watched TV in our hotel room as a family. During this time, I slept with Mrs. Willis while Sang slept with Mr. Willis in the double beds in our temporary hotel homes.

The gifts and attention won our affection. The desire to have a family was again awakened in us. Though we were the only children allowed to leave the orphanage with our new mommy and daddy, Mr. Ha began to find families for all the children here in America.

Between weekends, we all studied our sheet of simple words such as thank you, you are welcome, good morning and so on. I did not understand these words but memorized them by heart. Sang and I came to Mr. Ha's office to write letters to our new mommy and daddy. We waited to get the adoption paperwork completed. Then we could go home with them.

We adjusted to a new lifestyle at the orphanage. The Vietnamese children ate in the mess hall with the homeless American children but they separated us at one long table. We carried on our usual routines of learning English, the most important chore in this new land. We learned new games with other children, and the boys played soccer in the field with the American children.

We were all restless, not knowing what our futures would be in this strange place. Others felt Sang and I were the luckiest, the first adopted. My destiny was already determined. We knew that Mr. and Mrs. Willis wanted to keep us. So we stayed busy and had our bags ready to go at anytime to our next destination.

Our refuge at Buckner Children's Home in Dallas, Texas, 1975

CHAPTER 12
New Names, New Lives

My mother with her youth and beauty started her life again in her 30s. She remarried in 1972. We had been in the orphanage when she started her second family with her new husband, Nguyen Doc. We greeted our half-brothers and half-sisters, and we learned their names and ages. Tri, the oldest boy, 19, came home from the army for our visit. Tan was her second son. He greeted us at the airport and was 16. Her daughters were Ngoc Tu, 14, and Binh, 12. Her youngest son, Vinh, 10, weeded his way through the crowd so we could see him. The children were excited to be around us. The neighborhood kids swamped us, curious about our Western appearances.

Michael found Jason and me among the crowd.

"Now I know how you guys felt when you stepped off that bus in America," he laughed. The children climbed on him and gestured about his big size. The interpreter translated everyone's questions for us.

"Tell them that I am just 5-foot-10, an average height and size, compared to bigger Americans in the U.S." He held his hand over his head to signal his message as well. The neighbors asked us

*On the other side of the world,
my family awaits our return*

questions directly, and the translator had to tell them, "We don't speak Vietnamese."

"You guys blend in pretty well for a change," Michael joked with Jason and me.

"Yeah, but we don't understand a thing they're saying," Jason answered.

Our translator explained to them that we forgot our native language. With that explanation, we all could feel the elders signal their disappointment in us. Slowly, the newness from the three visitors in this small village began to die down as neighbors drifted back to their routines.

We set our packages down, and they took us to the back of the house. There, they served us hot tea. We gathered in the front room and all sat down around the coffee table. The front double door of my mother's home swung open widely to make room for the extra adults and neighborhood children still gathered around us. We sensed a conversation setting in, and this culture's social patterns during meal times and tea times became apparent.

Doan translated anything he wanted to his bigger audience, and he showed his delight at being the most important guy in the village. He demonstrated his ability to speak broken English to us while he gained credibility with those who didn't know the language. He answered many questions to our audience that he already knew from our previous conversations. Still, he wanted us to play the role of exchanging the words. Then he appeared to his audience that he fulfilled his role as an interpreter. The crowd slowly grew tired of the three-way conversations and withdrew. Finally we had breathing room.

I sat there observing my new large family, and thought how strange and wonderful it was to be called by our Vietnamese names. I became Hai again while Jason again became Sang. We'd come full circle from where we started in America. Our names were repeated over and over again like a mantra. The musical tones of our names became sacred chants in our minds. Our names were the only words we heard and understood among all the unfamiliar words. Our names anchored us in our new surroundings. Hearing our names put us in a trance. How often have you heard, "What's in a name, anyway?" Well, it was everything to us as our names shifted us through time and experiences. We reverted to our roots unconsciously.

I remembered the last time the Willises called me "Hai" before they replaced it with my American name. We had said goodbye to Mr. Ha, the staff and the other children. They watched us from windows as we prepared to leave. Mr. Ha seemed happy to see his children find homes, and yet we sensed his uneasiness that everything had happened so quickly.

"Too American," he would tell me later as an adult in his California home during my visit. "But it was for the good that you children have homes as quickly as possible in this new country."

1975 - 1976

Sang and Hai, they told us, were our old names. In America, the Willises told us, our names were now Jason and Christi. During the drive back to Houston to live in their house, they changed our lives. They made it a game in the car. We practiced pronouncing our new names correctly and soon we had memorized them. We said them incessantly on our journey to a new life. The drive to Houston with our new family on that day became another transformative time capsule. The drive put us to sleep easily in the back seats. The bright sun beamed through the windows and provided the heat from the cold winter. It created an incubator, a cocoon for these caterpillars' transformations.

Jason and I sat up in awe as we pulled into the driveway. We felt disconnected. We became new with this new suburban environment. The house, like other homes on the street, had shallow roofing and a well manicured yard. Our home and yard repeated the pattern of the rest of the homes and landscapes in the subdivision.

We entered the house together with our new parents leading. Our grandparents followed behind. Finally, we were under the same roof as brother and sister. We turned and looked at each other, meeting each other for the first time in this new life. The home had appeared small from the outside but inside was so spacious with many rooms. They pointed out many things and described each room with its own name in English as we repeated them. The clean, well-placed items made the house solid and orderly. Our tour ended in the family room as we shyly sat down on the large sofa. Suddenly, three dogs greeted us. They ran in when Mr. Willis opened the sliding glass door from the patio. The numbers and sizes of them startled us. The herd, including a miniature poodle, greeted us unconditionally into their home with liquid kisses. We dodged their wetness and affectionate puppy love as best we could. The concept of having animals in the house was foreign to us. The dogs were as big as we were.

We were in a world of our own. We absorbed as much as we could, not understanding a word they said. They scripted our new world, and taught us our lines. We needed no one else, they told us. Everything we missed in our refugee lives, they supplied. We would live in a big house with our perfect family with plenty of food and television. Mrs. Willis took our hands and led us into another part of the house. We entered the first bedroom. She carried my only belongings, the clothes that they bought for me during the orphanage time. She placed my bag in this room to indicate it was mine. I had my very own room with a large queen-sized bed! I pounced excitedly but then pulled back, reserved in my awe. She opened the drawers and showed me my new clothes and a stack of notebooks, pencils and supplies for school. I hoped school was optional in America. I wanted to go directly to movies like Shirley Temple.

Wow, I thought and smiled at them. I repeated the only word I understood—"thank you" —as I threw my arms around her waist. They were as delighted as I was with my new life. Mr. Willis stayed in the background for support but knew I feared him. He gave me friendly winks and smiles, stayed back, tried not to scare me, yet he let me know he made these things possible.

Next, we went past the bathroom in the hall to enter Jason's bedroom. He bounced on his bed too, and they showed him his new supplies and clothes. We all went to the bathroom to see everything, how to turn on hot water, cold water and how to flush the toilet.

The first evening we ate with our handsome new family in their formal dining room with plenty of food for six people, including our new grandparents. We could feed our orphanage with the amount of food on the table, and she brought more as we celebrated our first night as a family. Our meal reflected the Willises' lifestyle and formality. The ritual of this celebration of our first evening set the stage for future patterns in my life. It was quite lovely. The special attention to detail matched my Vietnamese sensibility and influenced my lifestyle preferences, which I practice to this day.

Mrs. Willis's taste left an impression on me. My enjoyment of dining begins with a greater appreciation for the ambiance than for the taste of the food. My experience of that night opened me to a side that I had never known before. To complete the dining experience, we learned a new phrase that became our expected phrase to leave from our meals: "May I be excused, please?"

Jason and I ran out through the kitchen to watch the TV that was now readily available to us. We no longer waited for special treats, and we could enjoy TV entertainment all the time. I also noticed there was free food in a basket on the counter when I passed by the kitchen available for us to eat anytime.

As we got ready for bed, Mrs. Willis turned on the water in the tub for both of us. They treated us like babies and gave us baths together. No one ever had given us this closeness as brother and sister. Being in the same tub with each other embarrassed us. We were so much smaller in size for our age than our maturity level and experiences. Our new American family projected their sheltered lives onto us. They decided for us how a brother and sister should be. This was the way to do it, and so we did it. How strange these Americans are, we thought to ourselves. We appeased them because of what they gave us, and we worked diligently to become part of their American culture.

We felt fortunate, and our new family was ideal. We could forget the horrible days in Vietnam. We could forget our past, they hinted, we were no longer abandoned. They said we were lucky, saved by their goodness. We became the perfect American children with them and behaved our best. Polite and quiet, we waited, and they told us what to do and what to wear. They dedicated their days and nights to us and focused on us as we adjusted to our new environment and responsibilities. They taught us to read and write our new names, Christi and Jason. Constantly busy doing paperwork for our new identities, we created new records for our new adopted family and country. We felt born again with new identities, rules, expectations and cultural traditions.

The bond of sister and brother through the years

However, getting used to our new way of life challenged us. Simple things like riding in the car often made us sick, and we frequently fell asleep. We ate strange food, unappetizing to our spicy taste buds. We drank milk that upset our stomachs. They soon discovered food that was more suited to us. We ate more spicy food than our adult parents did, but we also adjusted to the more bland foods that were normal and available.

They taught us how to hold our forks and knives correctly and how to sit correctly at the dinner table with our napkins and our left hands on our lap. They taught us to cut smaller portions at a time during our meal, and we learned how to leave the table gracefully.

We became two projects to perfect, two lives to mold and recreate. We represented the perfect children with the perfect family. They seemed well intended as they molded and sculpted our lives into new images. Exceptionally small in size and height compared to other children in the neighborhood, our American parents questioned our ages. No papers proved our age. The orphanage thought us 12 and 14 years of age. For a 12-year-old, I weighed only 48 pounds and stood about 50 inches tall. Jason was my same size at 14. The lack of vitamins and food had given us such small frames.

One day we visited a place with many chairs against the walls and a variety of magazines stacked on the coffee tables and in a large rack in one corner. A woman in white sitting behind a glass window greeted our new mom. We were at our first doctor's appointment in America. We were not sick, nor did we understand the intention of our visit. Jason and I sat there, quietly, mindful of our new authority figures. We shyly obeyed Mrs. Willis's rules and requests until they called our names. They gave us a very through examination, from our tops to our bottoms, from bone marrow, to our skeleton x-rays, which were lit up on the board in the doctor's office.

Afterwards we sat slumped in our chairs, tired from the waiting and the many tests we had gone through. My new parents conversed with the doctor, with speech we did not understand. Jason and I often still spoke in Vietnamese, whenever he would talk, despite Mrs. Willis's efforts to make us forget our language.

Jason never really changed much from the orphanage. He lived in his silence for too long to let anyone know who he was. The Willises explained to us that everyone thought Jason was retarded because of his silence. They also came to believe it because of his lack of responsiveness. When they caught us speaking Vietnamese, they reprimanded us and told us to only speak English. Then we would improve with our new language better and faster. We had much work to do in order to catch up to other children our age. The language issue became another excuse for Jason not to talk at all. Mr. Willis tried to improve Jason's limited world when he bought plane models for him to occupy his time in silence. They let him alone without too much fuss, and he disappeared with his new venture. Jason returned from his room and gave Mr. Willis the completed plane model. They were amazed that he could put the models together so quickly without knowing how to read instructions. Mr. Willis bought Jason bigger and more complicated models, yet he continued to stay in his silent world. They never questioned his ability or intelligence again.

The doctors "scientifically proved" our ages to our new family. They declared Jason to be 12 and me, 9 years old. They gave me my first birthday celebration soon after that on April 18. It was the same month and date from Mr. Ha's report. My first birthday celebration ever was grand. They made a beautiful cake especially for me with "Happy 10th Birthday, Christi" on it.

My party continued with five other schoolgirls who slept over night. Mr. Willis entertained. He filled the party with laughter and giggles as he sat with us at the picnic table outside, making faces and playing games. He was the perfect daddy, I thought. He made my friends laugh and brought happiness with his smiles. My friends liked my new daddy greatly and did not fear him as I did. Soon I began to befriend this giant, my daddy.

We quickly created rituals. I often jumped on his lap to watch TV, and he clipped off my toenails. That always made Jason and me laugh. We played silly games with him and watched clever tricks he taught to the dogs. He found his niche in our lives while Mrs. Willis continued to orchestrate our programs to become perfect American children. He became our entertainment, a fun outlet as we carried out our roles. In this house, everything was to be like that. Each one of us played our parts perfectly, including the dogs.

The first year was like Christmas every day. Neighbors came to visit. We attended "big baby" showers where they gave us clothes, shoes, toys and school supplies and plenty of English learning books. The Willises sent out announcements with hearts and our names and told hundreds that we now were a family. The *Houston Post* newspaper came to the house, interviewed my family, and took pictures of this Houston family who had adopted the poor Vietnamese children from the orphanage. Updates from the media and churches encouraged Mrs. Willis's perfect plan for our development.

For our first Houston Christmas, we woke with a toy store under the Christmas tree! Santa brought all the other things we did not have at the end of the year. Two beautiful bicycles tied in red ribbons captivated our imaginations, and we continued to be entranced with the many boxes of gifts from relatives and family members we had not met.

Our house became our first school with Mrs. Willis teaching us. That gave us time to adjust to our new culture. No matter how many comforts and gifts they gave us, I could not release my conditioned fear.

One day Mrs. Willis helped me put away my clothes as part of my lesson in tidiness. She opened several drawers and discovered that I had been hiding food in my drawers, mostly fruit and dried food easily overlooked from the kitchen. At the end of each day, I saved a piece of fruit and stashed it in various hiding places in my room. Whenever I felt hungry at night, I climbed out of my massive bed, felt my way in the dark and ate. It reminded me of my warehouse crimes in the orphanage. I crawled back into my bed and sat there eating my apple happily in the dark. This brought childlike comfort, to not be hungry anymore. It was then that I slept the deepest and relaxed for the night. I feared her discovery, but she just hugged me, and we sat on the bed as she explained. "Christi, you will never have to hide your food again, understand?"

Then she took my hand and we walked toward the den through the kitchen. I reluctantly followed, thinking she was going to punish me for stealing. We stopped in front of the refrigerator. She called Jason into the kitchen and opened the refrigerator door. She explained, "There will always be enough food for you and Jason. You are not in Vietnam anymore." She gently smiled at me, which signaled my safety.

"Okay," I said and ran to watch TV with Jason as I grabbed another piece of fruit from the kitchen counter.

We spent our days running errands, and Mrs. Willis's English lessons at home prepared us so we could register in a public elementary school in Houston. Jason and I enrolled at the same grade level.

Our introduction into the American school system started out in the fourth grade. Mrs. Mallory was my first and favorite teacher. As I sat in her class feeling isolated, not comprehending my assignments, she made fitting in more bearable with her soft-spoken gentle understanding. Her well-placed, snowy white hair, perfectly layered on top of her head, and her round features made her appear wise and gentle in my eyes.

She gave each student a goldfish in a bag. I took it home, not understanding why, and concluded that we must raise it for food. When I handed it to Mr. Willis, he showed excitement for a project we could do together. Jason and I began to watch him as he took over this area of our learning with more authority. He took us to the store and bought everything necessary, like tanks and trappings, for our pets. We discovered that pets were very important in this society, and pets were very well treated.

The fish lived in Jason's room, as Mrs. Willis thought it better for a boy to have a goldfish as a pet. I negotiated daily visiting rights since I could not have it in my room. Soon, the fish died from natural causes, and Mr. Willis flushed it down the toilet. I accused the boys of murdering the fish and trying to flush the evidence. While everyone laughed about it and saw it as a cute reaction, I only felt one more thing that I loved had been taken away by death.

Our days were filled with learning, practicing and training in English. School became our emphasis from early in the morning to homework at 3 p.m. until dinner at 6 every day. Mrs. Willis cleaned the kitchen table after school so we could spread out our school assignments. We all practiced and corrected until Daddy came home from work.

Math proved easy for us, and English was the most frustrating subject. Many times we studied after dinner until bedtime. My memories of the kitchen table and my tidy room are imprinted in my mind. Those places were where I studied so hard and adjusted to become a part of my new fair-skinned friends.

It was not easy for me to live in a silent world like Jason's. To talk and socialize with my friends, teachers or anyone else was like eating and breathing. It was part of my life. It was a difficult time for me to not be able to converse freely, to be cut off from knowing what was going on around me. My language barrier kept me behind. I wanted to flush away my old language like the goldfish and learn the American one. Riding in the car, I saw the billboards with big words and new words I did not understand. I would point and ask, "How do you say that?"

My greatest vice was a talent for memorizing my vocabulary assignments by heart and in order, yet not necessarily understanding the words. My thirst to learn drove the family crazy with my non-stop questions and "diarrhea of the mouth," as Mr. Willis called it.

My learning could not catch up with my yearning to know, and my frustrations started to build up. "Who said learning English would be easy?" a voice from within teased. I had at least 12 years of learning to catch up on! I did not like being behind and clueless. I wanted to be good at something; however, I was not good at anything. At least in Vietnam, I could sing and dance. Each year, the school in Vietnam honored the smart students. They graded each class by the number of students in the class. If the class had 30 students, they graded us, from one to 30, placing a number next to our name. Hai was always number 30, bottom of the class. It seemed that way with Christi, too.

As usual, my homework started right after school at the kitchen table. It had an opaque round glass top set on a mustard wrought iron base with four wrought iron chairs to match. It was my other chalkboard. After going through great pains to understand the meaning of my homework one afternoon, Mrs. Willis and I became enemies as her short temper crossed my hard-headedness. Her fist landed on the glass top, shattering the whole glass top to pieces. Broken glass scattered around the floor and on my lap.

Determined not to be beaten by this, I slowly picked up a large broken piece of glass on my lap and raised it in the air in the middle of the now-empty table and let it fall onto the floor as I walked off to my room and slammed the door. It was the day my frustration toward my new family and my strong will surfaced.

CHAPTER 13
Perfect American Girl

*H*e all went toward the back of the house to the dinner table. A blackboard against the wall of the room with "Happy Reunion Family" greeted us. Of course, all the others understood that the structure of the Vietnamese language reversed all words, so Doan said, "Family Reunion Happy" with his translation. During our many questions and answers, we desperately searched for words in the children's dictionary, and we overcame the language barrier with sign language as well. I excused myself to go get the gifts we brought for the children and returned with a Vietnamese-English Dictionary.

I pointed toward the children to indicate: "You all learn English, okay?" Le accepted the dictionary and looked up more words to communicate to us. With a big smile, she said, "Cam On, 'thank you' in Vietnamese." Her eagerness to learn more words reminded me of my own eagerness to learn and to adopt a new language. I had absorbed my new surroundings and culture around an American dinner table. With her actions and mannerisms, Le mirrored what my life could have been as my mother's daughter. While Le helped Mom set the food on the table, I saw myself learning my daughter routines with my American mother as I struggled to become an American.

1977- 1978

I searched to find my special niche, which was no longer my singing and dancing. To be special, I was going to be the Perfect American Girl with slanted eyes. Remembering my days of always being number 30, I always worked a little harder to make my As and Bs. I had so much to learn in order to catch up with my peers. I could not read a one-year-old's bedtime story, let alone fit in with the crowd.

I learned to help in the kitchen and do my chores, walked the dogs, folded clothes and set the dinner table correctly every night. I took lessons in etiquette. I practiced walking with my feet pointed straight instead of pointing to the sides the way Asians often do. My grandmother or mother always walked behind me, constantly telling me to point my toes. They allowed no gum because chewing gum was unladylike. They picked out perfect clothes for me to wear, only the best dresses for their little girl. I learned to walk and sit with good posture and greeted guests with the good manners taught to me by my family. One secret part of my Vietnamese culture I kept—holding hands. Holding hands, such a natural part of Vietnamese culture, they accepted because they thought it only showed affection toward the family.

Our transformation into a new culture, America, 1977

We became an American family. While Jason withdrew into his silence, I became a perfect American young woman to all my teachers and to all my family's neighbors and friends. The family's pride and joy, I showed my friendliness and happy ways with a smile always on my face. Jason became lost in my shadow. After two years, our family's lifestyle only improved when we moved to an even larger home in a new development. While Mommy raised the children, Daddy started a business in homebuilding and land developing. We moved to one of his subdivisions and lived on the biggest corner lot. He built the majority of the homes in the subdivision including the clubhouse and recreation area. He was the big man in our new society.

Everyone knew Daddy for his "life of the party" charisma. He was always a funny man and lively to be around. His tall, lanky build communicated the perfect image of a tall, dark and handsome Texan. Many mistook him as the "McCloud" character on TV shows. Everyone admired and liked him. During college, he was a young band director, and his band members idolized him. A talented writer of music, he had a passion for the trumpet. I heard many stories from him about taking the hopeless high school bands to being "winner bands" in the state and national competitions.

Of course, football was also part of the macho image that goes with being an American daddy. He loved to watch football games on television and told us of the times he played in the band. To help the "hopeless" become the "hopeful" in the school system was not financially rewarding, so he learned another trade after school hours, visiting construction sites. He bought a fixer-upper home to start his new career. He only started his new career three years before he began his new family. He designed houses for people with an understanding of their wants and needs. He understood aesthetics and human nature.

Mr. Willis, still young at 32, and his wife, at 29, adopted two tiny yet grown children to make a happy family to overshadow a slowly declining nine-year marriage. They told us that they had tried to have a baby all these years but could not have one. They originally filed for adoption of an infant through various institutions but that didn't work. One night Mr. Willis read an article in the newspaper about the need for volunteers to help at an orphanage for Vietnamese refugees.

So they came and "fell in love" with my smile as I walked out of the bus, as they often told of our family beginning. The rest was history, my family story.

"It was meant to be," they said, as I thanked them repeatedly for adopting us. Jason and I lived with the constant reminder that all this was done for us and that we were to repay them by becoming their perfect children. They carefully wrote the script, and we were to follow it no matter what.

Mr. Willis worked hard to support the household. Every day he came home in his dirty jeans and white shirt after supervising at the construction sites. He picked up his "joy," and I sat on his lap during his time to wind down with a cold beer. I became his "little angel" and often greeted him at the back door whenever he got home from work. He quickly made me know I was special, and because of him, I was happy and safe.

We had everything, including a beautiful two-story custom built home that gave Jason and me a private playroom with our own kitchen located upstairs near our large bedrooms. From our railing, we looked out over a large two-story den, filled with dark woodwork molding that reached up to a tall two-story cathedral ceiling.

My bedroom, designed especially for me, had a private sun deck with its only entry through my sliding glass door. A wrought iron circular stair going down to the patio connected with the master suite and den. Daddy fed my greatest need to be special with many special treatments. He convinced me that he understood me and did special things for me that caused Mrs. Willis to become irritated.

We entered junior high school at the same time we moved to our new home. We caught the bus every day at the corner by our house. Our ideal set-up gave us everything that we ever wanted. Jason and I became convinced that every American family lived like this. With a larger home, our list of chores around the house became longer. They were our contributions to life in this fine house, and we felt fortunate. Mrs. Willis became complacent with her four dogs, her naps and hair rollers. She sat around with an iced tea in her hand, and her temper easily ignited. Mr. Willis came home later and later from work and then only to sit in his library watching TV and drinking his beers. Our absorption into their world was complete, and the excitement and uniqueness of being there had long gone. They created their own perfect place through us, and now they returned to their old boredom.

"Keeping up with the Joneses" created more luxury, but also more frustrations and fights. Our three-car garage was filled with Cadillacs and, depending on what day it was, Mrs. Willis might not like her new car and exchange it for another one. It seemed as easy as exchanging a sweater.

My world gained more power as other children from the subdivision befriended us early despite our differences in appearance. I enjoyed having acquaintances and friends from the same subdivision going to the same school. As part of their image of the perfect parents, Mr. and Mrs. Willis became active in our school and that helped us adjust to the new system much quicker. I was involved in choir, and my parents attended the programs. They encouraged me to run for class office and gave us all the support we needed. We were still the perfect family with our perfect image.

Mrs. Willis continued to perfect our manners and appearance with her strict rules. Obediently, we followed them. Mrs. Willis permitted no unladylike behavior. Either Grandmother or she would still walk behind me to correct my walk, making sure I pointed my toes and kept my heels straight. They even checked my purse for banned gum. While jeans and denim were popular with my classmates, they were not part of my wardrobe. Mrs. Willis only permitted dresses and, on occasion, dressy pants. Her strict rules often clashed with my own desire to wear other styles and sometimes thwarted connection with my peers.

Mr. Willis continued to be my ally and often helped me balance out our differences. Jason and I often hung around him for his leniency and unstructured lifestyle. During one particular trip to the mall, I pulled Mr. Willis's hand to get his attention and pointed toward the store's mannequin. I pointed toward a pretty, colorful floral sundress with spaghetti straps and smiled.

"Daddy, can I have that pretty dress, please, please!" I pleaded. "I don't look like other girls with the clothes Mommy makes me wear." I made a face to let him know my dislike of Mommy's taste in clothing for me. He understood and agreed as he smiled at me and back to the dress. Mr. Willis bought that dress for me. I proudly held on to the shopping bag that contained the prettiest, and now my favorite, dress in my wardrobe. But Mrs. Willis forbade me to wear the dress after she saw it and stated, "It's too old for you."

My world became larger in scope while dealing with my own growing pains. There was a greater mix of students from all levels of income and ethnic backgrounds. I became more aware of differences. Mostly, I was at home with the fair-skinned students, and not with the Blacks or other Asians. For these past four years, I had only been surrounded by my parents' kind, and I did not understand anything else. I saw other Asians or Blacks but never befriended them because I felt different from them.

One day at school, I waited in line for lunch. Surrounded by my fair-haired friends as usual, I accidentally bumped a person in front of the line. A black student in front of me turned around and said, " Watch yourself, fucking chink, VC!" He stretched his eyes and face to mimic mine. Vaguely, I knew the word was low-class slang for Asian, and he had insulted me directly because of my looks.

My friends around me groaned and watched for my reaction. I fumed inside as my hot temper rushed to my head. My blood boiled and made my face hot. I desperately tried to think of something to get even as my friends waited for my response. The only thing I remembered came from different conversations I'd heard from Mr. Willis and on job sites in adult conversations.

I hissed back, "You damned nigger!" I hoped to release my hurt. I did not feel any better, but I pleased the crowd backing me up. I felt so hurt inside. My world from that point had awakened to bigotry, discrimination and racial differences. This confrontation taught me about diversity. I lost my appetite. No matter what I thought or how I felt, I was different from all my friends. It hit home that I looked and stood apart from what I knew.

"It does not matter how I see myself and how hard I try to fit in among my friends, I will always be categorized as the Asian, a foreigner with the face of an enemy. Someone smart in math, boring, a nerd and always a follower because they work all the time and never lead a life," I said to myself.

The rest of my day was filled with hurt and frustration. This incident crushed my sense of belonging in the "middle-class American blond-haired, blue-eyed race." I was different no matter what. I needed to learn to accept it. My middle-class friends would never say such things; however, I wondered if they believed it.

I hurried late to my last class. The hall was empty, and I turned the corner to reach my class. The same boy, hiding around the corner, stuck out his foot and tripped me. I fell hard on the concrete floor and skinned my knees and arms. My books flew in every direction. Then he ran away. I picked up my books and fought my tears, not from the pain of the fall. My pain was the pain of a sinking identity that I might never regain.

I picked up my books to go to the office to get bandages and reported the incident. Soon after, Mr. and Mrs. Willis came to the school, picked me up, and talked to the principal. I never saw the boy again and never faced another problem with any of the black students.

I became very visible in my junior high school after that incident. I began to excel in every class except math. I always sat in the front of the classroom. I ran for class offices and won as the eighth-grade secretary. My position required me to make announcements in the morning to the school with the other officers. Terrified to speak because of my accent, I feared they might not understand me or might set me apart as a foreigner.

Reading the lunch menu over the public address system, as part of my normal announcements, took every ounce of courage I could muster. I forced myself to do it every time I had the chance. My hands shook every time. I could now call English my language despite the rough spots. Less and less did I think I needed the skills of my former life.

Several months later, my classmates voted me "student of the month." That award placed my photo in the trophy cases. I continued my mission to gain my own identity as the Perfect American Girl. I won regional choir soprano solo singing competitions for the school. I practiced to pronounce my words more clearly to lose my accent.

Every day after school, I locked myself in my room in front of the mirror. I sat in front of my dresser, exaggerated my every word to train my lips and mouth to pronounce each word clearly and exactly. I wanted to sound like my American friends; I wanted to lose my accent and everything that might make me feel different. I even begged my American parents, "I want my slanted eyes operated on to look like you and my friends here."

Mrs. Willis responded, "Honey, I love your eyes, they make you beautiful. Don't be silly." She didn't take me seriously.

"I hate them. They laugh at me!" I screamed. "How much does it cost anyway?" I continued to campaign for this operation.

"Too expensive," Mr. Willis chimed in.

"I can afford it when I get older. I can save the money now. Won't you help me, Daddy?" I pleaded, turning on the charm to get my way, but even he would not relent.

The more I worked hard toward my goals, the more I felt isolated from my friends who could not understand me. I did not have any time for life anymore. I became always cordial to everyone yet always distant. My teachers were my only friends.

Finally, we said goodbye to our junior high school years and looked forward to our high school years. At our last award night for all the eighth graders, my school shocked me. They honored me with the top award. They pinned a metal from The Daughters of the American Revolution on my chest. As I walked to the stage, I said to myself "I am not number 30 anymore."

CHAPTER 14
Death of a Family

My mother cooked a feast that first night. We came in the square room off the open space from the kitchen. The children carried the food and placed it on the table. Michael and I sat together while Jason sat on the other side with our newly found stepbrothers. The room had double window shutters which we propped open. The evening air refreshed us as we looked up the mountain in Ky Do. Continuously, new faces popped in and joined around our reunion.

All three of us heartily ate the wonderful and tasty food and forgot our lack of appetite at the Saigon restaurant. The conversation built to cheerful laughs, between our sign language and Doan's mixed-up explanations. We listened carefully as Mom told him different stories about Jason and me when we were young. Doan's focus always aimed at talking to Michael in his broken English.

The children laughed before I could get the translation from our expensive but distracted translator. We sat and anticipated the lengthy, funny story. The children laughed as Doan explained the gist of the story.

He explained how when we were children we would... He

searched for the words to translate. We felt his frustration. In our own frustration, we had gathered in the beginning that Doan tended to sum things up in his translation. If it was good, he said "A-number one" or bad, he gestured, thumbs down and said, "No good... number 10."

After this story, he finally added. "You know... all fucked up!"

"What!" I screamed out while Michael and Jason laughed loudly.

"Where did you learn that word, Doan?" I asked, surprised to hear it here. We all laughed, and the family could only guess that we got the point of their story after all. Another story was saved by the unexpected outburst of our translator.

"I learned English from GI...." he responded. "I speak English good, yes?" He looked toward Michael for his approval but mostly to save face.

"Yes, Doan, actually that's one of the most effective words when no other words can do the job," Michael answered, patting Doan's back as he glanced our way. Jason and I nodded in agreement with Michael. Doan gave us the biggest grin and began to speak Vietnamese to my family again. Still today, I have no idea what the story was about.

We cast a spell over the village that night with our reunion of laughter and happiness around the family table, which was full of food and desserts.

The children helped courteously, and all honored their parents. Their parents quietly wielded their authority as everyone pitched in to clear the food. Soon afterward, the children brought in hot tea for all the adults.

We became one around that table. The gathering brought a warm closeness of a happy family again. We all laughed and bellowed out our enjoyment as we accepted Doan's limited English. I thought of the simplicity of this wonderful sharing. In my past, I had lacked this kind of sharing and yearned for real family. I compared this family to my American family, and I envied their uncomplicated lifestyle.

We slowly settled down for the night. I wanted to capture and hold that moment for a lifetime. As I rested my head on my pillow, my thoughts drifted back to the wounds of my heart.

1978 - 1979

Darkness shrouded our big home. The battles in my American family worsened every day. Jason talked a little more as a necessity, yet never enough for me to understand his trials or his pain. When anything bothered him, especially when Mrs. Willis yelled at him, he quietly went upstairs, closed the door and watched TV. Television became his form of escape, the way he numbed out the world.

My brother and I experienced the growing pains of being different and discriminated against by our own peers. Too often our friends, influenced by their parents, saw in our young faces an enemy from the unpopular Vietnam War. Jason held the pain of this injustice within his quiet, small frame. He was a man, camouflaged as a shy little boy. His anger would surface up, and he would lash out at his oppressors whenever they picked on him.

Riding on the school bus, Jason always sat quietly in the back. He stared out the window. As always, I sat in the front and talked to friends all the way to school and back home.

Suddenly, a commotion started in the back of the bus, and we turned to look. Shocked, I saw Jason and a boy with long blond hair locked to each other and sending fierce punches back and forth. I was terrified for my brother. The boy was twice his size and was known as the "bad hippie dude." He lived outside our subdivision, and we passed by his home every day as part of the bus route.

Never before had I seen such anger from this small, silent stranger who I called my brother. His face was red from his heated blood. His fists gave no mercy to his attacker. The bus stopped in a panic when the bus driver recognized that this was not just another kid fight. He slammed on the brakes, throwing them both on the floor of the bus. I gripped my seat in tears and yelled, "Stop it! Stop it!" as the bus driver ran back to the commotion.

I knelt on the bus seat and kept an eye on my brother. The crowd swarmed toward the back and forced me to stand on my seat at the front of the bus. My heart pounded heavy and loud in my throat as the hitting kept going. The yelling and the encouragement from the other kids built the intensity of the fight. My heart and mind were frantic. I plugged my ears to block out the cheering. Helplessly, I saw my brother in the midst of his own war. Time stopped.

The bus driver separated them with the help of the other boys. My brother's face showed no fear. His stone harsh look masked the anger and hatred he felt toward his enemy. The hippie boy crawled back to his seat, breathing hard with a pale red face. His face showed defeat with a bloody nose and a couple of red blotches on his neck and face imprinted by heavy punches.

Jason sat back in his seat quietly. Sternly he waved away any helping hands. He sat, held his breath and controlled his anger. Unbruised, he only stretched and tore one of his shirt sleeves. The bus grew quiet when the hippie boy got off the bus. He glanced with hatred toward me, called me "chink" and ran down the steps. The bus driver heard him and yelled, "Get off my bus. " He slammed the door shut. Tears welled in my eyes as I looked down.

The rest of the ride to our stop was filled with deadly silence. I hid my fear and tears as I got off the bus with Jason behind me. Relieved for my brother, I never knew I would feel that connected with my flesh and blood until that day.

We never exchanged our feelings for each other about that day. We lived separate lives at the orphanage and separate lives in this family. We never learned to be brother and sister or show any affection toward each other. We kept our distance like strangers as he dealt with his own emotions and I dealt with mine. Jason staked out his territory in our playroom upstairs. I did not know how to relate to the silence. I went downstairs to the family's library room and watched TV with Mr. and Mrs. Willis.

I often sat on Mr. Willis's lap. He scratched my back all night which was my favorite treat. We would get together to watch a movie. Mrs. Willis popped popcorn during the commercials, and I yelled to her to let her know when the commercial was over. Mr. Willis was happy to have me curled up in his lap. He depended on our cuddle time. It was his "winding down time" after work—that and the beers he drank. He often whispered in my ear, "I love you, angel." I was his anchor, and he let me know how much he depended on me.

Mr. Willis was physically there, but he often drifted away in his beers and fell asleep in the chair until morning.

Jason and I went through puberty. We couldn't stand to be around each other as we painfully lived through our teenage years. Our family grew more difficult to relate to as well. Mrs. Willis and I fought more often during these difficult times. As always, Jason excused himself and went behind closed doors upstairs. Mr. Willis drank his beers and watched TV in our library room. The men avoided us while Mrs. Willis and I fought.

After each fight, I got a wink from Mr. Willis. He never fought with Mrs. Willis on his own. Always he showed great admiration for me that I stood up for myself in fights he desperately avoided. Each time I became stronger. Soon I was stronger than any one of them. The more beer Mr. Willis drank, the less powerful he became in my eyes. He accepted his defeat by Mrs. Willis and let her have her way. Stubbornly I fought harder to stand my ground.

Eventually, our ritual of sitting together with me on his lap was no longer a gift. I no longer cared for the long back scratches from Daddy that became filled with careless touches, too often on the side of my developing breasts. His touch left a crude and bad taste. His drinking became more and more of a crutch. The bickering with Mrs. Willis about his drinking was too much for him to handle. He chose to drown himself in even more beer.

I disliked the alcohol smell on his body, and I began to feel uneasy about my safety. I had developed into a young woman with little understanding. I had no real interest to explore or ask questions even though I knew my body was changing. I stopped coming to greet him, as Mr. Willis's absences became more apparent in our home. He and Mrs. Willis became distant and hateful to each other.

Mr. Willis continued his drinking, and Mrs. Willis continued her constant "bitching." Jason disappeared deeper into the TV screen, and all I wanted was to make things better for all of us. I became the only tie that would get Mr. Willis coming back sometimes at night to be a family. Coming home already drunk, Mr. Willis continued to drink at home and hid his empty beer cans under the car seat. Wanting to be my friend, he bought me a diamond ring in a heart shape. But his gift brought more terror into our house from Mrs. Willis. Confused, I wondered about her anger toward him. Was it because of his drinking or because of his special love for me? At every chance, he told me, "You are my sunshine, angel. I only come back to see you."

Mrs. Willis constantly came down with headaches, and took naps with her dogs. In our home the laundry piled up on the sofa. I folded it when I came home from school. We argued over everything I did.

The final "pretend" family function occurred at my 13th birthday dinner. Mr. Willis came to that dinner with his happiness derived from heavy drinking. He celebrated my birthday. Mrs. Willis's family tradition made a 13th birthday important. It marked the day I was no longer a little girl. I had reached my teen years. Mr. Willis gave me a diamond necklace and showed me I was worth any expense. What a way to start my teen years! However, the implications of the gift had a greater effect on the family.

That summer of 1978, Mr. Willis came back for the last time. He found the house lock changed. All his clothes were gone. Mrs. Willis opened the back door and allowed him in. She handed him the keys to his new apartment. In the next year, they prepared for a divorce.

Not long after, they told us Mr. Willis was very sick in the hospital in Galveston. We drove there to visit him, and I saw a frail, weak man in bed. A large bandage on his forehead covered the injury—an injury caused by a fall during his heavy drinking. I never saw Mr. Willis with so much life sucked out of him. I didn't fully understand the cause. They labeled him an alcoholic. I felt sorry and helpless for him, yet I stuck ever so closely to Mrs. Willis. He ceased being a strong force in my life. I later found out in my later years, he had gone through a nervous breakdown and received shock treatments.

Early one morning in the summer of 1979, we drove to the courthouse. Waiting for the divorce proceedings to begin, we watched for Mr. Willis's car to show up from the windows of the courthouse. Mrs. Willis had us on each side of her along with her parents. We peered through the window to get a clue from something down below. She pointed toward the car, as a beer can dropped out into the parking lot.

"He's still drinking, even this early in the morning," she said.

When the trial began, Jason and I waited in a witness room with a doctor. I asked him, "Are you going in there, too?"

"Yes," he replied.

"Are you going to say that he is crazy?" I asked.

"I am going to testify for your dad," he replied. "He's been sick, but he loves you very much."

Finally, at the very end, they called us. The policeman took our arms and walked us on either side of him toward the front. We said nothing and just sat there. We were pawns in a very sophisticated adult game. We were the determining factor of who would win. Two sweet, adopted Vietnamese children, well-dressed, too small for their ages and still not fully speaking the language, would again have their lives decided for them.

After seeing the children, the judge ruled in favor of Mrs. Willis as the custodial parent for both of us. The judge gave all the money to her and her adopted children. He left Mr. Willis penniless.

The summer ended. Jason and I entered our freshman year in high school. It was supposed to be an exciting time for us; however, we knew it was only a matter of time before we would move. We stayed in our Houston school for six weeks of our freshman year before Mrs. Willis announced that we would be moving to Greensboro, North Carolina, the next weekend. We didn't know where it was, so she had to get a map out to show us. Excited to start a new life, she showed us a newspaper clipping about Greensboro.

"Great, we picked out our new home from a newspaper ad," I sarcastically said under my breath.

Mrs. Willis glanced my way with a harsh look and said, "Just be ready to move."

Bitter and distant, I felt like a pawn. I was torn about how I was supposed to feel. I didn't understand fully, but I knew I was caught in another battle zone. I learned to cut off everything so well during those years of fighting. I tried to cut off Mr. Willis completely from my life and mind. I had to get on with life.

I wondered what kind of life I would lead?

CHAPTER 15
Flights and Fights

Just then Doan blurted out, "Snafu, totally! Short for situation normal all fucked up." Michael laughed robustly. Their noise woke me up. The misplaced accent and surroundings made me realize I was no longer in my American family but in my Vietnamese family.

Michael came in the room and touched my shoulder, saying, "Christi Hai, wake up. We all are waiting for you. I hated to wake you up any earlier after you tossed and turned all night. Are you feeling okay?"

I slowly breathed in and replied, "Bad dreams, I guess. Oh, just the past, the far distant dream of the past." I slowly moved my tired muscles. I propped myself up on my pillow and added, "I am exhausted, though."

Michael sat on the bed with me. I had a deep need to reach out and hold him.

"Oh Michael, I miss my daughter terribly."

As he held me, I imagined having my daughter to hold. I couldn't fight back the tears. I whispered in his ear, too exhausted to talk with strength, "I'm feeling an emotional roller coaster in me.

I'm going through a lot of emotions right now—reliving my whole life on this trip. This is my past and present, passing in front of me."

"Tell me what it's like to be here, get it out," he prompted.

"Everything I am experiencing now in my Vietnamese mother is demanding that I face my past, and it is torture," I said. "I am screaming out to tell my mother but… but… I can't. I'm holding all this inside me, and I can't say a word that she understands."

I felt as if my emotions would explode as I continued to let out my feelings.

"She has no idea about my life in America. Does she think my life was perfect in America?" I questioned. "How can I share with my mother when we came from two different continents? I can't talk to her about my life." I choked out the words. "I want to tell her that I have waited all my life to share and ask for her motherly advice. I want to tell her what my life has been like without her."

I took a deep breath and continued.

"I want to tell her I had the right house, the right car, the right job, the handsome husband, the American Dream. I had things that people die for, that people lie, cheat and steal for, and I had it so young. I had it all, including my beautiful daughter." I paused as my heart began to reveal itself to me.

"And I gave it all away to live again," I said with a sudden realization. "I needed answers from my own flesh and blood to guide me, Michael. This is home."

I stopped and apologized, noticing the glazed look on Michael's face.

"I know it's not easy to get to this point, only to be unable to truly communicate," he said, empathizing with my frustrations. "You're still young and will get the answers from this trip and many more in the future now that you know your mother again."

"We still have two weeks here," I said.

"At least you are smart enough to get to this point quicker than most of us, to ask that question, is this all there is? You are in it. Be present with it. The journey reveals to you what you need to know," Michael said. His eyes were understanding as he looked down at me.

"Yes, I understand. I know, I have my own inner war stirring around," I acknowledged. "Thank you, my monk, my priest, my lover, my friend and my therapist!" I smiled. "I feel better and ready to get out of this bed."

We laughed. The children soon piled in bed with us and surrounded us. No privacy was ever possible or needed in this house. My mother glanced at me with understanding and appreciation of my special affection toward Michael. I was still in my pajamas when she signaled that she had prepared some hot water for my bath. I went to give her a hug, as my thank you without words and with no need for translation.

As Jason and I relived more memories and soaked family feelings into our souls again, my mother and sister Le became extensions of the "me" I never knew. The language barrier prevented us from communicating all our thoughts and yearnings; however, our time together retied the bond.

Jason and I learned a little bit more about our native language, culture, customs and the wonderful food from my mother. She represented everything I dreamed my mother would be. She cooked for us day and night. She made up for all the lost time. She ran an orderly house for her other six children and the lost ones she now welcomed.

The perfect mother and hostess in our eyes, she made things happen around her home. Her endless energy and caring was carefully placed during every meal. She continued to feed her lost children more food than we normally ate. She paid careful attention to our favorite foods and made them available whenever we wanted them.

She showed us off to the neighbors and officials in the village. We stopped at many homes for tea to pay our respects. Our presence enhanced my family's social position. A local police officer stopped by the house unexpectedly several times to socialize and conducted our "paper checks" every day for three or four days. It was all done as a status inquiry.

Our mom and stepfather demonstrated more of their fondness for one another as time passed. A quiet man, my stepfather was respected by his peers. Their marriage, despite the start forced by necessity, now seemed ideal. They structured the family's foundation on the solid ground of discipline. The children continued their chores and went to school even while having three visitors from the other side of the world imposed on them. Traveling with us, they discovered the motherland away from the farming areas. It became the most exciting event in their young lives.

As our journey continued, we no longer depended on Doan to speak for us. I shared pictures of Lauren with my mom and the family. I explained, "Lauren is now four years old, and I am going to have a tough teenager on my hands." I reported her personality to my mom. She laughed as she remembered me when we were young in the orphanage.

My mom shook her head as she looked at her granddaughter.

"Very pretty baby," Doan translated.

"I need to bring her back to Vietnam to ensure she will appreciate her life," I assured my mom. "I refuse to have a spoiled brat on my hand."

"You didn't turn out that bad!" Michael defended Lauren and me.

"Yes, but Lauren hasn't had our training ground here in Vietnam," I added.

"Look who she has for a mother," Jason teased and reminded us all that I gave her tough love sometimes.

"She'll be fine," Michael encouraged. "She has Vietnam as her other world to help remind her of her fortunate life in America. I don't think her mom would allow her to abuse her privileged life."

I held my daughter's pictures close to my heart as I breathed in deeply. I thought about how smart she was, how she taught me her children's rhymes and fairytales that we didn't grow up with. I couldn't relate to an American childhood at her age, but I hoped to close the gap as she got older.

We prepared to tour South Vietnam and loaded up the van. The children showed excitement at being away from their normal environment. I remembered the opposite emotions when I was their age. I was in too many new places, starting with the biggest place of all, America.

1980 - 1984

We moved along with Mrs. Willis's mother and dad, who always hovered close by. Whether it was their RV parked in the driveway or if they traveled between houses, they were always nearby. Finally, they moved into an apartment in Houston. Now, we all lived together.

Mrs. Willis flew to North Carolina. She looked for a house and brought back high school jerseys and pamphlets. She wanted to get us equally excited with our new high school jackets. We waited for the house to sell before we packed our things.

We drove to Greensboro and moved into an older home with a full living basement. It served as our grandparent's living quarters. We lived upstairs as a family, with three adults and two children in the household. Mrs. Willis attached herself to her parents, especially her mom, while her dad kept his distance and freedom. He chose to not interfere with the women's plans or relationship. Mrs. Willis grew up as an only child and an Air Force brat. Having only her mother constantly beside her gave her an incurable idea of what she thought she needed to be: "Mother knows best."

As the only child, she was her mother's puppet from day one. Her mother took care of her every want. Her mother remained the strongest force in her life. Grandmother had an incredible power over people. She had a grace and charm. I always admired her strength and charisma.

Mrs. Willis wanted her adopted Vietnamese children to be as enthralled with her as she was with her mother. She took it as a challenge to have us see her in the same light. We did not and could not. Our history made no room for her concept of parental worship. We had walked a path of living hell to reach her throne. She never knew what to do with Jason's silence except to be silent back. I became her hope to mold and alter. But my high spirit and stubbornness kept both of us locked in war.

Our fights became increasingly worse after our move. She now fought her own battles of living single for the first time since her high school years. She never developed a credit record of her own and had no marketable skill. As her world became more insecure, she fought harder to gain some false authority over me to give her control. She became the breadwinner, while Grandmother and Grandfather filled the role of parents.

I now had two mothers. Her mother became my first mother, the one who cooked for and fed us. After school, I filled in the first mother on my day's events, and at dinner I did the same for Mrs. Willis, my second mother, when she got home. Grandfather observed, and Jason kept silent. With her inability to understand Jason's silence, Mrs. Willis gave up and sent him back to live with Mr. Willis after one year. Jason left, feeling unwanted and misunderstood.

My world became too focused on me with three adults who sucked all the new experiences of my life from me during my discovery of high school and the teenage years. My mission to be the Perfect American Girl continued with more adjustments as I adapted to another new environment. I made the most of living in a very small town. I was the only Asian in our high school of 2,000 students.

Moving from a big city like Houston to Greensboro showed me many shades of differences from one world to the next. I absorbed my new surroundings. I made new friends and aimed at new marks. I tried out for cheerleading and made the Junior Varsity Team during my freshman year. I flirted with the "in group" and rushed high school sororities. I met new friends who were often the underdogs.

My best friend was an overweight, talkative, lively girl who dwarfed me with her 5-foot-7-inch frame. Going through my sorority initiation, my new sorority sisters discouraged me from hanging around my not-so-perfect friends. Discrimination was my introduction to this social system. I wasn't interested in their biased views and grew more distant from the in-group while I pursued the ideal student "image." My friends became the teachers and staff. I sang in choir. I also entered the school beauty pageant and was runner-up.

My mother became my new rival as she fought for both her own mother's attention and mine. I became more open to my

The American girl with slanted eyes
High school years, 1980-1984

The growing pains between
adolescence and womanhood
Sophomore Year

grandmother and grew tired of repeating my day's events twice. I refused to subject myself to my mother's endless questions. Her enchantment with being single again manifested itself in endless dieting. She tried to go from a size ten to size six, to being perfectly dressed "ne plus ultra."

Struggling to understand why boys at school would not ask me out, I discovered none dared to step out of his comfort zone to approach me and deal with my differences. I needed to find a way to fit in. I looked for any outlet. I attended activities at the neighborhood church where my family did not want to participate. Church brought me more acceptance, and I continued to go to church without the family. I did not understand why my family did not want to attend church services anymore. Brought up in a Christian environment in the orphanage, we faithfully continued our worship at the beginning of our adoption. But now, my family had moved away from what Mr. Ha taught us.

My rebellious stage with Mrs. Willis also involved fighting for my right to pick out my own clothes, to dress myself without supervision, and to be able to wear minimal makeup and clear nail polish.

In the summer of 1982, I met Beau, my first normal boyfriend. He was willing to depart from his culture's fixation with blond hair and pale skin to take an interest in me. For once, this part of my life seemed normal, from the milk shakes on dates to the make-out sessions in the car. That summer marked a significant place in my life, the innocent years of puppy love. Beau became not only my high-school sweetheart but my escape from many tiring fights I had with Mrs. Willis. My world took a normal shape with Beau, yet I was distant and too skeptical to believe in it. My relationship with Beau created more rivalry with Mrs. Willis. My world seemed less strict only when she dated, too. I had more freedom when a new date occupied her. Unfortunately, her prudish attitudes and strict rules prevented me from approaching her with my own discoveries and questions.

My sophomore year was filled with growing pains. The adult family stayed interested in my world for its liveliness, while Mr. Willis's letters began. His letters arrived for me with more persistence. I tried to ignore them.

Mrs. Willis and I were both friends and enemies, and we struggled to deal with our own battles. Our final confrontation finally arrived. During a heated argument, I forcefully stopped her from striking me, and in that moment, I gained my freedom. Hoping looks could kill, I screamed, "Don't you ever hit me again. I hate you!" The very words cut the air like a razor and marked my freedom from her rule.

She sent me to my room, and I answered with a door slam loud enough to wake the dead. During this period, Mr. Willis came back into my life. He knew from adult experience how to flatter and win over an innocent heart. He catered to my teenage whims when Mrs. Willis would not. He showered me with expensive gifts and spent money on me at Christmas. He gave me the gift I had wanted for a long time, the one that eliminated my hindrance as a cheerleader: contact lenses! He opened the doors to communication. First, I thanked him for the gifts, and then I accepted his letters.

Beau and I remained sweethearts until he left to go to college. He was my hope to reach some normality in my teen years. When Beau tried to move in the direction of sex with me, I asked Mrs. Willis why I was not curious enough to explore. This met with her approval, and she told me it was good to be a late bloomer. That conversation was the extent of my sex education.

Fortunately, we moved before sex became much of an issue with Beau. Soon I said goodbye to another home again. This time we moved to Florida. The unexpected move took me to another school in Winter Haven, Florida, for six weeks at the beginning of my junior year.

Mrs. Willis and I moved to Orlando soon after that, and I attended yet another high school. The separation from her parents gave Mrs. Willis and me a chance to get to know each other and get along better without any outside influences. We promised that we would work together and be "just the girls." We depended on each other more now as she struggled to start over in her career in the city while I adjusted to my fourth high school. This time it wasn't important to be part of anything since I didn't believe we would stay anywhere too long.

We suddenly switched roles as she voiced her questions and doubts to me after school. She asked my advice about her relationships with the men she met. She dieted more than she ate. Her desire to be thin always included me. I became her gauge, and we competed to see who would lose the most weight.

Our ritual of eating only salads and cottage cheese was standard, and occasionally we interrupted it with a dessert treat of yogurt with strawberries. She waited for me to get home every day, and we ate together around 4 p.m. We walked after each meal to work it off. We ate no dinner except maybe a small snack to prevent calories sitting on our hips and thighs.

I found it tiring and painful to go through the rituals and the dieting menu that became part of my life for three years. I had no friends or interests left. My many "starting overs" created a growing distance from making new ties. My only relationship was the one I had with Beau on the phone, in between his college girlfriends.

I had no friends, and my world became small with just Mrs. Willis. But opportunity beckoned as I turned 16, ready to look for my first job. Florida newspapers advertised auditions for Walt Disney World, working evenings in the Electrical Parade. I had nothing to lose as summer approached, especially with no extracurricular events taking place in my life.

I tried out against 500 other candidates for whatever job I could get. I didn't realize I had to learn new steps and dances during the interview, so I showed up in my pants, silk shirt and heels. While others were in tights and leotards stretching and warming up, I took off my shoes, rolled up my sleeves and tried out with them. They were swans, and I was burdened with two left feet.

My love for dancing and entertaining during my earliest years was rekindled. I felt so elated, and my spirit soared. It had been so long since I felt this alive, full of childlike joy and determination. Disappointed, I thought I did something wrong when they took me aside. I readied myself for rejection. Then the judges approached me and asked if I could work morning hours as Mickey Mouse and Minnie Mouse greeting guests. My size proved to be an advantage for the first time for something. I felt ten feet tall in a 4-foot-10-inch body, and I had gotten my very own first job. I worked at Disney for the next six months.

It was a great job. That summer of 1983, I learned about my love for work. I looked forward to work while Mrs. Willis emotionally drained me at home. A natural pattern developed, and soon Mrs. Willis showed an interest in working at Disney World, too. She wanted the excitement of being a part of Disney and sold ice cream at Buena Vista Village for a short time. She soon quit, however, aghast at the foul language and crude behavior of her co-workers during off time. I approached life with hard, cold realism, much better suited to harshness than hers. She thought the grass was always greener on the other side. And so she planned for another move.

We moved back to her parents' home in Winter Haven and decided where our next pasture would be. We finally came full circle to where we started— Houston. I quit my job and got ready to move back to Houston ahead of her because of school. Mrs. Willis talked to Mr. Willis and Jason, and they agreed I would stay with them to start my senior year on time. Mrs. Willis still had to sell her parents' home in Florida to move back to Houston. I was excited to hear that we were moving back. It represented the stability of my beginning roots after I landed in America. Also, in the many letters from Mr. Willis, he painted a picture of a fun, carefree, plenty-of-spending lifestyle that I missed. There were constant reminders from Mrs. Willis about being poor because our lifestyle changed with her income. The struggle and pressure Mrs. Willis felt limited the luxuries we once enjoyed.

Feeling that I was the biggest burden God ever created on this earth for Mrs. Willis, I went out of my way not to ask for too much. I was very grateful for anything. I accepted cheerfully the second-hand nightgowns and the home-sewn prom dress made for Beau's senior prom, as well as other small items. Because I was too small to wear anyone else's clothes, she bought me what she could. I gladly accepted any special gift that Mr. Willis freely sent, and he showered me with many.

Another move. At least moving back to Houston represented a glimmer of hope in my young mind. Mrs. Willis and I drove to

Houston and met Mr. Willis and Jason. I moved my stuff into the small front room that had a rollaway bed made for my unexpected stay. The house was clean and nicely furnished, an indication in my mind of the good life in Houston. Life with Mr. Willis promised to be easier than my burdened life with a single mom.

Little did I realize how my life was to unfold.

CHAPTER 16
Making Choices

e left my mother's early one morning to drive to Cam Ranh City Orphanage. Jason and I anxiously started our journey to rediscover our orphanage home and revisit our past life as orphans.

As we arrived in Cam Ranh City, a dirt road lined with palm trees and a row of houses greeted us. We turned the corner and caught a glimpse of the mountainside ahead. A long yellow wall on the right side brought back early memories of our school days. Jason and I laughed and smiled at each other. We remembered at the same time the many days we skipped school there. School was our least favorite place to spend our days. Passing by the school, we approached the front of the orphanage. The metal gate no longer marked its entrance, but the old worn-down concrete pillars still stood.

We tried to locate the many familiar spots from our childhood. Michael carried our camcorder to capture the images of the torn-down remnants of our fugitive home. Jason and I tried to locate the rock in front of the gate, but it was gone. My mother helped revive our faded memories and pointed out the different areas where our sleeping quarters once stood. The tin-roofed shed was no longer there. Wild, tall weeds covered most of the evidence of our past. My soul connected with Michael's as I shared the part of me that grew up in this wild, foreign land.

"Now we're even. You've shown me where you grew up, and now, I get to show you where I grew up," I said sadly.

Jason was quite moved. "How different this place is now from what I remember and how different our lives have been in the States," he said.

I looked across the road to see my mother. Jason walked ahead of us and found the various sites of the only childhood home we knew. Curious children swarmed around the area, preventing us from exploring further. Michael sensed our frustration, and his patience grew short.

"Doan, tell the children to stay the hell back, would you?"

Mom and my stepfather put themselves between the crowd and us so we could have some solitude. Jason and I were grateful and relieved to get a little breathing room. Then Jason continued ahead, climbing up through the thick jungle.

"Where is he headed?" Michael asked.

"He's looking for the boys' dorm on that hill. Come on. Let's go." I wanted to recover more of my memories. I pointed out one of the concrete slabs with heavy weeds around its frame as one of the girls' dorms. "I think that's where the bathing house used to be... I can't tell anymore. This has become a wild piece of land again," I said, disappointed.

"I'm sure after the war everybody salvaged any good material," Michael said, turning over a piece of plaster on the ground.

We caught up with Jason. He found the field and the four cornerstones of what was left of the boys' sleeping quarters.

"I remember the well down there and the creek," Jason said, pointing with his finger.

Somehow, a smaller group of children again managed to catch up with us as they climbed through the hills. I noticed all were barefoot, going through the rough, prickly landscape. Wherever we went, they followed.

"That's where we used to play soccer during dry season," Jason said, using the camera to record the sandy steps down from the

Re-visiting the site of
Cam Ranh Orphanage

Home Sweet Home

The skeleton of the metal gate
we called "home"

The Past

The Present

main level of the orphanage.

"Yeah, when it rained, it would be full of water, and we would catch catfish with our hands. The water would bring them in from the ocean," I said, delighted that he brought that memory back to me. I noticed the smell of the tainted creek. Jason and I stopped there silently and tried to put the orphanage back together among the weeds to locate the storage shed. I began to walk forward, remembering the many times I ran up and down the steps from the girls' dorms and toward the main building.

I walked around my old world again and realized the importance of this piece of land to us. No one could understand the meaning of this site unless they lived here once. I saw the barefoot village girl in me that was here as if it were yesterday. She lived here. Where did she go? Can I find her again? The time machine continued to show me my past. How would I put the pieces together? Over 100 orphans' lives changed here. I was alive as a result of the place that sheltered and fed me as a child.

"Oh God. What is it that haunts me here today?" I prayed. I walked slowly and took off my shoes. Le Thi Hai surfaced. I felt the hunger, the loneliness, the sadness and the pain. I heard the sounds of war around me. I saw my headmaster. I saw smiling faces around me. I also saw hope. I saw safety for children. I saw a home full of children here again. We walked ahead, back to the front gate to meet our party.

Jason and I found our mom at the gate. She finally came back to get us. Family again, we hugged her. I took a last look at the skeleton of the front gate. Then we left the orphanage behind us as we walked hand in hand with our mother. I had waited for these steps for an eternity.

The cool air blowing through the van's windows was a welcome relief. I looked back at the pillars as we drove away from the site. The brightness blurred my vision of the past and the future all into one. The heat from the visit weakened me, and I soaked in the cool breeze. The drone from the van put me adrift again.

1983

That summer was Mrs. Willis's first time back to see Mr. Willis. We all pretended to be a "whole" family again for that short period of time. Mr. Willis looked healthier, like a born-again person with his crisp heavily starched white shirt, sports jacket, black pants, and a handsome tie. His new, improved appearance magnified his good looks, especially compared to the frail, sickly, worn-out man we saw four years ago. Mrs. Willis wore her new size-six dress for the occasion.

I was glad to be back. Mr. Willis and Jason impressed us with their home. They lived in what I perceived was a decent environment that indicated stability—a good life.

We ate as one family again, a family of four, that evening. At the restaurant where we went for dinner, Mrs. Willis eyed Mr. Willis longingly. She acted as if she was on her first date with all her formality. Mr. Willis played with her seduction and enjoyed his small victory over four years ago. She put a quarter in the music box and played "You Were Always On My Mind" by Willie Nelson. But Mr. Willis showed no reaction, and we left the restaurant. Attempting a final dramatic goodbye, she started to drive away, only to stop for a second, as if to give Mr. Willis a chance to change his mind. He wasn't interested.

She left town, and Mr. Willis, Jason and I carried on endless conversations to catch up. Mr. Willis and I did most of the talking while Jason half listened and watched TV. He hadn't changed. I felt free from Mrs. Willis's dependency on my attention. This day liberated my spirits.

Over the next few weeks, Mr. Willis showered me with compliments, shopping trips and expensive dinners. He filled our days with fun, and I enjoyed a completely different lifestyle from that of the past three years. So emotionally drained from the pressure of making Mrs. Willis happy, I needed a fresh environment to take care of my emotional needs. Daddy fulfilled it all.

He always managed to have some fun readily available. It was go here, go there, buy this and buy that. He re-established his role as my scriptwriter, and I gladly handed him my pen. Here was the man who knew me the best, the one who would shelter, protect and provide for me.

School started, and I entered my senior year with Jason. We drove to school together in his car. Like our days on the school bus, the car trips reminded us of our brother-sister relationship. But Jason was now more temperamental with me as Mr. Willis began to give me too much time. I had taken his place. Mr. Willis's attention was focused on me entirely, since I came back. It had been Jason's before.

One afternoon Mr. Willis surprised me with a gift that I'd seen during one of our many shopping trips. He set up a bamboo brass mirror in the living room for me. I felt so loved and wanted. He made the gift a special "just because," he said. We sat on the floor, admiring the mirror, and I saw our reflected images. He sat Indian-style, and I sat inside his long, crossed legs. His arms sprawled over my small frame as he gave me robust, yet tender hugs.

He understood my naiveté and hunger to be loved, and he charmed my 16-year-old ego. When we stayed up late to talk, he often told me his secret hope had always been to get Jason and me back.

"No matter what. I never stopped trying to get you back. I knew after getting Jason back, I would get you back, too. I never gave up hope on you, Christi," he said during his winding-down time on the sofa.

During one of our conversations, I was surprised to see him drinking a beer.

"Why are you drinking again?" I asked.

"This? Oh, it's not that big of a deal. I only drink a couple to help me wind down in order to sleep at night," he explained casually. He carried a Diet Coke in his hand from morning to night, and after 10 he drank a few beers.

One night, the phone rang and I answered. It was Mrs. Willis. She wanted to know what was going on with us. I told her I needed a couple of things I had left behind.

"I'll bring them to you when we get there," she said.

"No, I need them right now," I said.

There was silence on the phone as if she knew this was going to take place. Then she spoke. "I don't know what is going on in Houston, but things have definitely changed. You haven't written once. I know you're busy getting to know your dad again, and I know y'all are having a really good time, but surely there is a little bit of time for me, too?"

"I've been busy..." I stammered.

"Look, you've been an everyday part of my life for so long, now suddenly you're not here." She paused. "And when I do talk to you, it's like talking to a stranger."

"I've decided to stay with Mr. Willis and Jason from now on."

"What's happened?"

For once, I could think of nothing to say.

"Has Mr. Willis bought you any bedroom furniture?" Her voice didn't reveal the intent of the question.

"Not yet. We haven't talked about it," I said, determined not to let her sway me. "I've got to go."

"Then if you're not going to live with me, there's no need for us to move back to Houston," she said and hung up.

I received a box from her a few days afterwards. I opened the box to see my birth certificate, letters and cards that I gave her through the years. Everything from my school report cards to the wallet-sized pictures I gave to my grandparents was in that box.

I was devastated. I screamed and threw the box into the closet corner. I crossed her out of my mind and my life. She had deserted me as she felt I had deserted her. They never moved back to Houston, and I never heard from her again. To this day, I am sad for the two of us.

CHAPTER 17
The Loss of Innocence

Michael, my family and I continued in the van toward the coast and Nga Trang. We'd heard it was paradise with an ocean view. Eagerly we looked forward to another new place in Vietnam. A special closeness bonded us together after leaving Cam Ranh City. This time we left as a family, as one.

In the van I felt my mother's hands on my neck. She pulled my hair back from my left ear and inspected me carefully. I wondered what she was doing.

"She look for your scars," the interpreter explained.

Then she lifted Jason's right arm and saw the large scar underneath his bicep.

"Wow, she remembers. What happened to you?" Michael asked, looking at Jason's rough scar.

"I'm not sure actually, I think it was a blood vessel got clogged up when I was a kid," Jason answered.

"I went to the American Air Force base on a helicopter when I was little in the orphanage. Doctors operated on me," he said, sharing his memories.

"That's one hell of a war scar there, Jason," Michael said.

I often wondered what other war scars Jason still carried with him in his silence all these years. Mom commented often that he was quite like our father. This reunion gave him an important role in our family. Mother understood and accepted him in his silence. He enjoyed his status of being the oldest son and still a bachelor. Our mom introduced him to many beautiful, eligible girls in the village. With the attention, he smiled more and raised his dark thick brows. His actions indicated his fondness for meeting pretty girls.

My mother turned back to me and looked at my ear again, determined to find something. Doan explained what my mom said while she searched my ear.

"She says when you a little girl, you eat bowl of rice. You fell and broke the bowl and it cuts your ear off. Your mom rushed you to doctor, and they sewed it back again."

"You're kidding!" I burst out with surprise. How could I forget a big incident like that? My mom nodded her head and gestured that it was true. I smiled at her, felt my ear and made sure it was still intact.

"Ma, cam on," I said, thanking her in her language for saving my ear.

The children were very quiet and too carsick throughout the trip to stir around too much, yet they managed to laugh at my American accent using their Vietnamese words. My mother continued to search for the scar with more determination. Michael helped her and pulled up my hair on one side. They both bent my ear back toward the light.

"I see it, it's barely there," Michael announced. "It's just a thin white line on the bend of your ear in the crease."

The examination continued. She pointed to more scars. She remembered. She cared. Now she looked for newer cuts and scars on me. It was her job to know her daughter. She wanted to know all my scars. She wanted to take me back as her daughter.

I liked her hands stroking my hair and arms to find more scars on me. I held her hands close to my face and adored the sweetness of her motherly touches. I wished I could tell her about the many scars I carried deep within me.

I took her hands, wrapped them around mine, and pulled them

against my chest. I held them there tightly as if she could reach inside my heart to find the other scars. I mentally recounted the invisible scars and silently revealed my deepest secrets to my mom while her hand soothed my beating heart.

1984

Mr. Willis was ready and waiting with all his tricks and his magic wand to make things better for me. The war still existed. Mrs. Willis surrendered. Mr. Willis won. I was the prize. I never understood this peculiar rivalry. They placed me between them in their adult games, which I did not know how to play.

"I told you I would get you back again one day," he said, enjoying his victory.

Our philosophical talks often took place as he wound down from the day with his six beers. I talked away to his attentive ears. It was a treat for both of us to converse since he lacked any openness with Jason.

"What do y'all do, then?" I asked.

"You're looking at it," Mr. Willis said with a laugh. "We watch TV, and he doesn't say a word, no comments about anything he sees on TV. He might say something if I press enough for a comment," he explained. "Better yet, he'll go to his room to watch something else. He doesn't talk like you do."

"No, seriously," he said, reaching down to get a handful of salted peanuts as he looked up at me. "You went away from my life as a little girl but now you've come back to me as a woman. I am very proud of you, Christi." He reached out with his long arms and hugged me.

Our evenings were filled with great entertainment. We talked and joked. He easily captivated a teenager who needed a lot of attention. He continued to drink to wind down. Every morning since my incident with Mrs. Willis, he wrote me sweet notes and fed me nurturing words:

Dear Christi:
Good Morning! I Love You So MUCH!!!!!

> *Tonight, I couldn't go to bed without telling you what a special person you are.Christi, no matter where you are, or where you go, YOU BRING BEAUTY into the life of those about you!!! You are soooo Beautiful!!!!!!!! The Radiance of your SMILE and the twinkle of your EYES just brings life into the world!!!*
>
> *I've never met anyone that in any way measures up to You!!! Angel, you have brought so much happiness into my life that I constantly look for ways to repay you!!!With you at my side, there is nothing I can't DO!!!*
>
> *I'll probably dream about you and tomorrow I'll be thinking about you all day!!!Christi!!!! Thank you for coming into my life!!*
>
> *I'm sooooo excited about you being here that I can hardly sleep at night!!!Just remember you're my #1 and I LOVE YOU!!! HAVE A GREAT DAY & I LOVE YOU!!!!!*
>
> *Craig*

I felt so important and loved. I trusted him to take care of my future since Mrs. Willis crossed me off. I needed all the assurances I could get, and Daddy filled the bill. He made me a part of his home.

The spare room was a place for their storage. My staying with them was a last minute decision so I put all my stuff in this room and slept on the couch. A rollaway bed created a space for me among their boxes.

I used his room to talk on the phone. I often laid across the bed, talked to my girlfriends, and caught up with my junior high school class. I had come back to the same junior high school class of '80. They just moved to the high school next door. Soon after my phone calls, Mr. Willis and I began our own conversation. All giggles from the phone calls, I was happy to be back.

My life seemed carefree, simple and safe here. I hugged one of the pillows as Mr. Willis talked to me while sitting on the bed. I talked endlessly, never short of subjects. I propped the pillow behind my head, and he listened to the enjoyable conversation.

Suddenly, one night Daddy bent down and kissed me ever so slowly and gently. Shocked, amazed, and confused, I felt his mustache brush against my lips. A torrent of sensations ran through me.

"Why did you do that?" I whispered.

He softly touched my long black hair with his large hand. My head rested perfectly in his cupped hand, and he gently replied, "Because you are so beautiful!"

He cast a spell over my teenage mind. I did not question him as he leaned down to kiss me again. I melted with his love. I was in a warm place as if I were back in my mother's womb. My cheeks warmed up as my mind went to another place, another world. I was lost in a honeycomb maze, sweet and confusing.

Endlessly patient with me, his every move was cautious. He assured me with his tones, and we continued to carry on our conversation deep into the night. Then he slowly undressed me. I felt confused and overwhelmed with new sensations. I was in awe. I felt beautiful as he painted this picture of me. I was spellbound. He charmed and bewitched me. His desire grew intense, and he penetrated me.

Suddenly, in an outburst that sounded out of place in the stillness of the mood, I screamed "Ouch!" and he quickly withdrew. I felt pressure, a puncture inside me. Something tore in me. I ran to the bathroom, shocked by the pain. I saw blood, my blood.

He seemed surprised when I returned.

"What did you do? Why did you hurt me?" I asked.

His face was white. He put on his pants. He took a deep breath.

"Well, sometimes you bleed if you haven't had sex, but you..." he hesitantly said. He seemed puzzled.

"I haven't," I responded quickly.

"Surely, you and Beau, after you dated all that time?" he asked.

"But we didn't," I answered, annoyed with him for questioning me. I walked out the room. It was 2 a.m., and I could feel my body drooping from tiredness. I did not think seriously about what had happened. The curiosity of a new venture, and the seduction of his words blinded me. My body felt different. I felt new sensations that I had never experienced before. Something awoke in me. Aware of my body and my curves, I felt my breasts for the first time and realized they were developed like a woman's. I fell asleep thinking about what Mr. Willis had told me: "You're not really my daughter, you know. You went away a little girl, and you came back a woman." His words echoed in my head as I faded into sleep.

The next day there was a gentle knock on the door, and Mr. Willis entered my room. I sat on the rollaway bed and combed my hair.

"How do you feel?" he asked.

"Fine," I said, combing my long hair over my head. I avoided looking at him.

"Are you ready to eat lunch, then?"

"Uh huh."

"Where do you want to go today?" he asked.

At lunch, he continued with his flattering.

"I really think you are very special, Christi. I would never hurt you, you know that, don't you?"

In a world of my own, I answered, "I know." I trusted and believed him.

Every morning Mr. Willis taped love notes in the bathroom. He wrote them the night before. He reassured me about how wonderful I was.

"You are sooo GORGEOUS!!! and I'm SOOOO PROUD TO BE SEEN WITH YOU!!!" the notes would say. Young, naive and so impressionable, I needed and believed his words.

During the day, I followed my usual routine of going to school. At night, I went to his bed. With Jason home, we had to be discreet and made it into a game. I met him in his room after Jason went to bed. And every morning, he reassured me again with love notes. He made me the most important thing in his life and set me up on a pedestal.

> *Dear Christi,*
> *I had been sitting here awhile wondering what the future will hold and I walked into our bedroom and sat beside you for awhile and looked at you sleeping and Christi, my heart just BURST!!! You're SO BEAUTIFUL!!! NOT JUST A BEAUTIFUL GIRL but a BEAUTIFUL PERSON!!!*
> *I wanted to kiss you but I was afraid I would awake you!! Christi , you're the GREATEST person I've ever known!!! You*

hang tight in the GOOD TIMES and TIGHTER in the not so GOOD TIMES!!! You're really a fabulous PERSON. You're the one I DREAMED of finding for so long!!!

You're a tough little CHARACTER!!! Angel, so often I wonder if you realize what a SPECIAL PERSON you are. Only one in 10 million people does God create someone like you!!! I saw that 10 years ago the first time I saw you I KNEW IT!!! It is like I told you I can read people quickly!!! and I saw in you such a special person so long ago. In August, you asked me "How long have you loved me this way" and I said "A long time" and I should have said, "10 years." I loved you then and I love you now and it still gets stronger each DAY!!!

I LOVE YOU.

Craig

I took it in as part of my breakfast medicine. I brushed my teeth and read the love notes reflected back at me from the mirror. He taped them where I stood to get ready. He fed me what I needed most, love. He showered me with gifts and non-stop pampering. I felt embarrassed to talk to anyone else and did not know what to do. As my free time disappeared, my peers began to say that I was a spoiled brat.

My world was distorted with contradictions. I became aware of it dumbly. While my days flowed with childish routines, my secret life with him occupied the rest of my time. My secret life distanced me from all my schoolmates. I had no time for them. Daddy planned my schedule. He picked me up from school as soon as the last bell rang. He always had my favorite snacks or treats ready for me in the car, and we would take off to an activity.

My repayment was to be there for him. His greatest fear was being alone. I was seen as "Daddy's little girl" or "Angel" by his friends and coworkers, who saw us together constantly. I visited subdivisions with him and met his buddies. I sensed that his closest friends knew of our game when his friend Tom made a comment about us.

"At least, she should stop calling you Daddy," he said loud enough for me to hear from the other room.

So, he became "Craig" instead of Daddy.

Mr. Willis bombarded me with messages while I became isolated from the rest of the world. I did not study how to get out of situations like this in my classes, and I felt trapped and lonely. His notes tried to reassure me: *"For 3 years I have loved you from afar!!! Now you are here. Seeing you each Day is UNREAL!!! I Love You!!! Soooo Dearly!!! Thank You for Coming Back!!!"*

Daddy filled my evenings with many stories during our usual talks, and I listened. The story of how we first met was his favorite. He told me how the adoption took place and reminded me how lucky I was.

"You can have anything you want and need. I gave you all I have and I will in the future," he said. "I brought you from rags to riches."

Mr. Willis's attraction sucked the life out of me. He needed so much, much more than I could give. His pleading confused me. He forever squeezed more from me to quench his needy demon. His slow and subtle incisions left scars on me in places I could not locate. They were deep within. What could I do? Where was my life leading? What kind of life was this?

CHAPTER 18
Confession

Joan tapped my shoulder and translated my mother's question: "She says she feels your heartbeat is racing, do you know what it is?"

I could only nod silently, fighting back the tears. There was no way I could share the horrors and pain of my personal war. I squeezed her hands, still across my chest. Then I leaned down and kissed them to bring her comfort.

"I am glad to be here with you, Mom," I answered.

I blanked out the beeping of the van horn and the other voices. Mother's touch on my hands reminded me of my hurts and scars. The excessive pain built inside me and needed release.

"You weren't there for me, Mama," I cried out to her in my heart. "I wish I'd had you to guide me. I was lost without you."

1984 - 1985

The relationship continued, and Mr. Willis gave me more authority over the house. He gave me a checkbook and credit cards issued in my name. Jason increasingly hated me and blamed me for everything that was secret around the house. We grew even more distant. I didn't like being there either, but I couldn't even talk to my own brother about it. My brother obviously had questions, yet he never talked about it. He ignored everything at home and did his own thing. We coped the only way we knew how.

Soon I grew bored with the game. I disliked the secret I had to keep and the pretend life I led. I was isolated from anybody my age, and even my own brother had deserted me.

Jason and I had a major fight about something. I can only guess the reason we were fighting. I wished he could just talk to me. I needed to talk about it. He needed to show his anger. He kept his silence. It was an unspoken dilemma in our family. Was this normal? It took 10 years for my brother to tell me he had tried to confront Mr. Willis on my behalf.

"It's not right. You know better!" he said to Mr. Willis. But Mr. Willis just ignored him or belittled him in some way.

I had no time for myself or even to date when there were other boys. I didn't realize the magnitude of the situation until I was deeply mired in it. It was difficult to get out! He played on my guilty conscience so that I would not leave him alone. Trapped in my guilt, I forsook my life as a teenager to complete his world.

After a while, I became disillusioned with pretty things. The generosity disguised his intentions. When the money failed to lure me, he played on my guilt and made it my responsibility to make everything better. Weak and constantly upset, he said he needed help with certain things around the house. He became ill when I wanted to leave. I became restless and frustrated. I grew bitter as I stayed around the house and envied Jason's freedom. I wanted to date boys in my school and go to parties. The more I wanted to get together with other students at my school, the more explosions occurred at home.

My senior year came and went. I skipped my senior prom to be at home with Mr. Willis. Jason dressed in his tuxedo and picked up his date. I stayed home. Mr. Willis played father. He took his camera out and took pictures of Jason's big night. I felt like Cinderella, forbidden to go to the prom. Unfortunately, my fairy godmother never arrived with her magic wand.

My most painful years

That evening, he rolled up the long sleeves on his starched shirt to his elbows. I witnessed the two large scars on both wrists, furiously slashed on an angle across his veins.

"Oh, my God," I said, caught by surprise. My voice quivered, "Why?"

"All the letters I sent to you in North Carolina were my last hope," he sobbed, "and you never responded."

I became his life-support system as he opened up to me with harder and heavier information to absorb. Whenever I wanted to escape, I thought back to the two large, jagged scars on his wrists. He had given me everything, I reminded myself. He truly loved me and needed me. I could not confide in anyone else, especially not Mrs. Willis! I had no one to talk to. Misery set in. He never bought my bedroom furniture. Slowly, I used a few drawers in his room to store the clothes that were still in my bag. I suffocated within those walls that once were my comfort and shelter. He had no friends, and my world became as isolated as his. I was not ready to be a mother, a daughter, a wife and a lover all in one!

During 1984 and 1985, the real estate industry suffered terribly in Texas, especially in Houston. Savings and loan Banks went broke. Overbuilt homes stood vacant. "For Sale" signs stood in rows and rows; everyone reduced prices to pay back the high interest rates. This bad turn in the market provided a diversion for my jail keeper and a chance at escape for me.

Mr. Willis headed to Dallas to look for a new position. He telephoned all the time and left the impression that I would not even dare think of going out with someone else. But he was not around to stop me, and on my 19th birthday, I decided to fly to Georgia where Beau, my old high-school boyfriend, was going to college. He was my only link to reality! I made no friends at school, and I was so alone. Fearing Mr. Willis's reaction, I waited until the last minute to go. I showed up at the airport and wrote a $500 check at the counter for a first-class ticket. No amount of money for a weekend at a college in Athens, Georgia, was too much for me. All I had was money to buy my way out, to escape!

Beau greeted me at the airport when I landed. His youthful face beamed. I was so glad to see him. It had been so long since my sophomore year of high school. It felt like a lifetime. I realized how much I changed. I arrived in my expensive clothes and $100 shoes, while Beau was still the typical college kid in his best grungy attire. We met again as if we were back in high school. We went through all our high-school flirtation and childish jokes. It made me feel 19 again. He helped me to forget my world and the older person I had become. I had so much to hide, and he helped me pretend it was not there, at least for a weekend.

His persistence showed he had not changed much from his high-school years. His curiosity about sex with me was as strong as ever. We reminisced about our freshman and sophomore years in high school.

"You were the toughest girl I have ever dated," he reminded me. "I couldn't get anywhere with you."

At college he lived in a dorm and was in his third year. I loved it! He took me to meet his friends, all gathered in a room, wearing cut-offs, smoking, drinking beer and eating pizzas. The environment was like medicine to me. It was so normal for them. I guess this is what 19-year-olds are supposed to be doing, I thought. I felt out of place in my silk blouse and skirt and my high heels. It felt uncomfortable to be around his friends for too long. We walked along the hall to say hello to more of his classmates. Then we walked to the next dorm room that was dark inside. Groaning sounds of kids making out heated our passions.

Beau took my hand, and we walked in the opposite direction. He smiled. We went upstairs to his dorm room. Beau fit in so well. However, he had left his friends to be with me. I was glad not to have to stay and fit in. I felt so grown up.

"You can go back to your friends if you like," I told him. "I think I need to lie down to get rid of my headache." I changed into my silk nightgown. I wished I had a T-shirt to slip into for the evening. So preoccupied watching me undress, he barely heard what I said.

"Oh, no, no. I'd rather stay here. We have a lot of catching up, you know," he said and smiled with anticipation. I felt young and normal again with Beau as we climbed into the top bunk bed. We talked like two school kids, lying on our stomachs, with our feet swinging back and forth in the air. We reminisced about our dating days. He laughed and reminded me how often he'd had to take cold showers after our dates.

"But," he added. "I understand. You were the nicest girlfriend I had. I'm glad we didn't…," he said. He said he was so crazy about me in high school, and I was always so standoffish with him.

"That's because I didn't know what to do. I was embarrassed to let you know I didn't know anything about sex," I finally confessed.

It was as if we were back in high school and innocent again. I thought back to how naive I was about everything, especially sex. Mrs. Willis and I never talked much about it, and I was never curious enough to test the waters. I was content making out with Beau on our dates. Now, we were ready for the real thing. He had been my closest friend in all my years of moving, and we'd managed to stay in touch. I needed to trust someone, and he was the closest person I had to trust. He was my only friend left. I still had feelings for him and he had feelings for me.

After five years of waiting, we finally spent our first night together without worrying about curfews. We stayed awake until 2 in the morning, enjoying the privacy and openness of being with each other again. He shared his experiences with me as I listened. We were like two kids comparing lunches. Then it was my turn to confess, to tell all about my life experiences since we parted. I wanted to forget, but I needed to tell him. I had to get it out of me. I was torn between telling him or not telling him. I thought, here he is, a sweet guy who cares about me after all these years. I can trust him. I believed he would understand and offer me solutions. I needed to unload. I needed him to make things better. I needed for him to still love me and still want me. I hesitantly began my confession.

"You can tell me anything," he said encouragingly. "It can't be that bad, can it?"

The radio music played softly, and the clock cast its light on us. It was now almost 3 a.m. I could see his face, waiting for me to open up. I was in great desperation, yet somehow I looked forward to getting it over.

"Well, my first sexual encounter was nothing like yours. Actually very odd. I really did not date anyone else after you. My first encounter was..." I looked for signs to discontinue or go on.

At my hesitation he said, "Nothing can be that bad."

"Well, it was Mr. Willis." I stopped, holding my breath for his reaction.

"Mr. Willis who?" he asked stupidly, and I eyed him oddly.

"You mean, the Mr. Willis, Mrs. Willis's ex, your father?" He sat up with a puzzled and half-disgusted expression on his face. I felt us disconnect, and the separation burned a hole though the wall in my guts.

"Oh shit!" he screamed as he pulled away from me.

"He's not my real father, anyway," I yelled, repeating Mr. Willis's words to me, repeating his script in my head as I tried to defend myself.

Beau had a sick look on his pale face, and I had a sinking feeling in my heart. He got out of the bed, and I covered my face, screaming inside, "Oh, God, what have I done? I was so stupid to tell him or anyone."

I heard the door shut as he left the room. I sat there on the top bunk naked, feeling even dirtier for being there and for having had sex with him. The whole room spun with a murky vision of stains and filth. I gasped for air. I choked. The air I took in was like breathing acid inside, eating up my lungs' tissues. I cried out my uncontrollable pain of humiliation. My body began to tremble with an enormous excruciating pain. My stomach turned with disgust and nausea.

My world turned dark. I sat up, hugged my knees close to my chin and rocked back and forth to comfort myself. I hated Beau. I hated me. I hated life! Beau, my last hope, had turned his back on me. I felt crucified in that dorm room. I now sat alone to face my own demons. I felt raw and vulnerable. I had been so naked with the one person I thought would empathize with my situation. What did I expect him to do?

I pulled myself back together. I straightened my back rigid and waited for what seemed like an eternity. The digital clock said 4:30 a.m. when I got up to put on some clothes. I went out to look for

Beau. The lighted hallway was quiet and deserted. I walked down the stairway to go outside. Beau was sitting on the stoop with his palms under his cheeks and his elbows on his knees. He looked like a hurt child.

I walked softly toward him. I did not want to startle him, yet he sat there as though he expected me. I put my hand on his back and asked, "Are you okay?"

He shook his shoulders and brushed my hand away.

"How could you?" he asked, as if I had hurt him by telling him my confession. It was not about me. It was himself that he thought of. I walked back to the room and slept on the bottom bunk bed.

The rest of the weekend we put on an act for his friends and for ourselves. His friends from the dorm waved at Beau as we passed by. One shouted, "Very healthy!" He smiled with pride.

"What does that mean?" I whispered to Beau as we walked by.

"It means that you look good," he said, glancing my way, eyeing my breasts and sighing.

"I'm glad someone is enjoying this trip," I said.

I paid for everything that weekend to get some decent food besides beer and pizza. It was apparent that I'd changed too much and that I'd been hoping to reach back for something that wasn't there. Beau and I did not talk about the confession again. I could not and would not trust him again. He lived the typical sophomore life in college. He was too young and carefree to understand what I asked and needed from him.

I gave him a weekend to enjoy on Mr. Willis's money. I felt devastated from my failed attempt to solve my problem with another person. Beau was not the answer. No knight in shining armor could protect me. Beau was a boy still playing with his wooden sword. He had not seen any warfare in his life. He couldn't understand my life. Where would I go now?

CHAPTER 19
A Different War

The palm trees greeted us at the shores of Nga Trang. The view on Highway 20 astounded us. We agreed Nga Trang was the prettiest area we had passed through. It was the gateway to other offshore islands. The French made it fashionable and popular, and American servicemen had also discovered it during the war. The evening arrived fast under a cloudy sky by the time we reached the busy streets along the coastline.

We visited the Po Nagar Towers. The temple was a monument of the Brahman Buddhists. Visitors and the devout came to make offerings and pray to the Cham Goddess. The towers allowed a spectacular panorama view of the city from their elevated vantage point. The whole town of Nga Trang opened before our eyes. On one side was the river and the mountains. The other side was the harbor, crowded with fishing boats. The boats passed out into the open sea and made a picturesque canvas. We began to see Vietnam for the first time as natives and as tourists.

We checked into our hotel and went to dinner before settling in for the evening. Mom and I stood on the balcony in front of our rooms, taking in the cool air and listening to the ocean waves on the beach across the street from our hotel. The new atmosphere and the quiet moments we shared away from the others felt healing for me. She held me next to her tiny body, and I wanted to tell her more of my complicated life. I desperately wanted to break the language barrier during these quiet, private moments. I closed my eyes. As the ocean waves rustled against the shore, I continued to tell her about my life in my mind. We held hands in silence as though she heard my thoughts and my cries.

1985

I accepted going back to my cage. I licked new wounds. I had tried to escape only to find I could not. I was relieved that Mr. Willis was still in Dallas when I returned. He was still looking for a new subdivision and land to develop. He called, and I couldn't lie, but my disappointment about the trip appeased him.

"We didn't get along. He's just a kid. It's over," I told him. I thanked God, he took it. He told me that we were moving to Dallas and he needed me to help him sell the house and get ready for the move. He wanted me to drive to Dallas to look at a couple of rental houses where we would live until he could build us a house. I accepted my roles again but now with more responsibility. I felt in control again. I was the wife, the authority figure, the decision maker, and I would choose where we lived. I became busy with the many changes taking place.

I finally found a buyer for the house in the declining market, and Mr. Willis drove back to do all the paperwork. With him in Dallas, the distance made my return bearable. The many things he needed for me to do eliminated the anticipated fights over my trip. I became important. I was an adult at 19 with adult responsibilities and adult habits; sex now became one of them.

When we moved to Dallas, Jason and I took college classes at a nearby community college. Soon we would choose what university we wanted to attend. Jason decided to move to Austin and attend the University of Texas. I envied him this freedom. It was his "out." Mr. Willis pressured me to pick a college nearby in order to help around the house. We moved into a five-bedroom house with plenty of room. Besides, Mr. Willis told me, he could not afford to send us both off to college when we had plenty of room there. I felt even more responsible to make things better and too guilty to leave. At the same time, I hated his devious tactics to limit my choices. He constantly reminded me, "You're lucky that we adopted you both."

"How many times do I need to thank you?" I shouted.

My world became smaller and smaller. I didn't know a soul there. My only chance to get away was through college in Dallas. I picked the most expensive and prestigious college to attend. I demanded to go to Southern Methodist University if I had to commute. Money was never an issue as long as I stayed in my cage. He gave me the run of his checkbook and credit cards. I paid the bills, and he never questioned them.

As we all adjusted to another place, Mr. Willis's predictable ritual of drinking at 10:30 every night continued. Unlike the first year of trying to please him, I began to manipulate him. We still shared one bed, and I took my normal place in the master bedroom. But things were more complicated than ever. Over time, our evenings became filled with small disagreements. The more trapped I felt, the more disagreeable I became. Each evening would stir up more tension, and many times the trip to Georgia came up. The fights became meaner and cut deep to my core.

"You stole my money to go fuck your little high school prick," he said sarcastically. I had known it would come up sooner or later.

We lived in the big house alone. While Jason stayed at college, I was a captive. I became more isolated, and Mr. Willis gained more control over my life. Ashamed of the secret world I lived in, I played many roles. During the day, I pretended to be a college student who had everything. I attended SMU, drove a Cadillac with a car phone, and had what few other students had: extra spending money. During the day, I constantly struggled to get away and have a normal life. At night, it was different. I was caught in a web. I didn't know how to untwist, unweave or untangle my situation.

Going to college was my only reprieve, yet I could not relate to anyone. Oh, how I longed to be normal. The SMU students were cliquish and heavily into their sororities and fraternities. My only friends were a couple of commuters who had their own problems surviving the high tuition. Too isolated and too different to make friends, I went to my classes and came home to the only place I knew. To prolong my freedom before coming home, I filled my idle time with shopping. It occupied my time. Spending was not a problem, since I paid the credit card bills. That was my only freedom! It started with a new $500 dress for college to lessen my feelings of entrapment. Soon even whole wardrobes never took away my loneliness.

I spent freely without understanding the value of money. I only knew I played with big numbers that Mr. Willis always covered. The more the demons set in, the higher the prices climbed. I molded myself into the Dallas style extremely well with my Neiman Marcus credit card and 24 other gold cards. My tastes became more expensive while my freedom shrunk. I sought after the very best that money could buy. I tried to cover my ugly life with the most expensive camouflage.

There were no more morning love notes or playing on my guilt. Instead, he turned to the evening's interrogations. He criticized everything about me and tried to make me feel less than important. With every fight, I learned more hateful words, words that I never knew before. They defined me in his eyes. He repeated them enough that he convinced me. I lost ground with the fights. I didn't know how to fight back with words.

He constantly reminded me how dependent I was. He never let me forget my mistake of taking that trip to Georgia. He told me that I needed to feel grateful for his forgiveness and his generosity for giving me shelter and support. College was now another negotiating item in my survival.

"Just remember who puts you into the best university—the best that money can buy!" he repeated.

Jason stayed away. He blamed me, and I accepted all the responsibility. I envied his freedom! I still had nothing of value. I needed to survive my college years. Graduation was my only hope. I had to get my degree, no matter what! My degree was my ticket to freedom!

My outside world became nonexistent while my secret inside

world ruled everything I did. I felt even more trapped in my situation. I used my past training to survive. I played my many roles with Mr. Willis well. My ability to switch off and on in one role or another became automatic. I did not even notice when I actually switched. Sentenced to this sophisticated war zone, I sharpened my survival skills. I became many people with different personalities.

I learned many things at 20 that only women in their 30s and 40s knew. I learned the art of seduction. I played the role of being a mistress. I learned new things in bed at an early age. Mr. Willis introduced lurid pornographic films into my awareness. I became a trophy, a possession, kept as a sex toy to wine and dine.

Mr. Willis photographed me for pleasure. Then I watched as he cut up the pictures and flushed them down the toilet bowl. I felt myself go down the drain with the pieces of photos. This ritual symbolically destroyed my self-esteem. I felt disposable. Mr. Willis also played on my fear of being homeless. I gave up my freedom and myself because of a fear that had been with me since I saw my first childhood home destroyed. I couldn't leave him. His was the only world I knew.

Within my fortress, my dragon laid low. Its oblique movements wrapped around my soul, and its fatal touches scarred me. It made me forever ugly and tainted with its marks. In the mirror, I only saw the image of ugliness. I did not see any good left in me. I could not even reach back to the simplest, happy memories of a GI holding me as a child. I sang no more beautiful songs to myself. Nobody gave me gum. No one sent me glittering castles on pretty cards. This was that glittering castle, and it had proved hollow. I never knew what the inside was like until now. I yearned for soldiers in a fortress to protect me. I needed my headmaster. I wanted to go back home to the only place I knew was safe… my orphanage.

"I'll kick you out," he threatened. His words paralyzed me with fear.

It seemed easier for me to stay and fight than to be out in the cold with nothing. He bound me with a fear that had never left me. I was alone in this world without a family of my own. My terror of being cold and hungry had never left me. I took as much as I could bear.

However, the price of my freedom increased, and my expensive tastes climbed even higher. I tried to fill my hunger for love with material things, but inside I was still the little girl with only a bag of rice to keep her alive.

Freedom was far from reach. Too embarrassed and ashamed to share my troubles with the outside world, I had no one to turn to. I would never again trust anyone who said they wanted to help me. There was always a price. Those prices I never wanted to pay again. I needed strength to fight this endless war. I was experienced in war. It was the only life I knew.

However, the battles became more brutal, and I lost ground. I moved out of the master bedroom to a room down the hall. When the fights became unbearable, I took the car and drove all night. I cried to God and questioned whether He was there or not. I waited until Mr. Willis slept. With nowhere to go, I returned to the only place I knew—my cage.

"Nothing is going to beat me," I promised as I geared up for another blow.

My many quick escapes with the car became history. He took away the car keys during our later fights. As I held the keys to leave the battle zone, he took them from me, and claimed, "This is my fucking car, my fucking house, my clothes on your body and in your closet. And you can pay your way through SMU if you like, you fucking bitch."

The atmosphere was painfully toxic.

Determined to never be beaten, I stood my ground with my head up high. I often remembered the earliest story told to me in my early years of learning English. I remembered the words of Sir Thomas More, "A coward dies a thousand deaths while the warrior will only die bravely of one death." I hung on to my Sir Thomas More bravery.

Finally, disgusted with the cruel and heartless teasing, I walked out of the front door in the middle of the night to get away. I walked aimlessly in the freezing cold and rain that night. I cried so hard to God and myself, and again I questioned whether He was there. I never showed tears of defeat to Mr. Willis. Only when I was away from the house did I allow myself to cry.

I walked toward the home of a girl named Emily, the only friend I knew. In my soaked clothes, I woke her up at 3 in the morning with a desperate plea to stay for the night. She grabbed clean towels and gave me her clothes to change into that night.

"Please let me stay. I'm afraid to go back," I cried.

She listened and suggested that I stay with her for a while.

Emily was my only college friend. We had met in an English course. She was getting her required courses in Texas for her teaching certificate. She was five years older than I was, yet we could relate. Early on she'd told me that she was "ABC," American Born Chinese.

"Emily, do you know that you are my first Asian friend, matter of fact, the only friend I have in this large state of Texas?" It surprised her to hear how isolated I had been.

"Where are your college friends?" she asked.

"I don't have anyone!" I replied, and she understood.

She agreed to let me move in with her. She lived downstairs while I lived upstairs in her new condo. I only had my clothes, and she provided me a fully furnished room. I stayed there while I continued going to school with Mr. Willis's checkbook and credit cards. I still paid the bills, and he paid my tuition. Mr. Willis did not dare do anything to disgrace his image to the outside world. He was always the supportive father. He pretended to be extremely nice and painted a perfect picture for the world by continuing to support me through school and by giving me money to spend.

With my freedom regained, I began to contact Beau again. He still was my only connection to the normal world. He came down often while I was Emily's roommate. We started a new relationship and seemed very happy. I needed him again, and he didn't mind visiting a new place. He ignored my secret and my confession. He figured that I was out from under Mr. Willis and my life included him only.

Soon Emily came to me with news. She and her boyfriend were engaged, and she would move back to Philadelphia in three months. I was happy for her, but the news sent waves of panic into my soul. Her move forced me to move back in with Mr. Willis. Getting ready to start my junior year in college, I figured I could bear the pain for two more years. I must get through my college years, I thought.

Things were somewhat pleasant before the next storm began. Eventually, we were back to the same tone, same beat, same place, and same time with just a little bit more screaming from me. Determined to stay unbeaten, I went on doing my own thing.

Because Beau was always broke, I would fly him into town. I set him up in a hotel room and spent a lot of time with him. He was still the same college kid with no money from three years ago. We forgot about my secret and tried to move on. I continued escaping to my teenaged years with him as much as I could. He was my only normal reality, but I knew he could not give me the reality that I needed. In addition to Beau, I dated boys my own age, but I did it secretly. I considered them affairs.

At SMU, I lived for my lunch dates, for school seemed so trivial to me, yet it represented my freedom. School was one form of escape, sex was also my escape, and shopping continued to be my biggest escape. Beau became my most expensive escape with a price that I willingly paid. I kept him available for whenever I needed him.

One evening when I got home, Mr. Willis was waiting in the dark for me. I sensed trouble in the air. He threw the checkbook at me. I knew the moment had come.

"You took my money and spent it on him, so you could fuck him! You whore!" he screamed in my face. He was angrier than anyone I had ever seen. He raged on and on in my face. He started to push on my chest as I fell backward. His massive body towered over me.

He started non-stop name-calling, accusations, obligations and on and on and on. I fisted my hands to my ears to block the torture. I could not stop my tears of defeat, for I was losing ground. Once again I was a defenseless child back in Vietnam, trying to act tough in front of others. I had to do something, but I didn't know what.

I picked up the phone to get help from Beau. He heard me crying, and he screamed at Mr. Willis. Over the phone, Beau offered to beat him up for me. I wanted him to do something, anything! I had nowhere else to turn. Beau screamed on the phone for me to "get the hell out of there." But I couldn't because Mr. Willis held the car keys.

"Steal the damned car and get out," Beau replied.

I had no one in Dallas to go to. Emily had moved already. I ran in my room and locked the door. As Mr. Willis banged on the door, I continued to talk to Beau on the phone in my locked room.

"Beau, don't hang up. Please stay on the phone with me. I'm so scared," I pleaded, not wanting to be alone. I gripped the phone, sitting on the floor in the corner. I needed to keep talking. Beau talked to me all night. He suggested I get out and move to North Carolina where his sister lived and where Beau had transferred to a different college. Wanting desperately to drive there right then, I couldn't, but I was relieved that at least I had somewhere to go after this storm.

Awake all night, I plotted and planned my escape to be with Beau. The next day, I canceled all of my classes for the semester and packed to leave for Chapel Hill. During the day, I was strong enough to fight back, and Mr. Willis went back into his usual denial of all that had happened the night before. Like Dr. Jekyll and Mr. Hyde, he acted as if nothing had happened. He camouflaged his manipulations with helpful, supportive handouts for my financial needs. It was his way to discredit any attempt I might take to enter the outside world.

Quickly, I moved to another state. I left with only my clothes. I could not steal his car as Beau suggested. I bought a one-way ticket with a credit card, stashed several hundred dollars, and cashed in my expensive jewelry for my security. The old Vietnamese way was innate in me to buy jewelry and gold pieces for security. I now understood the old traditional concept of women wearing gold as a way of showing off their wealth. They had common sense. The gold always could buy safety, even in times of war. This was my wartime, and I traded my gold possessions for my safety.

I thought back to my childhood days and how the war surrounded me in Vietnam. The orphanage no longer provided food, shelter, education, or guidance for me. I was alone, and Mr. Ha was far away. He had saved me once, but how could I explain this war to him? I did not have anything that did not belong to some other person in this country. I had no female role models to show me how to do better. My resources were so limited.

The plane ride was my escape. I left before night fell. The safest time for my escape would be when the sun was still out. I felt anxious to be gone and afraid of the unknown. I did not plan anything except to just get out! I hoped that my next refuge with my high-school sweetheart would be better.

CHAPTER 20
The Escape

*M*other's house again filled with laughter. We made new discoveries. Between their chores and school, the children taught us about Vietnam. We visited my family's friends. We dispelled many misunderstandings in the way the Vietnamese, including our own family, perceived our lives in America. Despite the language difficulties, we spoke about everything. Doan's English became the lighter side of the family discussions. We all made it a game to figure out what he was trying to say. We mastered a new form of pidgin English. It proved more useful, and we got our messages across.

We talked over long dinners and over hot tea around the coffee table. Talking was a big part of their customs. Visiting with just our family was rare because visitors continually stopped by to meet us. As the crowd wound down one evening, we carried on our family gathering. They brought out the Vietnamese "Export 33" beers for the occasion.

"Why can't you stay here with us for three months?" my mother asked. Jason and I looked at each other and knew it was an easy question to answer. We explained our American lifestyle and culture to them and that time was a precious commodity. But it was difficult for them to understand something they knew nothing about.

"Because if we don't come back after two or three weeks, company not give job back to us. No money. No food. No house. Number 10," Jason said in a combination of pidgin English and Vietnamese terms for Doan to translate.

"Ah." Many heads nodded, and we wondered if they understood totally.

"Others come back. Tell us many great things. All Americans rich. All bullshit?" Doan asked us.

"Yes, some bullshit. Not true." I took another sip of tea.

"We work very hard to live there. No naps and sometimes we eat fast at mealtimes, sometimes no three meals. Life very busy," I explained, noticing Le looking down at the floor. Her perception of my life was shattered with this new information.

Mom changed the subject, directing her questions to me now.

"Your mom wants to know when you have another husband and make another baby."

She shyly smiled at Michael. I jumped in to erase that thought from my mother's mind and Michael's.

"Not ready. No husband for long time this second time. Friends okay," I laughed. "Jason's turn this time."

They all looked at Jason, who shrugged and drank his beer silently.

"Also, too expensive to have another baby right now. I need more money to afford..." I said, turning to Michael. "Look up 'afford,' would you?" I asked, and Michael shuffled through the dictionary. "Cost of having baby approximately seven to 10 thousand dollars to deliver baby in hospital and expenses. We all have to work first."

Doan moaned, "Wow... ah ... ahh." He shook his head to add emphasis to his translation. "In Vietnam, few dollars to have babies."

"Another husband not that easy," I said and covered Michael's ears with my hands, teasing.

"Hopefully one day again, Mom," I said, acknowledging my mother's hope.

"Lauren needs a little brother one day," she answered with a smile. How haunting that my mother sensed my struggles about that part of my life. I knew I could not have another child right after my divorce. Now I would like to have a second chance to be a mother again with a little boy. I have this incredible need to know joy in marriage and in motherhood. In the past two years, I experienced motherhood under the adverse conditions of divorce. Would I meet my lifetime mate for sure this time? Would I ever have a second chance to know the joy of being a mother again?

"Don't worry, Mom. I'm still in my early 30s," I said, giving her a big smile, "still young and filled with more questions about life." I gently squeezed Le's hands on my lap to comfort her. I knew she often wondered what her life would have been like if she had been in my shoes. I wanted them both, my mom and sister, to understand and know the truth that my life was not always as safe and easy in America as they thought it was.

1986 - 1987

I was on my own in a world I had never experienced. Where was I going to get money to live? What about my school? Who was my family now? I felt so lonely in the world, and I thought of my real mom for the first time in all of those years. I closed my eyes and visualized being back in the safest place… Mother's womb, all warm and safe again. I wished I had a real home to go to so I could lick my wounds. But I had to face and create my life the best I knew how on more borrowed ground.

The trip to Raleigh proved long and gave me time to ponder my next move. I was only a purse string away from Mr. Willis's dysfunctional family affair. He had been my security blanket in this big universe.

Beau and his sister Jenny met me at the airport. I gathered Beau had told Jenny about everything to get her to help us. He was happy to see me, and I was grateful for the support. But we were also nervous and fearful.

We drove to Jenny's nice, well-decorated contemporary condominium. Our room was not ready for my unexpected arrival.

The wardrobe boxes I sent by bus arrived later. Nothing marked my room with any familiarity except the teddy bear that I gave Beau for Christmas in high school. He had kept it all this time. I thought of it as my warm welcome. A stack of blankets and pillows would serve as our bed until we could buy one.

I thanked Jenny for the room on such short notice. We arrived late, so going to sleep was a relief. Beau and Jenny helped me settle in her place for our first night. She was the only American girl who was my size that I ever had met. Beau was the only boy and the baby of the family. Beau stayed the night with me as we spread out the blankets by the boxes on the floor.

Once we were alone, Beau started to unbutton my pajama top. The evening developed naturally as we expressed our insatiable desire for each other. I escaped reality with Beau that hot, steamy night.

The next day I was a lost soul, trying to find myself. I literally started over with nothing except my clothes. I had no concept of what the real world was like. I was still that Vietnamese orphan girl, learning the American version of reality. This time for real!

I could not get a job with a salary anywhere near what Mr. Willis just gave me. Jenny, who followed behind me to turn off all the lights, paid light bills. I had always had jobs, but they were for fun and extra spending money. This time the motivation was different. I had to eat! Jenny became my teacher about the hard facts of life now that I was no longer a captive in wonderland.

Sunday morning, we sat around the condominium since we were off from work. Jenny took the heavy stack of the day's newspaper and went through it thoroughly. She showed me its usefulness. I sat there with scissors going through the coupons.

"Do these things really work?" I asked, revealing my ignorance about real life.

Jenny looked up and smiled. "Try them next week buying your groceries, okay? And by the way, make sure to turn off the lights in each room," she casually suggested as she continued to cut the coupons.

I felt silly not knowing these simple things, yet it also made me feel insecure as money became something to earn rather than spend.

I took a job at a high-end woman's clothing store at the mall. I enjoyed being around only the best of clothing. Comfortable in that environment, I knew brand name clothes and how to give the best service.

During the day, I worked at the mall serving wine, cheese and cookies to my demanding clientele for a small salary and commission. In the evenings, I drove the 25 miles from Raleigh to Chapel Hill and saw Beau. He had moved into an old three-bedroom home with his two fraternity brothers as housemates, and it became my hangout as well. Since I did not want to interfere with his school and fraternity activities too much, I would patiently wait for his free time. I was in a handout position with both Beau and his sister. However, I was able to offer Jenny a meager contribution toward expenses to stay in her good graces.

They let me stay with no questions about my situation. I felt ever so humbled. Jenny let me borrow her car to drive back and forth to work and to drive down to see Beau. My life was very different, and it was difficult for me to adapt. I needed Beau to help me lose my dependence on Mr. Willis. I believed his education was important to our future, but I delayed going back to my college until I knew what to do next.

An abused princess who had everything in a prison fortress, I'd become a peasant with no home to call my own, constantly borrowing from others. I hated the feeling of being poor, and the loss of the luxury of buying this, buying that, eating out, and having my car phone. I learned to get by paycheck to paycheck with a small, tight budget. I survived.

With Beau, who had been very attentive when I first arrived, my waits soon became longer and longer. Busy with his fraternity activities as an officer, he failed to notice my desperate need to be closer than ever to him. I was a fish out of water. My retail hours permitted me to stay overnight and drive back the next morning by 10. For the first time in my life, I learned to borrow money and purchased my own used car to get to my job. I had finally gained some independence. I was out of my cage. I continued to learn from Jenny, my first female role model.

Slowly, I transferred my clothes from his sister's condominium to Beau's closet as I began to stay in Chapel Hill and live with Beau and his fraternity brothers. Three boys and I shared the three bedrooms and one bathroom. We took turns in the morning. Beau and I hung around one another like a couple. A long-term relationship since my sophomore year in high school at least gave me a sense of stability. We went on with our forever dating, living-together rituals, not knowing what to do with our futures. I depended on him and hoped for a normal future. He drifted back to his partying, fraternity lifestyle and avoided any responsibilities.

I had learned how to cook, and I managed to have a nice surprise dinner for him for our special anniversary of seven years of dating. But Beau did not bother to show up that night. Crushed, I ate my meal alone in the fraternity house. I served all the food to his roommates. My emotions expressed themselves more as Beau became more distant and a "royal jerk" for a boyfriend.

"What did you expect?" I asked myself. He was a typical college boy who wanted to have fun with the boys, drinking at beer bashes. He played his role perfectly. I grew bored attending his many parties and fraternity functions. All their parties were alike, a lot of drinking and a lot of smoking. You can smoke only so many joints. I realized I did not fit this world either. I saw it was not any better here.

I stayed in touch with Mr. Willis from afar. I needed more money to survive. My wages did not make a dent. Each month there was a check in the mail with his plea to come back. I happily accepted the checks, more now than ever, to live. They were my only security blanket since I lived on an hourly salary. My salary seemed less than what I spent carelessly on meals with Mr. Willis.

My moods changed easily. I felt down about everything now. I was depressed one day and delighted the next. Perhaps it was the pressure to survive at 21 while surrounded by carefree college students. With no degree of my own to get a real job, I learned the value of education. It was hard to swallow the fact that I had left my own college to be a sidekick at a fraternity house in Chapel Hill, North Carolina. I disliked the directionless aspect of my life. I no longer envied their carefree lifestyle to just party all the time. Both lifestyles trapped me.

One time I had to hang around in Raleigh for a week while Beau and a couple of his fraternity brothers went on a hunting trip. "It's a 'Southern' thing to do," Beau explained to me before he left. I began to notice my disposition changed. My body had shifted somehow, and I gained a little more weight. I was depressed. I could not get up in the mornings and make it to work on time. I was more tired. In an attempt to feel better, I changed my diet and lifestyle. Every morning I felt sick and then was fine the rest of the day. I waited to get over my illness, but it would not go away.

One morning I woke up in a panic and jumped in my car to go to the store. I had to throw up in the nearest bathroom on the way. I bought two home pregnancy tests. I took the two tests in our room the next morning. I was terrified, praying to God to let it be negative. Later, I noticed someone had moved the test box. Jenny must have come into the room to get some of her things since we often borrowed from one another.

I stayed home that morning and waited for the results. I was too sick to go to work. I paced the floor and went into the kitchen to eat something to settle my nausea. I hated breakfast but lately I learned it helped my sickness! The test was positive. I panicked. I tried the second test, hoping the first test was incorrect. It was positive again, complete with pink rings around the valves.

"Oh, God," I said softly as I retraced my time with Beau. The night we arrived in Raleigh, we had no plans. Too caught up in the passion of seeing each other that first night, we did not think.

"I have to tell Beau," I whispered. Shocked by the news, I held it inside me. Beau wouldn't be back for three more days. I sobbed and paced with my nervousness. That night Jenny asked if everything was okay, as though she suspected something was wrong.

"Yeah, everything is fine," I answered, grinding my teeth, panic stricken, anxious to tell Beau first.

The day he came back, I drove down to see him at the house. He was not around, and his roommate told me "the hunting party is at Crazy Zack's." It was their hangout for loud music and cheap beer. I went in and fought through the crowd to find him. I spotted him with the guys in camouflage outfits, rough looking, sitting at the bar. They all looked awful and unshaven from the past week of hunting. They looked like something out of a war movie.

The three hunters sat in a corner of the bar drinking beer when I walked up. I chuckled at their appearance. "Oh my God, you look like hell," I said, laughing at how rough Beau looked compared to his normal clean-cut, blond-haired pretty-boy look. Now, his rough beard showed maturity on his baby face. He stood, crossed his legs over the bar stool, and put his arm around me. He mimicked, "Hello, darling," in a John Wayne style to fit the scene.

"Hi, guys. How was the trip?" I said as I hugged Beau back. I was ready to leave the loud noise and felt out of place. I whispered loudly to him over the music, "I need to talk to you outside."

He signaled to his buddies, "I'll be back. My woman wants me." He was playing his part. I rolled my eyes while leaving this bad movie scene.

We went outside where it was quiet, and I waited to deliver the news to Beau in the car. I sat in the driver's seat and wondered how we were going to handle this situation together. I breathed deeply and let it out.

"Beau, I'm pregnant," I blurted out. I felt a sense of relief from finally getting it out of my system.

"Really?" he responded, half proud and happy about it, but then he changed his tone. "Are you sure?"

I expected more of a response. I expected some empathy and some concern. He was not thinking of the magnitude of the situation, but I'd had a lot of time to think about this. Maybe he thought it was an accomplishment, a manly thing for his ego to hear. I cried. We decided to leave his friends at the bar and go back to the house.

"Here, I'll drive. You shouldn't be driving," he said and got out of the car. He held open the passenger door for me. He was so gentlemanly. Then he confidently got behind the wheel and took control. I was surprised and impressed with his reaction. He drove carefully and was so gentle with bumps on the road, as though I would break. He looked over at me, smiled, and explained his caution.

"I feel like I want to protect you," he said as he touched my stomach.

His caring moved me. I thirsted for any kind of affection he gave me after our rocky last month. I was scared, and his special attention to the baby that night made it bearable. I was hopeful that everything would be okay. It was like a spell over us. We knew we were pregnant with our baby, and he accepted it pleasantly. While he showered and shaved the week-old beard and changed clothes, I stayed behind to be with him in "our" room.

Beau sang in the shower as I lay down on his bed and touched my belly. I felt some peace, seeing he handled it well. I was filled with excitement and grief at the same time. Beau came in with a white towel around him and dried his hair with another. I rolled over on my side and propped my elbow on the pillow to hold up my head.

"Feel more civilized now?" I asked.

"Yeah, but it was an awesome trip!" He was still full of excitement, like a kid. He sat down on the waterbed, and the waves made me feel queasy.

"Oops, sorry," he said as he gently controlled his balance. He then took his towel off and unbuttoned my sweater. His muscular body showed evidence of hard work. Lots of baseball games kept him tight and lean. He seemed taller than 5 feet and 9 inches, but young with his taut and narrow body frame. Many times, people mistook him for a younger boy because of his baby face. He grew a mustache to give him an older appearance.

Beau had worked as long as I could remember, even back in high school. His parents were divorced, and his mother raised four children on her own. He had become independent early to lessen the burden on his mom since he was the only boy. All his sisters did well for themselves, and they learned to be independent.

Beau put himself through college with his work. He had managed to get some help from his father in the later part of his life. The need to work kept him in college longer, and he was now in his fifth year. Beau was always different from the other boys; he fought harder for things. I admired and connected with the ones with more history in their character. Those with soft, easy lifestyles who did not have to fight so hard held no interest for me.

He was always broke and lived from paycheck to paycheck. While others went to the movies, our dates consisted of watching

TV at home. I did not mind, actually, because it meant more to me when he could afford something special for me. I had never understood the value of money. Now I wanted things that money could not buy. I wanted happiness and freedom from my cage. I wanted the two of us to create a family, to create a future.

He fell asleep rubbing my stomach as he lay across my chest. I lay there, combing through his blond hair with my long nails, and stared at the ceiling for answers. We spent the weekend talking about the baby.

"What are we going to do?" I began to ask the obvious questions. "We can keep the baby, but how are we going to raise it? You're still in school. We can't afford to take care of ourselves, let alone another mouth." I needed him to give me some solution or a plan. Give me hope, Beau. I prayed.

Silence.

"Do you really know how much it takes to have a baby? I'm not ready to get married. Are you?" I asked, looking for a reaction or a solution.

He said nothing about the baby and did not even respond to my question of marriage. I knew then that he refused to consider the possibility of keeping the baby. I analyzed the situation hundreds of times in my mind before I told Beau the news. He just had not had time to think about all this yet. Give him time, I told myself.

He stayed silent through my questions.

I struggled with all the logical reasons to not have this baby while the natural instincts of being a mother set in. I faced the biggest dilemma of my young womanhood. I felt something so special growing inside me. I wanted to be a mother as badly as I wanted to have a mother. I could be the good mother I had dreamed about.

This child was something of my very own that I could call my family. We would never be lonely again. I wanted to pour all the love and affection I had toward my own baby. I could trust and protect it as no one else could. I knew how special that bond was. Even though I lost it with my mother, I could have it with my baby. My baby could be my hope to live and fight with a good reason. The baby quickly became my reason to live, since my life was not worth much in my eyes. Torn with the happiness and the burden of being a woman, the suppressed fear of a lost child surfaced in me. This war tested my womanhood. Now the world tested not only my survival but also the survival of my baby.

Beau gave no indication of wanting to marry me, and he provided no plan to solve the situation. He sought advice from his best friend and his sister. Jenny advised against keeping the baby, for Beau's sake. I got irritated that he talked to so many people and not to me directly. I did not want them to know yet.

"Why don't we just wait and find out for sure Monday, when you go to the doctor," he finally said. His tone indicated that he now hoped it was a mistake and we would not have to go through this.

The doctor congratulated us as we walked into his office. He then looked at us and realized how young we were. Beau dropped his head low and stared at the floor like a child admitting his mischievous behavior to the doctor. I hated his reaction! We sat down across from the doctor and listened as he talked about the importance of medical care in preparing for the baby.

"What if we don't want this baby?" Beau asked.

The doctor closed the door.

"An abortion is an alternative," he said quietly.

I voiced my concerns. I felt the baby growing inside of me, and I did not expect Beau or anyone else to understand this battle. I had faced life alone, and I would face this alone, too. I felt my growing pain and faced God Himself. My strength rose within me.

"I want special care to prevent any complications during, after and in the future. I still want to have children later."

In that case, he said, he could put me in the hospital and do it privately.

"How much?" I asked the most pertinent question for our situation.

"Approximately $600, plus hospital expenses." We did not have that much money! I looked at Beau. I wanted him to say something, anything. He withdrew even further. Did I need to handle the financial problem too? I never hated being poor as much as I did then. I swore never again to be this low.

"Well, I don't know if I'm comfortable publicizing it with

hospital care." I did not know what else to say and looked toward Beau for a response, any response. I pleaded in my head, help me here, Beau! Where the hell did you go? He sat there like a little boy, motionless.

The doctor looked at us and stood up. "Well, you both think about your decision and let me know," he said and showed us the door. Beau had nothing to say. He became a boy in my eyes.

In the car he said, "I've mentioned this to a couple of my friends, and..."

"What! Who else have you told?" I screamed. "Do you want to advertise this?" I was embarrassed that he had said anything. I remembered his first reaction and realized it had led to his spreading the word. Our pregnancy was an ego trip more than anything. He had proved his manhood to the other small boys.

"Would you let me finish?" he screamed back. "I can borrow some money from them or even my dad for the abortion." This statement showed me he had contemplated abortion all along.

"No!" I was angry and humiliated. "Don't ask your dad. I don't want him to know, too. I will figure out something." I was upset and I cried. I was angry at my lack of security and for being in this situation in the first place. I stared out the car window in silence through tears, preoccupied with my dilemma.

We drove back to his sister's condominium.

"Will you be okay?" he asked with the engine still running. He was in a hurry to get back to school.

"I'm fine!" I said, the anger still in my voice as I got out of the car.

Jenny handed me the phone that evening. Beau was on the line. I went to my room to take the call. I had not said anything to anyone else, but I suspected his whole family knew by now. They never said anything to me during that time.

"Well, I did talk to Dad about the money, and..."

"You what!" I screamed as my hot temper boiled. "I told you not to. Is he proud of you now?"

I knew he had always tried so hard to win his dad over by being macho. I still resented his lack of responsibility at the doctor's office. I vented my anger, hurt, betrayal and disappointment toward him. I had learned to street fight with my tongue from my past, and in this league, he did not have a chance.

"Don't even bother to ask him or anyone for the money," I demanded, embarrassed that he could not bother to try to take care of his own mistake without calling for his daddy.

"I'll get paid next week and I'll go to a public facility instead. I'll take care of it," I said. I slammed the phone down. I went to bed thinking of my decision while he went to get drunk at a party.

My survival instinct switched permanently on to be tough, and I took charge that day. I could not afford the emotions of being fragile. Everything seemed doubtful in my world that night. I thought of so many alternatives besides going through with the abortion. I played with the idea of keeping the baby and going back to Dallas. It meant that Mr. Willis would have to help me even more. I knew he would love the idea. Yet it was just another entrapment of my own making to stay in my cage forever. I would have to sacrifice everything, even my own freedom. What about the baby's welfare? Is that situation a healthy life?

My baby and I seemed destined for sadness and suffering in life. How cruel would it be for my baby to suffer the hatred that this world has for us? I cried. My thoughts ran like ice through my veins. I could just see Mr. Willis's face as he told me, "I am not surprised, you're just a tramp." His voice and face danced in my head all night. I tossed and turned.

My life and my baby's life would become victims of the same circumstances that had trapped me before. No! I would not let it happen, not again to another innocent soul! I could bear all the pain that my heart and flesh endured but I would not do it to an innocent life. I could not live with myself. That thought eliminated the only hopeful choice for the baby.

"God forgive me." I prayed and wondered if He ever heard any of my pleas.

I decided that night. I took off two days from work for my appointment. The only thing I asked of Beau was to be my transportation and pick up my check at work. We drove to a nearby clinic to wait for my turn. My heart sank sitting there, waiting.

"At least I was relieved for a brief time," I thought to myself. I knew I loved something enough not to drag it through the grief in my life. I knew this was the best decision. I affirmed my decision to be stronger than ever. I answered myself, reassured myself, and hated myself all in one moment. My mind collapsed with exhaustion with no real options found. I was here.

"Have courage to go through it, Christi," I demanded of myself.

Waiting in the public health facility, I observed the large room filled with chairs and sofas around a TV. There were two young couples on the other side. I wondered how many young couples walked through these doors? How many babies did they terminate? How many humiliated and desperate people came here? How many tormented hearts ended relationships at this point? How many unknown experiences in this room was I now a part of? Another story, another mistake, another ignorant action by people with their own power to create life, yet end it instead?

One boy sat in front of the TV and watched cartoons. His girlfriend was behind the closed doors. I felt a sense of irony that a young boy—still a child himself—could create a baby and then watch cartoons, reacting to them rather than his own life.

The other couple sat close to one another and waited patiently as she cried. I beat on myself brutally. I felt ashamed and stupid for letting something like this happen to me. I thought I was smarter than that. But it was as though my fate had been decided that first night I came back. It was exactly three months since that evening. Now I faced the consequences and the memory of my decision for the rest of my life.

Beau and I did not say a word to each other.

Finally a nurse took me behind the closed doors. I heard the vacuum machine while I walked down the hallway, and I thought how strange it was that someone would be vacuuming at this time of the day. We went into an office where I began to fill out some forms.

The counselor asked me, "Why are you getting an abortion?"

I felt relieved that someone had actually asked.

"Because I can't give my baby a full, happy and healthy life," I stated. I guess I passed the test. She asked me to wait in the other room for the doctor. Sitting on the examining table, a cold chill came over me. It was sterile, still and lifeless in the room.

The doctor came in wearing his surgical gloves, ready to do his duty and nothing else. He was as cold as the room with no words exchanged. I lay down and stared at the ceiling. I became transfixed on the ceiling, and I detached from reality. He rubbed my stomach and put a cold cream over my belly to read the life form inside me with a sonogram. He turned on his equipment. I heard the vacuum sound. No one could ever forget that sound.

I twitched with fear as the vacuum sound came near my body. I felt stupid and ridiculous for not knowing enough to realize what I heard before. It was my baby's life being sucked out of my body. I closed my eyes as tears ran down both sides of my face. I held my hurt in. I disappeared from that room and the humiliation I felt. I was cold, lonely, embarrassed and hurt and just wanted to die.

"Please let this be over soon," I prayed to God or anyone who would hear my plea. My body stiffened with my pain and my tears.

"Relax," he finally said. He continued his task. He reached deeper inside of me and poked and pushed inside of me while his other hand pushed down my stomach. I felt every pull of the suction from the cold steel. The devil himself was inside me, trying to rip away my soul and heart.

"You're done," he said.

I wanted to open my eyes and find all this was only a nightmare. I saw the doctor before he took off his gloves and went out. The room was cold with no human touch before, during, or after. I shivered from the cold, the isolation, and the loneliness, and I got dressed, feeling completely drained. My spirit left me. My baby was no longer here.

My clothes did not make me feel any warmer. No clothes could make me feel warm again. I walked into the lounge as Beau awoke from his nap. Cautious with me as though I was going to break, he kept his distance. I walked out of the building, pushed the front door open, and showed him I did not need his help. I went out tougher than when I came in. The hot sun through the car window did not warm my coldness as we drove back to the condominium.

I took my pain medication and laid down. Beau tried to be helpful. There was not anything else he could do. He looked at the clock. I remembered that he and his family were getting together that night for pizzas and to plan his mom's move back to Greensboro over the weekend.

"Go ahead. I'm fine," I said. I waved my hand toward the door. I pulled the blanket over me as he left the room.

"We'll all be back later, okay?" Beau said, anxious to get away.

I still shivered. I had not thawed out since the morning. My feelings clamped shut. The pain in my stomach was more bearable than the pain in my heart. I closed my eyes to let the medication fade me out. I prayed that I would never have to end another life in me.

"Why didn't you just let me die on that street in Vietnam?" I cried to God.

CHAPTER 21
The Gift of Pain

The next morning we visited our Aunt Cuc's family for a celebration. We walked together on dirt streets, hand –in hand with our brothers and sisters. The five miles to Aunt Cuc's home took two and a half hours with us stopping to visit and talk to workers and neighbors. We dodged buffalo and oxen waste on the roads as we walked further into the countryside. We caught a small boat across the rusty river water, pulled by hand with a rope tied to iron pipes on both banks. We enjoyed our adventure. We joined their daily lives and used the basic forms of transportation like walking and riding oxen carts toward the working fields. We passed many rice paddies and impressed on our minds the breathtaking views of the mountains in the distance. We experienced the local ways and loved the part of our journey that let us share their daily way of life.

Aunt Cuc's home was a grass-mud hut, the kind I'd read about. A long table was set up for the party in one room while we talked in their family area. They took down the only photograph of our grandmother, our mom, and us from their wall where it had hung untouched for years. They gave it to us to keep. The aged, yellow newspaper left its mark and imprinted its age on the frame.

In the later part of the war, my mother convinced her sister to send her youngest son, Hiep, to the orphanage to save him. American parents adopted him, and he had recently graduated from college. He could not return with us, but we carried news of him to his mother and father and celebrated their hopes. Hiep was too young to remember them at all, and he showed no interest in seeking them out. But we wanted to keep their hopes up as long as possible.

We went to the kitchen to preview the main course. It was a small kitchen with heated clay pot burners and some cooked meat on the butcher's table. Raw meat hanging from the wall stunned me.

"They killed cow this morning at 6:00 for party," Doan explained.

"How many cows do they have?" I asked.

"Two. This one is dinner." He smiled, ready to enjoy the feast.

"Oh? Just for us? They should not have done that." I felt heavy. I realized the cost of the celebration.

"No problem. No problem. Vietnamese way. Enjoy!" he said, speaking Vietnamese to the family about my concerns as we left the kitchen.

The party started, and all three of us ate, feeling guilty that they'd killed one of their two cows for the occasion. Everyone else enjoyed the party without a worry, and I learned the Vietnamese held the attitude of "eat and be merry today, because you might not be here tomorrow to enjoy it." After dinner, the parents wanted my sister and me to sing the song I remembered from my childhood. We sang and danced with our hands to my favorite song, which every little girl knew. We cried at the memories and joy. I hugged my sister and felt at home at our big family celebration.

We thanked Aunt Cuc's family and left before nightfall. We walked back the five long miles and enjoyed the sunset and dusk of Vietnam.

Back home, we gathered around the coffee table for tea and to again visit with our family. Our talks brought Le and me back to our childhoods, and we continued our singing hand-in-hand. We became closer, and she opened up more to me. The younger

Aunt Cuc's Family

*Celebrating hope —
Our reunion at Aunt Cuc's*

children slowly grew tired of our discussions. Mom and Le sat with us late into the evening. They tried to understand more about our lives as we learned more about theirs.

Le finally opened up, and Doan told us that she was once married. Her mother-in-law made life difficult for her, and she returned home. The news came as a big surprise to me. Vietnamese girls get married only once in their lives, and custom expects them to respect their husbands and stay in the marriage no matter what fate might bring. In Vietnam, a wife no longer belonged to her family but became a member of her husband's family. She accepted all duties and responsibilities toward her husband and in-laws.

"I didn't know. I'm sorry." I hugged her, knowing it is very rare that Vietnamese marriages end in a divorce. I knew her life was not easy afterward.

"How is your life after the divorce?" I asked, knowing she might not share her pain with us. She shook her head, not wanting to tell us everything, and we accepted her decision. She sat there, sadly reminded of her fate.

I held her, and we became sisters to each other while our mom touched our hands. I understood her pain and her loneliness isolated in her dilemma. I wished I could comfort her during those times as I relived my own pain. I wished this moment of comfort among all sisters and mothers. Even in America, we all needed this comfort, probably even more so. I remembered my cries for comfort, as my greatest pain continued to resurface.

1987

I was dead to the world and did not move until the next morning. The sun was bright, shining through the window that Saturday morning. It was quiet, and I lay there listening for any voices or movement in the house. I looked at the clock. It was 10 a.m. I got up, only to be reminded of the abortion from the pain in my lower stomach.

I walked into the empty living area. They had already left to move Beau's mom. I felt so alone, and the place seemed so empty. The isolation gave me too much time to think. I changed into moving clothes and took off in my car for his mother's place, an overnight bag on the seat with a change of dressy clothes. I drove up just as they were putting a few final items on the loaded truck. Jenny's boyfriend was carrying the vacuum from the house.

"Hi, John," I said, walking toward the house to find the others. Victoria, the oldest of the three sisters was cleaning up the empty house. Jenny and her mother wrapped a couple more items inside a box. I looked for Beau and offered to help.

"Can't I help y'all do anything?" I asked, feeling a bit uncomfortable from the gazes. I wondered if they all knew of our situation. Nothing was mentioned.

"No, Christi, we're just about to go. Thank you, though," his mother said. I had known her a long time yet never really knew her. She busied herself with two or three jobs, providing for her family. I admired her spirit and determination. Her eyes often showed dark circles from her hard work, but she always had a cheerful attitude.

I walked outside to search for Beau and found him in front of the truck. Surprised to see me, he came close to greet me and whispered, "What are you doing here? They said you were not to drive, especially with a stick shift." At least, he showed a little concern.

"I'm fine," I said, and changed the subject. "Are y'all all set to drive to Greensboro?"

"Yeah, as soon as we stop somewhere for a burger for lunch. We're leaving now."

"Then I'm going with you," I declared.

He looked at me as though he felt I shouldn't go. My expression told him that I was going. He knew he couldn't win over my stubbornness.

"Fine," he said. "Mama is driving one car, Vic and Jenny are taking the other car, and John and I are driving the truck." Each car was filled with stuff for the move.

"Then I'll follow in my car," I said. When the procession pulled out, I remained the last car and trailed the herd. I was eager to get on the freeway because it did not require me to change gears and eased the tension in my lower abdomen.

The zooming of passing cars on the Interstate and the music on the radio brought me to a new environment from the deadly silence of the condo, at least for the day. I feared being alone with nothing to do except to think. I wanted to stay busy and forget.

We reached the new place, not too far from where they had lived when he was in high school. It brought back simple memories. As they unloaded, I could not lift anything. I felt helpless and in the way. After moving his mother, we drove to Leslie's house. She was the youngest of the three sisters, already building her future with the ideal all-American family. She had a year-old daughter, a wonderful husband, and the perfect first home, something you would see in a fairytale. Her stable life was what I'd wanted for my future with Beau. Now it seemed out of reach.

I waited there for the moving party and played with the one-year-old daughter. The harder I tried to forget, the more things surfaced around me that reminded me of my loss. We planned to stay at Leslie's that night and go to church the next day. It had been awhile since I'd been to church or had done any normal family activities. I looked forward to being part of it. Everyone ran around, and I tried to quietly fit in on my own. I was in a house full of people, but I felt so lonely.

We settled for the night. Leslie put Beau and me in the downstairs guest bedroom while the sisters stayed upstairs. I craved being close to Beau. I wanted to lie down in bed and cuddle with him. Since the day before, we had grown ever more distant. I realized there was no connection left when he took one of the pillows and a blanket out the door. His cruelty plunged like a dagger into the deepest part of my heart.

"Where are you going?" I asked, surprised by his move.

"Well, it's my sister's house, and it would not be right if we stayed in the same room," he said, trying to explain.

"Oh?" I sarcastically uttered. I followed him to the den as he made a bed on the couch.

"What do you think Leslie thinks we've been doing?" I asked, still amazed. He ignored my plea and closed his eyes to go to sleep.

I felt abandoned like the little girl under the shed in Vietnam, waiting for anyone to give a damn about her in this world. It was pointless. He would never understand. I held my pain inside.

With everyone too busy to notice, I retreated to my empty bed. It felt good to lie down. I curled up, again feeling cold and lonely, my heart crushed by the rejection and the grief. I closed my eyes, feeling sorry for myself, for my loss and my emptiness. I wiped away the tears. I pushed all the pain that I could bear deeper within as if I had swallowed broken glass. It cut into my soul as I tossed and turned all night.

The next morning came early. Everyone stirred about for breakfast and got ready for church. I got up and put on my casual clothes from the previous day and packed to leave. As they started to leave for church, I came out of the room, all packed to go.

"I have to work today, and I need to be back to make sure," I lied. They left the house for church as I drove back to Raleigh. Beau showed no concern about my decision and left for church with his family. I got in my car and turned the radio up loud to drown out my own thoughts. I kept my head up high. Determined to be strong and firm, I pushed forward.

I came back to the same empty condominium I'd left the day before. I went to the kitchen and got something in my stomach. I found some cheese and crackers. Directionless, I paced, walked, and kept busy. I finally sat at the table in front of the bay window with my snack. The sun felt good on my face. I stared out at the wooded backdrop of the property. I sat motionless, not hungry for food but for other comforts. I peered through the trees, lost in my own world.

I felt the twitching of my stomach muscles and the sharp pain in my gut releasing itself into the silence of the room. I bellowed out all my restrained pain in a loud cry. My weeping broke the deadly silence in this place and in my deadly soul. My pain was so great that I couldn't hold it in anymore. I cried to God, to the angels, to the devil himself with my pain. I could not stop my tears. My emotional volcano erupted. The tissues piled up on the table, and tears soaked my T-shirt as I released the endless pain.

I gasped for air as my stomach twitched with excruciating pain. I never knew there could be so much pain in me. I cried to be cleansed of whatever was left in me. I felt dirty, ugly and ashamed. My hopelessness took over my existence. I wanted to tear the skin off my body to find something to hold onto. I thought of my past and saw my future passing me by. I had nowhere else to go except back to what I knew before. My captive cage, my dragon was my only other option. My search for love had led me to the worst places.

That thought brought me more grief, and I gasped for air between my bellowed cries. I was tainted. Nothing good was left in me. Throughout my life I had sold myself in so many ways for simple security, food and shelter. I hated myself for not being strong, not being able to turn away from the money that bought me food and security, the fear that kept me choosing less for myself. I was a captive in every situation.

I could not trust anyone, not even myself. I went to the bathroom and stripped off my clothes. I wanted to wash my flesh and soul in the steaming shower. I cried my way through all the hurt and pain. I cried to God to take away all this pain. I grew weak from the pain in my heart, the puffiness of my eyes, the aching stomach that reminded me of my loss. I lost all hope. I had sucked away the only thing that was ever really mine. I lost my soul when I lost my baby.

"Why me? What do you want from me?" I screamed to the heavens a scream that shook the ground where I stood in the steaming water. I wanted cleansing of all my sorrows and hurts. What would ever wash me clean?

I painfully cried out, wanting my baby back! It was my only connection to another soul in this world. I had no more energy as the hot water scorched my skin. I got out and wrapped a towel around myself. I went to my unmade bed and crawled into a ball.

"I want to go home, God," my weary soul pleaded for relief. "Did you forget the little girl you saved from Vietnam?... I'm still here." I sent all the "SOS" energy I could muster. "You helped me once on the China Sea. Now I am lost in another kind of war zone."

"Can't you see me anymore?" I asked as I cried myself to sleep.

I woke up when I heard the front door shut loudly. I knew Jenny and John were back from Greensboro. I had slept through the day and was hungry for dinner. I freshened up myself a bit to hide any pain I had left. I entered the living room to greet them.

"Hi, guys, how was everything?" I asked, sitting down on the formal white sofa as we chatted across the open bar into the kitchen.

"How are you feeling?" Jenny asked, suspecting the obvious.

"Fine!" I responded as though I'd awakened a different person from this morning.

"Did you have to work after all?" she asked.

"No, I just called and quit today," I answered casually.

"Oh," she said, surprised to hear the news. "What are you going to do now?"

"I don't know... I'll find something tomorrow." I felt assured that everything would be just fine.

I felt different from that morning. I had broken down the weak side of me forever, and I became a stronger force to conquer whatever was ahead. Did God give me strength while I was asleep? Toughened from the pain, I understood my decisions. What I needed to do about my life was finish my college education. I donned the armor of Sir Thomas More and began again.

I had a few more months left before the next semester began. I stayed in Raleigh for two more months and worked at a Bennigan's Restaurant. I continued to accept Mr. Willis's "supportive father" supplemental checks each month. Finally, I called him to let him know my decision to return.

"I'll be moving back to start college next semester, okay?" I said. He was more than pleased, and I was ready to fight any battles to finish my education.

Beau and I remained friends and hung out together more loosely since we were again carefree during the next three months. Beau became a buddy, someone I had known forever. We were more comfortable in a non-committed arrangement. He went back to his normal fraternity rituals, and I didn't interfere. He stayed busy with frat parties, and I stayed busy waiting tables for my little wages.

Waiting tables, I came to appreciate even more the need for a college degree. Never again would I want to do that. Three months was long enough to earn my dislike for being on the other side of the table. It was hard work, and my size was a handicap to reach items in the kitchen to do my part well.

I looked forward to heading back to SMU. I wanted to be a college student again. I stuffed my car full of my belongings, then waited for Beau to call. He never called, and it was getting late. I hugged Jenny and thanked her for everything. Then I headed toward Chapel Hill to pick up the rest of my stuff from the fraternity house. Upset that Beau did not call, my temper rose the closer I got to the house. I arrived at the house, but Beau was not around.

"Beau is at one of the party houses," his roommate told me.

"Nice having you as a roommate," he said with a smile.

"Thanks," I answered. "Tell Dave I said goodbye, too. You guys were great roommates."

I headed toward the party. When I got there, I stormed in asking for Beau, and they said he was at another party. I fumed. "What do I care?" I asked myself. I charged out to my car and drove straight back to the house to get the rest of my stuff from his closet.

When I got there, he was back, drinking with his fraternity brothers on the porch. I was infuriated at his lack of consideration, his not caring enough to call when he knew I was leaving the next morning. He met me at the gate as I passed him to get my stuff.

"I needed to comfort my little brother with his broken heart," he said, half smiling.

"How nice," I countered. "Then you and your little brother can spend the rest of the time together." I pushed my way into his room and grabbed my clothes. I stormed out of the house as he tried to stop me from going.

"You inconsiderate bastard!" I screamed as I slammed my car door to leave for Dallas.

"It's one o'clock! You can't drive all night!" he said, talking through the rolled-up car window.

I was not about to stay the night with him as I spun the car around and headed back to Dallas.

"Just watch me!" I hissed back.

My anger and frustration gave me the momentum to drive 12 hours straight to my cage. With one nightmare over, I geared up for whatever waited for me in Dallas.

CHAPTER 22
Survival Instinct

oan shed more light on Le's situation, telling us what he knew.

"Bad rumors. Not good for her life. Her husband says she cannot give him babies. She tried to kill herself. She take poison."

I knew of the stories of women without male heirs who are by tradition disgraced and abandoned by their husband's family. I held her even closer to me, wanting to heal her pain and heal both of our womanhood experiences. Her story broke my heart, for I was once again reminded of our similar pasts. We bonded as sisters in our pain. Our lives mirrored each other from opposite ends of the world.

"She's still young. She's only 25 and very beautiful," I said, shocked by the new information. "Surely, that old wives' tale can't still exist today. At least she can return to her own home with Mom." I comforted her. Le sat there reliving her pain, while I envied her refuge home.

Doan changed the subject. I blocked out his voice as I became more sympathetic to my sister's history. A bond we had apparently carried in our separate lives had brought a common ground into our newfound sisterly relationship. I was happy that she had Mom to come home to, while I relived my own memories.

Sister, sister... together again.
A mirror image of East & West
Le Thu & Christi Hai

1987 - 1988

I came back to the house I'd left six months before. I returned to settle back into my old life with a new perspective. Jason was still away in Austin finishing his degree. It was helpful that Mr. Willis was out of town the weekend I came back. I went straight to bed after my long twelve-hour drive from North Carolina. As I put my stuff in my own room, I prepared for my new life.

When Mr. Willis came back from a business trip, we gradually resumed our routine of conversations over dinner. We never ate at home, and we rarely used the kitchen. Instead, we went out for dinner. We were civil to one another. I shared little of my trip and did not tell him about my terrible ordeal. I had come back stronger, and he accepted my terms. He knew I'd fight back.

I kept my bedroom door closed and locked at night. I never again put my foot in his room nor him in mine. Because he would rather have me around the house than for it to be empty again, he never forced the issue. I knew he'd been lonely, living by himself.

Then I geared up for whatever fights were necessary for me to get my diploma. I slowly assumed my role again of paying the bills and handling the household chores. I hired a maid to do cleaning. I kept the house looking lived-in, instead of like a cold, empty shell. Mr. Willis needed me to bring some life into the house—good or bad. Jason only came home occasionally, so my return was welcomed with cautious kindness. Mr. Willis saw that I had the strength to be able to leave and be on my own for six months.

Beau continued to stay in touch. To avoid any conflict with Mr. Willis, I would only return Beau's calls late at night. I suspected my conversations were being monitored, but I wasn't sure until a dinner conversation when he chided me for "crying to a kid."

Over time, the familiarity of our old habits returned. Mr. Willis and I got along fine, as long as I kept my guard up at all times. I was still suspicious of him and watched my back. I had one mission— to graduate by 1988 no matter what. I was behind one semester, so I crammed each semester full to graduate by August, including 18 credit hours in summer school. The work at SMU was tedious and not really reflective of real life. However, it offered me my freedom. I used my time and resources wisely, planning and plotting my escape.

I began to spend his money, without taking a noticeably large amount at any one time. I had my credit cards back. I stayed in the house and kept him company. I'd sharpened my skills at getting my way. I learned to cover my bases. I had learned to survive while I was in Raleigh.

My new strength made me even more attractive and exciting to Mr. Willis.

I became street smart from my outside exposure to real life. Carefully befriending those I needed to know, I cultivated relationships to ask for what I needed to accomplish my mission. Talking to adults was my focus; attracting older men was my specialty. I became resourceful. I learned to juggle many situations while I kept Mr. Willis content with my new attitude.

But inside I was still lonely and empty. My life was like a bucket with a large hole in it, and I tried to fill it with material things. It was hard to put any money in a savings account without Mr. Willis's knowledge, and he always encouraged free spending.

Our Christmas gifts grew to a couple thousand dollars cash each year, along with other gifts. I stashed money in various secret places. The little Vietnamese girl who hid food now hid money for her security. I charged all my credit cards to the limit each month and paid the minimum to camouflage the large, expensive taste I'd developed. Arguments again became part of our lives as he kept trying to break me down and keep me under his control. It became a world that I'd accepted. Each fight brought into clear focus how much he wanted me to be near, even at the cost of supporting my expensive tastes. He was willing to pay any price to keep me home with him. He was so afraid of being alone. I had found his vulnerability.

Mr. Willis never quit his drinking habits in the evenings. I accepted that as part of the battle. Each fight became predictable. To disarm him, I would yell, "Go ahead, tell me everything that I am! I've heard it all by now!" I was now de-sensitized to the angry words and vicious insults.

Having me under his control became his obsession. The more spirit I showed, the more determined he was to break me. Both of us became keen-witted with his obsession to have me. I filled my idle time acquiring expensive designer clothes from Calvin Klein, Jones of New York, Vakko suede dresses, 14- karat chokers and diamond rings. At 21, I had everything a woman in her 30s or 40s could want. My fondness for shopping fulfilled my need for revenge. It became apparent to his friends and workers that I had expensive tastes, and the amount of money I spent on shopping became a joke.

Mr. Willis called out from his home office one day as I walked past.

"Christi," he called. "I need to talk to you for a second." I poked my head in the door and saw he was going through the bills.

"Don't you think $35,000 on shopping this year is a bit ridiculous? I'm not made out of money, you know!"

"I know," I answered with some affection. "Things are expensive nowadays." I was acknowledging the price we both knew he paid for keeping me around. "I'll try better next year." I sweetly smiled at him intentionally to avoid a battle.

Mr. Willis was a very complicated individual who thrived on challenges yet never drifted too far from his comfort zone. I kept him challenged and entertained. He was a man with many hang ups and quirks. Looking good was the most important aspect of his image. He spent hours in front of the mirror in the mornings.

He also had addictive tendencies. It seemed that every other month, he ordered hundreds of custom made pin stripe shirts to keep his image intact. Being in Texas, he rarely put on a sport jackets. However, he always bought the best suede and the finest quality coats for his closet. The cuff links and ties were in endless supply. In contrast, he kept a lifetime supply of his old faithful polyester pants, which he preferred because they didn't show wrinkles. He maintained his crisp, all-together persona, an illusion to hide his many weaknesses. His obsession with maintaining his slim figure drove him to make unwise choices in what he ate and to vomit after his drinking.

He carried a large amount of cash with him at all times. He had a great need to be superior as he freely voiced his opinions during the many free lunches and dinners he provided. Using a pocket full of cash, he controlled others. Around the construction site, he was loud and crude in his jokes and expressions. But he always wore executive business attire to distinguish his position as president and owner.

His dependence every night on alcohol was part of his life; he never missed a beat. Cases of beer were stored in the garage for his convenience. His many illnesses became his secrets, and he read medical and psychological books to find his own cures. He distrusted doctors. He was a man who inside was an empty shell with no feelings. Trapped in a place of nothingness between life and death, he tried to isolate me and suck me into that nothingness zone with him.

Being his life-support system was too much weight for me to carry, especially while I tried to keep my own soul safe from being like his. I fought to move on campus the next semester. I wanted to do normal things, and I managed to charm him and get my wish of having a room to myself in a campus dorm. I spent his money to decorate it right down to the matching curtains that coordinated with my comforter. It was a taste of freedom that he allowed as long as I was accessible to him. He would still pick me up for dinner.

Our lives continued as he catered to my need to feel free yet he would not free me completely. Being on campus only made me realize even more my differences from other college girls. I lived a separate life and never fit into their world. I dated guys who commuted to SMU and struggled to pay their own way. They were more challenging to be with than the well cared for fraternity types.

My life became private and discreet. My secret war at home became more complex as I tried to portray a normal college girl. Dealing with reality can drive anyone toward drugs, alcohol, sex or other forms of escape to make it through the bad days. I discovered

body-building workout routines and jogged on the track endlessly to stay sane and to make it through my final year of college. Through the discipline of body building, I was able to create a tough shell to protect the insecure, fearful little girl inside. Pretense became my armor but it created more problems because Mr. Willis found this new more developed version of me even more attractive.

I thought I had freedom, yet I discovered I was still under Mr. Willis's watchful eyes and even ears! Our ritual of eating out always consisted of small talk about his business and about my school activities.

What outer shell do we create to protect the inner shell?

"So how is everything at school?" he asked at one of our usual dinners.

"Fine, I really like having a room there. It beats fighting the traffic commuting every morning! Thanks," I replied cheerfully. I was careful what I shared. Mr. Willis asked a lot of questions.

"So, have you met any friends yet?" he asked, watching me carefully for my answer.

I was wary about where this was leading. "Some, why do you ask?"

"Nothing. Just making sure you're enjoying yourself," he lied.

"Yeah, right! What are you up to?" I was suspicious and knew how to read him.

"Nothing," he answered again as the meal arrived, and I dropped the subject.

After the meal, we splurged on dessert and ignored the previous conversation. He drove me back to the dorm and tried to kiss me on the lips, but I turned my face and kissed him on the cheek instead.

"Tell your friend David I said, hello," he then said with a smirk.

"What are you talking about?" I was disturbed that he'd picked out that name. How in hell does he know about David, I thought to myself. It wasn't the first time he'd mentioned the name of one of my male friends. I ignored it as though I hadn't heard him.

It wasn't until I came back to my room one day after skipping a morning class that I saw my answering machine rewinding itself. Someone was going through my messages. I stood there dumbfounded as I heard a message from David play back.

I was astonished at Mr. Willis's desperate attempt to suffocate me. I bit my tongue and decided not to confront him. I refused to add to his enjoyment or give him any satisfaction. That summer I stayed close to campus to finish the semester while he continued to provide my every need except full freedom.

I petitioned the College of Communications of SMU to allow me to take my required course that summer, which was not offered until next semester. I couldn't wait for the next scheduled time in 1989. The request was granted when I confided my life and death situation to the head of the department. I gave an incredible story about my family in Vietnam, which I had no clues about at the time. The department head was sympathetic and adjusted the schedule so I could complete school that summer. I did have a matter of life and death in my situation, but no one would have believed me or cared to get involved if I shared the truth.

The summer of 1988 was the beginning and end of this battle. My diploma was my ticket to freedom. I anxiously finished my last

My ticket to freedom?
SMU Graduation Commencement, 1988

exam, and then I was free. I ran down the steps to my car that sunny afternoon, drove back to the dorm and filled my car full of clothes—the only things I owned. I moved into an apartment and paid two months rent with the money I had stashed for my freedom. Mr. Willis was surprised and almost proud that I had the guts to do that.

The sweetness of freedom was here! I finally understood freedom since our escape from Vietnam. I knew it clearly for the first time.

I carefully selected my apartment to look out over a creek with a willow tree in front to create a normal setting for me. I sat on the floor of my apartment with no furniture, two closets full of clothes, tasting freedom alone. I cried.

Freedom terrified me. I was so alone and unsure of my future. I'd gotten so used to my old lifestyle that it had become an addiction. Mr. Willis's was alcohol. Mine was the security of what money could buy.

I dated older men and married men to keep from being alone while my apartment stayed empty. I kept my lifestyle of eating out and receiving expensive gifts. On a typical evening, I'd look at my diamond watch, also a gift, and realize I was running late for my date. I'd put on my heels and look at myself in the same bamboo full-length mirror, checking myself over for the last time when there'd be a knock at the door.

I loved to go out on the town. I felt free. My dates would treat me to an intimate candlelight dinner. I drank very little wine—one glass would last all night, since I don't drink alcohol. Perhaps I would ask him to take off his wedding band. They always obliged. After dinner, we'd walk hand in hand out to the car and talk more in the dark.

The feeling of being wanted transformed my world into magic. I was the princess waiting for my Prince Charming to come and take me away to his magic kingdom to live happily ever after. I was happy as long as he didn't ask me to come to his castle. I was afraid I would be trapped again. I kept seeing my married friends for infrequent nights of passion, but I kept my freedom. We were safe and yet we fulfilled the needs we couldn't fulfill elsewhere in our lives. I tended to keep away from needy men, not wanting commitments of any kind. Mr. Willis had forever affected my ability to form trusting relationships.

On the other hand, Mr. Willis always knew my situation no matter where I was. He sent Jason over to visit my new apartment with a credit card and a full line of credit as a gift to help me furnish the empty apartment. I went out the next morning, enjoying my day at the furniture store, and I picked out my white-on-white striped sofa and love seat, with oversized chairs and accessories to match.

I'd always enjoyed interior decorating, and I'd done many of Mr. Willis's model homes. I bought a queen-sized bed and bypassed the dining room set. My dining room was already filled with a full Universal workout unit that helped me keep fit and saved my vanity. I was again in my element when I shopped, and I scheduled my full furniture delivery for the next day.

My apartment was my first expression of who I was away from Mr. Willis's influence or control. I camouflaged my world in a sterile and clean white-on-white décor. My bedroom furnishings were pure white and feminine. The room was filled with hand-embroidered white pillows, a white goose-down comforter and a white net canopy over the bed. I loved sleeping there with the canopy covering my bed as though someone were protecting me while I slept. I had my first bedroom that reflected my own taste. I no longer had to share my space with anyone. Keeping my world in crisp white offset how I saw the rest of the world. In my world of whiteness, I could breathe.

With my taste and experience in furnishing model homes, I entered the home furnishing industry. I not only discovered my design talents but also my work ethic. I was driven to make my world better. I stayed busy with work and maintained my lifestyle with help from older men with money. Mostly the men with money that I met lacked heart or character. They often seemed to depend on money as a way to purchase power. This type of man can control the will of others and too often others sell out to their power to them. I was one of these women. I had never known a healthy, honest and loving relationship. Even though the affection was shallow, the temporary dating quenched my thirst for love and affection. I always managed to choose less than I deserved.

My world was larger now. I kept to my hard, honest work for a smaller salary while I figured out my future. Mr. Willis, who tracked my every move, was still my greatest challenge. He came over to see the apartment and to give his approval of my clean, good taste. He was part of my life no matter what. He enjoyed living through me as I ventured out, not knowing what I would do next.

"I'll never be surprised with what you would and will do, Christi," he said with some admiration. He supported my ever-changing madness to get my way. He enjoyed my spirit and spunk to face new challenges as long as he was included somehow. With the gifts and money he gave me, he appeared to be a very generous man to outsiders. Yet I was always under his powerful control, and I knew my price had been paid.

I was never free from him. One time he hired a private investigator to keep up with me. He consistently supplemented my income to keep me at a lifestyle he knew I was addicted to. This was his only way to stay in touch with me. Infuriated by his obsession, yet expecting his persistence, I didn't try to banish him from my life but merely kept him at arm's length. My life continued to be an extension of his life. We simply accepted the love-hate relationship we had. It was our norm.

After years of molding and then breaking my spirit, he had accomplished his goal— dependency on him. I was free from him physically. However, I was not free from the effects of his repetitious enticements over the years. He took my greatest fears— hunger and loneliness—and cultivated them so deeply in my soul that it was hard to shake off. His had become the only home I had, for good or bad. I'd hung on to it as my only base, and it had nearly sucked the life out of me. I hated my life and my dependency, yet he continued to feed me enough rope to keep me no matter how far I went. I hated Mr. Willis yet I needed him. I was addicted to a lifestyle I could not live without. All I had was the self-image given to me by this lifestyle, as I tried to satisfy my yearning for the security of food and shelter.

Every part of my life was affected by my damaged image of men. My life was filled with manipulation and lies and empty promises from those who were around me. I didn't experience anything different. Nothing had really changed. More secrets and more loneliness. What did I expect from the world at large?

I used men as men used me. While the men built their egos, I had to control my world to ensure I would not be manipulated again. Ironically, I needed them for a false sense of love and affection, yet bad relationships stripped my self-respect and distorted my concept of a loving relationship. My world contained plenty of temporary affairs that warmed my body but left my heart and soul cold. From the American soldier's gum to expensive gifts from rich American men, my childish perception of being liked and important was fed.

I was in a cycle with no end. But the flickering hope of my dreams for true love stayed with me like the fairytale lives we all wish for. How many frogs would leave their warts on me before I could find one prince?

CHAPTER 23
Self-Reflection

alone in her hopelessness, my sister sat quietly in her bedroom with a bottle of poison in her hands. Her chance to end her misfortune came in the emptiness of our mother's home. Just as she took the poison, a voice from an intruder in the open home startled her. She choked from the surprise, and the bottle shattered on the concrete floor. A young man from the village had dropped in to look for my mother and found my poisoned sister. He took her to the doctor and cared for her during her recovery. My sister decided to rebuild her life and begin a relationship with the young man. The relationship was her hope to have another marriage—a good, loving marriage. She wanted to break the normal Vietnamese fate of divorced women, who were usually resigned to single lives. But my sister's relationship ended when the potential mother-in-law showed her disapproval of their relationship. The young man's mother decided no marriage would take place. My sister was unlucky in their eyes. She accepted her fate. I understood her fragility more. I tried to overcome this outmoded way of thinking and told her, "It's not true. Some man will be lucky to have you as a wife."

As I saw tears gather in her eyes, I wanted God to give her back her self-esteem. The protective side of me wanted to fight her war for her. However, I knew she needed to face life on her own and reclaim it for herself. I remembered the many fights I fought and the hard truths I faced with my own dragon in order to reclaim my own soul. Our beginnings were similar. My battle started when I tried to be what others wanted me to be. I wanted to tell her my story to give both of us comfort in our sadness.

1989

While my diploma represented another step toward freedom, my dependent patterns proved harder to break. My life expanded into the real world as an adult of 23. Beau stayed in my life by phone and by meetings in both Dallas and Atlanta. While I continued to see other men, Beau remained my only real contact with people my age. Each time I would put him behind me, he would still be available when my needs became more than I could get from other relationships. We related on the most basic level. Some people base their relationship on love, trust, and respect while we based ours on sex. It was his main interest, and it also filled my needs.

Mr. Willis still dropped the names of the other men in my life to keep his hold. His private investigator was doing his job well. However, he knew that Beau took away his possible physical attachment to me. I felt trapped in a loop between these two men. They were not men to me; they were the dragons I knew too well.

One night Beau asked me to marry him. I said "yes," less out of love than to free myself. I wanted to leave my past behind me in Texas. After Beau and I became officially engaged, he did an official thing by going to the bank and borrowing the money for the engagement ring. I felt sure I could make it work with the two of us married and me freed from my captivity. I moved to LaGrange, Georgia, to be near him. The attraction of a new town and a new start appealed to me. Atlanta was an hour away, filled with fine restaurants, shopping and first class hotels which provided escape. I often went to the city on weekends and spent Mr. Willis's money in Atlanta hotels.

The engagement broke off soon after I moved all my furniture there and settled in. Even though we were no longer officially engaged, we couldn't let go of each other. Beau was there waiting whenever I weakened and let him back into my life and my body. When I needed an escape, I turned to Beau. When he became a trap, I broke away.

Often I thought of the little orphan girl who arrived in Houston a dozen years ago. At first, people treated us as if we would break. They acknowledged the scars and the trauma of war on our young lives. That little orphan girl no longer surfaced. She became the American girl who covered her fears and scars with expensive clothes and other people's money. I tried to break away from that dependency and that image I had created.

I wanted freedom and feared it. Freedom was outside the gate of the orphanage, outside the gate of my well-constructed illusion. Freedom meant risk. It meant going to a place I did not know and doing things I did not know how to do. So instead I held on to the known. And the known for me was Beau and Mr. Willis. The men in my life did not really care about my well being. So I became like them—users.

My move to Atlanta also meant career opportunities for me. I interviewed with Fortune 500 corporations for sales positions. They looked for enthusiastic young associates, and I needed better guidance and normality in my new free life. I needed to find a $100,000 a year job to feed my lifestyle.

While I waited for one of the jobs to become available, I returned to Dallas to visit Jason and Mr. Willis. This visit was peaceful, compared to those of the past. I felt more confident about my future, and I started to hope that the day would come when I would break my financial cord to Mr. Willis. He had created a need and desire in me for luxury. Convinced that money was the key to my happiness, I knew I had to provide for myself those things he had given to me.

I got on the plane with new commitment and courage that day. I knew I would survive with or without Beau. Hope grew in me that I would make it. I flew from Dallas to Atlanta with great hope

The barefoot village girl, Vietnam

The American Girl, USA

and satisfaction in my heart. My life was now free of Mr. Willis's pressure. He accepted my move. But he still held me from a distance. He pretended to be a concerned family member, and I claimed a healthy family structure in my interviews. For the sake of my prospective employers and my new friends in the real world, I pretended to have a normal family who adopted me and I offered few details of my home life.

I believed society would not accept or understand any world other than an ideal one. I transformed into what others wanted me to be. I fit into this world, but I remained secluded in my private life as I structured and defined a new identity.

A simple life with Beau appealed to me after living in Dallas with Mr. Willis. LaGrange provided a quaint, small, homey scene. It was an ideal way to start my life over in this little town. Beau met me at the Atlanta airport when I returned. He did not speak during the hour-long drive to LaGrange. Not bothered by his silence—our history did not involve much verbal communication—I rode along lost in my own thoughts. I was glad to have the small victory of escaping from Mr. Willis's world. I knew I had hope with Beau. Little did I realize that my dreams would soon be shattered again.

Our long distance relationship had only given us time for a physical relationship in all our eight years. We could not relate on a mental level. After we called off our engagement, we still squabbled over the ring. I had made the arrangements in Dallas for Beau to buy the two-carat diamond ring at wholesale, without having to pay my girlfriend a commission. The ring was the last evidence of our engagement. Beau's sisters told him to keep the ring as an investment. But I gave him two options: either pay my girlfriend's commission and keep it for himself, or return it. I informed him I did not want the ring, and I could return it to my friend's store while in Dallas.

Pleased to be a thousand miles away from Mr. Willis and pleased to start life over again with or without Beau, it did not seem to matter. After two years of business experience following college, I was confident that I could find a career and start supporting myself. I willingly chose to forego the fine things for freedom. My resume was out, and I sorted out the last piece of the tangled web with Beau to begin again.

Beau and I drove back to my apartment, filled with the furniture Mr. Willis bought. Beau had a key. He often made himself at home there, since he shared an apartment with a roommate, just a few doors down. His apartment reflected his college years with little furniture, the bed on the floor, and clothes all over the room. It was only too easy for him to make himself comfortable in my well laid-out, fully decorated environment.

When we entered my apartment, I went into my bedroom. He followed me with my bag. I looked at my bed and froze. I felt the blood drain from my face. The sight left me cold and white.

"How dare you?" I screamed, turning around to face him.

"I thought you would like it," he said with a smile on his face. The look on his face was as degrading as the scene of my bed.

My white cotton bed, with my favorite lace pillows and other delicate things, was now scarred with four silk scarves tied to each post of my bed. The sight twisted my soul, and I realized what our relationship had become—more of the same humiliation. Mr. Willis had created an image of my mind and body, and now it mirrored itself in the scene created by Beau for my welcome home. Beau's desire for me was no more than an extension of what Mr. Willis created. He took it upon himself to take Mr. Willis's place in abusing my very being.

"How dare you think you can come into my apartment and do this?" I screamed as my frustration built. "Who the hell do you think you are? You don't have the courtesy to talk to me for an hour, and then you expect me to lie down for you, and let you tie me up! Fuck you! Get out of my apartment!"

I ripped the scarves from the bed. He ignored my anger and went toward the bed.

"Sorry. I didn't mean for you to think that. I'm really tired. Can we just forget it and go to sleep?" he said. He tried to cover his embarrassment and crawled into my bed to sleep, pretending that it was no big deal. I was even more humiliated that he thought nothing of it. He made himself at home in my bed as if nothing had happened. I couldn't deal with my anger and embarrassment. He had crossed the line into the core of my existence and confirmed my fear of what I'd become—a whore in his eyes.

"Get out of my place. Do you hear me?! Get out!" I continued to scream as he blocked my angry blows and kept his usual place in my bed. "How dare you think this is your place to stay when I told you to get out!" I nudged and tried to pull him out of the bed.

"Would you just let me sleep? I waited three hours for your flight. It's late! I just want to sleep. Would you stop making a big deal out of it?" he mumbled in a sleepy voice.

I couldn't get him to move as he shut me out to go to sleep. Infuriated, I felt powerless in my own apartment and in my own bed. There he lay, claiming his place in my bed. I continued to scream, denying him the quietness he needed to sleep, and my frustration built up to violence.

"You bastard! Get out of my bed. This is my bed. Get out! Get out!" I screamed into his ears. My anger built up even more that he didn't have respect for my property and claimed it for his own. He thought he owned me as well, and he had cruelly played out his fantasy with me. He thought he took Mr. Willis's place with his unsophisticated attempts to play on my deepest fears. The more I thought of his childishness and crudeness, the more disgusted I became with him and me for being with him.

I gave him too much credit and myself too much hope. I pretended that our past, our silence about my secret, brought us to a different level of understanding. I thought we had a private bond that I mistook for trust. He proved otherwise. Bondage was a game that he wasn't ready for, and our relationship wasn't ready for. A game that requires total trust. He had none in me, and I had none in him. He presumed too much to confront me with a game that takes total trust. The game required something he knew nothing about. And I neither trusted nor respected him. In reaction to my screaming, he slapped my face. I felt humiliated. He continued to stay in my bed without listening to my pleas for him to get out. I climbed into the other side of the bed, situating myself so I could use all the strength I could gather with both of my legs. Then I forcefully put both feet in his back to roll him out of my bed. It shocked him to get a blow, but he did not fall out of bed. He jumped up from his sleep, and he grabbed me and held me down on the bed to stop me.

I fought with my feet and arms, pushing him out of the bed.

"Get out of my bed," I screamed. His strength was twice as powerful as mine, and it made me tired of fighting. He grabbed my arms to hold me, and I could see his reddened face.

"Damn you!" he screamed, grabbing my throat and choking my last word to silence me. I gasped for air and panicked. I tried to scream, "I can't breathe! I can't breathe!" Caught under his powerful arms, I stopped lashing out. I needed to calm down, and to calm him down, from the heat of this nightmare.

I coughed as I fought for air until he realized his strength and that he was hurting me. He took his hands off me as I pulled myself away. I feared for my life for the first time. Again I cried to him, "Get out of my apartment!"

Enraged, he stormed out. I locked the door behind him, crying in fear. I picked up the phone to call home—Dallas.

"Beau just tried to kill me. He choked me... so hard... I lost all my air," I cried hard to the only person I knew would listen.

"Just calm down," Mr. Willis said. "Is he still there?"

"No," I said. "I tried to get him out of my apartment, and he wouldn't go."

"Just calm down. I'll call the bastard right now. Try to get some sleep." Mr. Willis comforted me, and I felt he was on my side for a change. I hung up the phone, relieved and maddened with the thoughts which filled my head. My throat was still tight from Beau's hands, and the implications of the four scarves lingered in my mind. This was the night that the American girl named Christi faced her dragon—the dragon of what she'd become to the men in her life: a whore, a sex object. My endless cycle of soulless relations finally reflected themselves to me from that bed.

I swallowed the sharp razor of reality that evening. I swallowed hard the thousands of sharp edges into my soul. I acknowledged what I had become—a scarred human being. Life forced me to look at those scars. I felt dirty and disgusted. I turned on the hot shower to help me feel cleaner somehow. Once again I stood under the shower immersed in its hot water, trying to wash out all the stains. Exhausted, I went to bed.

I took two sleeping pills to stop my mind from thinking. I

thought how liberating it would be to just sleep forever. I wouldn't have to deal with that person I'd become. I wouldn't have to live with her any longer. I closed my eyes and hoped I would drift away from this world forever. My life didn't seem valuable to me. It held too much grief and pain.

I saw the little Vietnamese girl named Le Thi Hai with her apple in her hand among the white clouds. She held an apple with both hands while the apple turned into a bitter fruit. The apple crawled with snakes, worms and insects. She stood there smiling at me, not realizing the rottenness of the apple.

"Can't you see your apple is not what you think?" I called out to her. My voice came out in very slow, dragged speech as it was hard to move my mouth. She stood there smiling, not understanding a word I said. Her childish smile haunted me as she moved her arms closer to her lips to bite into the apple.

"No! Don't bite into it!" I screamed, running toward her image as it drifted farther and farther away from me. I ran faster and faster. My legs, weighted down, never allowed me to catch up with her. "Hai, wait! Wait! I'm coming." I ran faster and harder in slow motion, reaching my hands out to her as she disappeared into the white heaven. Exhausted from my run, I fell down on my knees and cried, trying to catch my breath.

I woke up exhausted and remembered my dream of the two me's. My body ached as I moved slowly about my apartment that morning. I walked toward Beau's apartment to take care of business. His roommate answered the door, and I walked in, asking for Beau.

"He's in his room. Still asleep," he said.

I opened the door. "We need to take care of the ring right now," I said.

He moved slowly in his messy bed toward a wooden chest beside the mattress to search for the clock. It was noon.

"I'm glad you can sleep this late." I no longer had any toleration for him or his lifestyle. I thought to myself, "I needed him to escape? God help me." I looked around his messy room.

"I didn't get to sleep until late after talking to Mr. Willis for two or three hours last night," Beau pled in a sleepy voice.

"What?" I said. "Y'all talked for two hours last night?"

Shocked that the conversation had gone on that long, I asked, "What did you talk about?"

"Hell, he didn't blame me for scaring the hell out of you," Beau said, as though Mr. Willis had given him permission to do so. "I told him of your trips to Atlanta on the weekends and he said he wasn't surprised."

"How dare you talk about our relationship or my lifestyle with him," I said, bewildered.

While Beau felt he had a friend in Mr. Willis after their lengthy conversation and his understanding, I knew better. Beau lacked the experience of dealing with Mr. Willis's manipulation. I was sure Mr. Willis got everything out of Beau, not to defend me, but to strengthen his control over me. Mr. Willis had lured Beau into his web. Infuriated with myself for picking up the phone in my cries for help, I realized that Mr. Willis never offered me hope.

"How can you spend two hours talking to the very person I rightfully avoided all my life. You betrayed me to him for your own ego," I said. "Damn you!" I hit the wall hard to get out my physical anger. My hand ached, but I felt better from the release of my anger. "He got you under his little finger and got you to confess. You took this chance to throw as much dirt in my face as you could to make you feel better, didn't you?"

Speechless, he realized Mr. Willis had outsmarted him. He amazed me with his naiveté.

"I bet you didn't bother to mention the scarves," I said, knowing this game very well. "Do you really think Mr. Willis cares about our relationship? Do you really look up to him to justify yourself at my expense?"

He sat there, listening to my play-by-play of their phone call. "I know Mr. Willis. You don't. I would never throw dirt about you like you did about me."

Embarrassed for Beau, I saw him make an effort to apologize. I felt hurt for him for the first time. I knew so much more than he did. My world had become so complicated and so sophisticated. My real world was impossible for him to understand. While I fought many different wars to live my life and become stronger, he was still growing up. I felt bad for him, and I understood his feeling naive in so many ways. I'd been there, and I learned to get out the hard way. I never wished him to be where I was on the inside. He would never understand my war. He wasn't prepared for it, and I couldn't ask him to understand it.

"About the ring," I said, changing the subject. "I paid off your note at the bank. Look at it as gaining a good credit history. You need to stop by the bank to sign and close the note."

"I have to think about it over the weekend. I'm going home to visit my mom," he said, looking up.

"Fine. It's all taken care of. You can borrow more money at that bank in the future if you like. You have the credit history now. It's done." I'd become his teacher about finance and credit cards.

"Where did you get the money to pay it off?" he asked.

"I always have money," I said before closing his door. I walked back toward my apartment and thought to myself, I paid my way out of another unwanted web. All I had was money! While the money paid the price for freedom from Beau, I never had enough money to free me from myself. What price do I have to pay to be free from my tainted and damaged past?

I returned to my apartment asking, "What's next?" I had no one to talk to, and I didn't dare pick up the phone. I had no one I could trust. I went outside to my balcony to gain another perspective on my life. I stared toward the wooded area of my balcony view, looking for answers. Reflected back were only the kudzu vines that had taken over the ground and the large beautiful trees with their inexorable growth. Kudzu vines were that unstoppable vine imported from the Orient to grow in the South. Kudzu grows and grows and takes over everything. My life felt as if it was also being covered with kudzu, and it slowly suffocated my senses.

I grabbed my keys and drove off toward town, looking for answers. I finally stopped at a church with inviting red double doors. God was my only hope.

"God, please be there for me," I prayed as I walked toward the doors. They were locked. Desperate, I wandered to the side and tried the back doors. "I need to talk to you... you're my only hope... please let me in." Again, the doors were locked, and I regretted the many times I had forgotten about Him. Perhaps, He had forgotten about me, too.

I walked through the churchyard and sat on the bench. As night fell, I wanted to be near Him. I needed to feel his presence in my empty life. It had been a long time since I prayed to Him. I walked toward the children's playground and sat on one of the swings. His church was the only home I had left to find comfort. I needed to know someone still loved me. I needed Him to still love me while everyone in my twisted world turned against me. I felt so alone in the dark world. I felt helpless and lost like a child.

"If you can't hear me, I hope you get my message," I whispered as I wrote on the sand of the playground: "God, help me!" I sat on the swing, crying as I had so many times in my past, and again I wondered if He was there. I pleaded for Him to be there for me during this deadly silent evening.

The swing next to me moved, and I was startled by what I thought was a shadow. I raised my head up from my palms to be more alert to my surroundings and my safety. There was no one there but the mysterious movement of the swing by my side. My tears stopped, and I felt He was there. I accepted my answer. God was there for me.

My world was no longer silent as I swung myself, and the swing next to me moved with my motion in the dark. Screeching sounds from the swing set broke the silence. I welcomed the new sound and enjoyed the cold evening air against my face. I felt lighter. I felt comforted. I no longer wondered if He was there or not.

Thank you, God!

CHAPTER 24
Learning to Trust Again

Mom and Le often disappeared from our circles of discussion around the low table, yet they always joined us between housekeeping and fixing our meals. Mother supervised the arrangements with the maid, and Le helped Mom oversee the children and did chores around the house. They managed the household. Our stepfather tended the family's pregnant pig, watched their silkworm farm and watered the vegetables. They worked hard with their usual chores and still took care of our every need as their guests.

We appreciated Mom's desire and her accomplishments in providing for her family. We all understood that is how they had one of the bigger homes in the village. My mom often walked to the village market to do her shopping or sent the children riding on the family's oversized bicycle to pick up smaller items she needed for meal preparation. She represented the simple normality I lacked in my life, and I felt at home with her directions. I often walked with her to the market and watched her cook, between my talks with the men. I wanted to learn my mother's ways, to find the pattern in my life that I had missed. Though a grown woman, I was still her child and still needed all the basics of life. My life had taught me everything but the most essential things. It was not that long ago that I'd had to learn a new way of life in America. I hoped to learn more from her before I started my own family. I never had a role model to teach me how to be a daughter, a wife or a mother. The only way I could show her my childish needs was by following in her footsteps. We walked together silently during our many ventures, and I became that same little girl who was once spanked by her mother to make her go home from the field.

One day as she and I walked hand in hand to the market, Mom gave me a thumbs-up. "Michael. Michael, number one," she said, as she squeezed my hand to give her motherly approval.

"I'm not giving up yet. My right prince will come again to stay for good," I nodded.

It was my first reward as her daughter. She encouraged me to try again with her approval. After my father died, she did the same, and I was the same age she was when she started a second family. I related to her and somehow I mirrored her life from the other side of the world. I cherished her affirmation. I accepted our new, simple, and muted communication. No other language was as powerful as the silence we had in our relationship. No words diluted the depth of our connection. She saw no failure in my divorce. She saw only my successes. I had come home as a mother of my own daughter. In my dreams, I wanted for so long to be her daughter. Another dream came true for me on this trip. I realized I do have a family, rich with culture and history, to offer my daughter, after all.

Collectively, my choices, good and bad, brought me home to her, and my growth was a spiritual one to come home to God Himself. I was now home—a place where I could lick my wounds and heal. I had my heavenly Father and my earthly mother with me.

"Cam on," I said, thanking her and feeling happy to be with her again. We continued our walk to the market in silence. I thought back to my first marriage to see where it had gone right and the lessons it held for me during those seven years.

Priceless time with mom
Ky Do, Lam Doung, Vietnam.

Living my past...
A day at the market with mom.

1990

I was still young, lost and learning. I made one mistake after another.

I concentrated on getting a career started to free me from my situation. My hope of finding a connection with another human was what kept me fighting. But my patterns kept continuing. The more I searched for depth, the more disconnected souls I met, and that only brought me back to solitude. I wore my armor well as I faced the real world for my livelihood. Inside I felt like damaged goods, but I was determined to create my outer shell to be everything the human eye would envy.

I returned to my stringent physical routine to make myself tougher. I began at 4:30 a.m. and worked out at the gym until 7 a.m. It was my strength. I hid my sensitive soul behind the tough exterior. I cringed at the thought of trusting anyone again. I only trusted me to fight for me, and everyone else seemed to be my enemy. Fighting for me became my pattern. I grew hard toward those who wanted to be closer. I was the good soldier with an empty shell inside. I needed somebody to believe in me, yet I did not believe in myself. I kept my self-image and false confidence up, and confirmed the confidence shown by my new employer.

I accepted a position in sales with a Fortune 500 company. My career gave me a sense of worth. I desired to take care of myself and to thrive on the normality of the professional world. My bosses became my first mentors, and they encouraged me to develop my potential. While others saw great potential in me, I saw a beaten down, insecure little girl hanging onto her apple. Every day I feared failure and the loss of their confidence. I needed their hopes since I lacked hope. I needed their strength while I struggled every day to become the 4-foot-11-inch "tower of strength" I projected. I needed their guidance to live a normal life. I needed so much from them. I lacked the confidence that I could ever pay them back with my performance. My guard was always up, as I struggled with my interior wars.

My endless cycle finally concluded when my path suddenly

took a new turn. It started off simply enough—at a business meeting in Atlanta when I met a man named Joseph. At the meeting, his good looks and manners created interest in the other women in the room. But his blond-hair, blue eyes and handsome face presented an obvious and familiar scenario for me. Even though I tried to dismiss him from my mind, I was attracted to his spirit for life. His confidence dazzled me. He invited himself to sit next to me at dinner.

"If you don't mind, I would like to sit here to get to know you better," he began with all the confidence in the world. Amused, I admired his opening and played the expected part.

"Sure, it's all yours," I said and then asked, smiling, "So, tell me, how did you meet your wife?" Everyone I met on the sales force was married except for me.

"I'm not married," he corrected.

"Then I presume there are a couple of girlfriends who are very interested in you across this table?" I asked, eyeing the same women who surrounded him a few minutes before. I sensed the watching eyes along the table and suspected some intimacy or interest for him from some of the women that evening.

"Nope, just me," he bluntly stated.

I turned to my other side, acquainting myself with my other new co-workers, and I ignored his interest. Later, he showed up at the bar where I met with others. We talked. He surprised me with his intense conversation. I had underestimated his depth at 28 years old. His maturity and intelligence captured my attention. Later we danced. After a while, I excused myself and left him waiting. I never returned.

We met again a month later in Atlanta at a business show. I accepted his dinner invitation to celebrate his birthday. I found it was a special celebration. We shared many common beliefs. Passionately, we sought to find a soul greater than our own. It was refreshing to me that our conversations interested him more than the typical physical scenarios of my past.

He was very open, and I picked his brain for his knowledge of the business. He shared openly with me his great hopes for finding a sensitive soul as his partner. He was ready to commit to a relationship while I was ready to forego it all together.

"I'm not interested in developing any kind of relationship with you or anyone else," I declared many times. "I do appreciate your helping me to understand my new career, though."

We spent an evening talking in depth about his beliefs and passion for life. I talked about my passion to succeed in my new career. With his charm, he challenged me intellectually and questioned me with a keen sense of being able to read me. He openly challenged my shield and went straight to the point in our discussions. His was the most straightforward and stimulating style I had ever experienced. Nothing was oblique with him. In all my conversations, I buried layers of subtlety and innuendo. He understood me somehow. Did I dare tell him?

"Would you help me understand my new job?" I changed direction to business when the conversation became too personal.

For the next few months, he did just that as I learned my job. I was scared, and he knew it. His phone line was always open to me. I was unsure and full of thousands of questions. I had everything riding on this role to fulfill my needs and get away from my past. It was my chance to be free. He was patient and helpful and answered all my questions.

My past was right around the corner. As I geared up to move back to Dallas to work on my own, Joseph became my guide and my friend during my period of adjustment. I needed his help and knew it was important to cultivate his friendship.

As we talked, we learned more about each other and ourselves. He did not want any payments of any kind. I was a friend. I had never experienced having a friend before.

"Joseph, what causes you to spend a lot of your time with me? Is there something you want from me that I've been too dumb to figure out?" I quietly asked him during one call.

He laughed and said, "You are giving it back by talking to me." Then he paused. "I am intrigued by you. Don't get me wrong; this is not a line or anything. You just got it. You've got the spirit, the passion, the charisma and a glow about you that is attractive to me."

I took every nice word deeply into my soul like balm to heal my many scars. "He thinks I am all that?" I wondered.

"You've got a lot of excellent qualities about you that make you worth the investment of my time," he added.

He thinks I am worth it? How could this be? I wondered. I thanked him for the most wonderful compliment of my life. Joseph was the first friend without a price that I had made in my new world. Perhaps my luck had changed.

I opened up to him more about my beginnings as a Vietnamese refugee. He thrived on hearing my tales, which I had only shared with a few people. I thrived on his kind words as I learned more about myself again. He taught me that not everyone is like Mr. Willis and the few people I knew in my life. He shared. I listened. Our co-worker friendship continued with many long distance phone calls until a few months later.

While the rain teased its way down the evergreen of the mountainsides, Joseph and I ventured up among the thousands of trees. We climbed up the mountain, noticing the beauty of Mother Nature's creations as we enjoyed the fresh clean air.

It was a mysterious day to be up on top of this mountain. The fog covered the valleys as we stood there looking down on Blue Ridge, Georgia. There was a sense of magic in the air, and it seemed that nature was toying with our emotions. She had already mesmerized the mountains with her potion. She filled the atmosphere with a surprising mixture of mystery. The dark, heavy clouds weighed themselves down to the mountaintops, and the sun cast its faded rays to silhouette the heavens softly on a small town below.

I had never heard of his town until a few days earlier during a phone call. Then here I was, climbing up Blood Mountain where the Appalachian Trail to Maine began. Joseph told me the history of Blood Mountain. A site of a great battle between two Indian tribes, people said, the mountain on that day had so much blood running down the side that it earned its name. I heard the trail was long, hard and beautiful but one that only a few would attempt. How strange that this trail reminded me so much of my life. Blood Mountain was a metaphor for my journey. What lay around the bend? As I stood on Blood Mountain, my soul bled inside for answers. My search was like looking beyond those valleys, too dim to see but filled with promise and wonder.

I felt alone standing there, yet I was not alone. When Joseph asked me to share this weekend with him, I had been reluctant to come. It was another relationship. I thought I did not want to pursue any relationship. How could I trust anyone enough to fill my life with any substance? By now I had no expectations, yet a spark of life flickered within my soul and kept me hoping to find love and joy.

Joseph was different from others I had met. Somehow, he knew where to take me to get me to lower my shield and share my thoughts with him. The misty cold air made me shiver. Opening up made me shiver inside. I shared my thoughts about this mountain and the hold it had over me. He stood there in silence and let me talk as we both looked ahead and beyond, toward the other mountains.

"I have wished so many times that I could have this kind of perspective in life," I said. "You see, up here, I feel stronger and safe. I can see around corners, and ahead, and I can turn back to see where I have been. I want to put all of the missing pieces I've lost along the way back into my life."

Then I turned to him and asked, "Do you ever feel that there is something missing from your life?"

"Matter of fact, yes! My missing piece is not having that special someone to share my life with," he replied. He had a clear goal to find his mate. Surprised, I admired him for being completely truthful with his own feelings and thoughts. I listened as he continued.

"I grew up here. These mountains are home. It's been a long time since I've been back to Blue Ridge and to this mountain," he told me. "Actually, this is where I see things more clearly whenever I need to sort things out." He walked closer to me and put his arm around my shoulder. I relished his strength. He turned me gently to face another direction.

"Do you see that mountain on your left?" he asked. He pointed toward it. "That's Brasstown Bald. We'll drive up there tonight, and I'll share my secret with you." He took a deep breath to begin. I watched his chest expand to inhale more air. "You see that's my haven. I go there, and it re-energizes me from the stress in my life.

I go there to find my peace, to be alone with the wind, the owls, the stars and moon, to think."

He moved me around in a circle to catch a panoramic view of his roots.

"There is something for me up here in these mountains that you have never experienced. I will always have a place to go home. I run here to lick my wounds," he said. He took pride in his haven while I ruefully noticed his accuracy in detailing my loss.

"You and I are very similar, you know. Our needs are very much alike, even though we came from very different backgrounds." He turned to me and looked straight into my soul. "You're not like other women I've met before. Your soul runs deeper than you let on to the world."

"I bet I'm your first Asian female acquaintance and the first Asian person to set foot in these North Georgia mountains, right?" I laughed to divert his attention from his search into my soul. "So, what's a guy like you doing here on these Georgia mountains all these years? You don't even sound like a Southerner."

"Well, you are looking at one of the rare natives. There is a saying here, when God created Earth, he started in Blue Ridge," he smiled.

"Can I confess? I never would have thought you came from a small town. New York, maybe, or Chicago," I said. "What happened to your southern accent?" I teased him with my Southern accent with the Asian twist.

"I stayed in Blue Ridge until I was 18. I left to go to Southern Tech in Marietta and paid my way to school and then, later I went on a baseball scholarship to finish it. It's not that far, and yet it was a world apart from here. I guess I lost some of my accent somewhere along the way," he said and laughed.

We sat down on the rocks, propping our backs against one another as we looked out over the mountains and talked. "I appreciate and understand what this small town environment gave me the further I go out in the world, Christi."

"And what is that?" I leaned back, my head bumping his.

"Oh, very basic rules on how to live a better life. I know what I want out of life. I respect hard work and do my best. Be kind to neighbors and hold onto lifelong friendships," he answered. He turned around quickly and caught my back before I fell on a rock. I screamed in fun, and he smiled.

"When I was a kid, I used to hunt and trap animals for their furs. I sold them for my savings. I thought of that just now," he beamed, sharing with me his young adventures.

"Oh, yuck! And you think that was fun?" I made an awful face. "I knew there was something strange about you."

He played his Daniel Boone part well to my imagination. My path kept sending me Southern men.

"Well," I admitted. "I hope to find a place like Blue Ridge in my life. I am tired of running around searching, you know? I want to have a place to call home where I can really be me. You're right, I don't have a home to run to in order to lick my wounds."

He read my thoughts, "Things haven't been so perfect in my life either, but I've been looking for a lot of my missing pieces ever since, so I can honestly say that I do understand your search. Being a roving salesman allowed me to travel, and I learned a great deal. Since college I can happily say I know who I am for the moment, whether I'm in Blue Ridge or Europe."

"How do you know who I am?" I asked. He paused before he answered.

"You got to go on a hunch," he answered simply and smiled. "You got to trust."

His statement jolted me. How much he could see of my inner thoughts. He said so many things I wished I understood.

"Trust, huh?" I repeated. "You know, you're the first guy who actually came through my front door instead of through my bedroom door."

Never had I come across another soul like his. He soothed my fears with his understanding, yet never tried to get past my shield. We continued to talk about life, values and aspirations while sitting on top of the mountain. We respected one another from the first day we met as co-workers. I was the rookie of the business, and he was the rising star. I approached him hesitantly because of the tangled webs of my previous life.

I recalled when he had invited me on this trip. I was training in

Spartanburg, and Joseph called to invite me to come visit his hometown where he was going for the Mother's Day weekend. He thought it would be more interesting than being stuck in a hotel.

"What? To meet your mother and visit your hometown?" I was firm on the telephone. "No, I'm not interested."

"No, no, it's not like that," he explained. "I bring my friends there often. My mom is accustomed to it."

"Look, like I said before, I am not interested in getting involved with you or anyone else. Relationships are the last thing on my mind." I was constantly raising my guard so I wouldn't get involved.

"Then be my friend. That's all!" he said so convincingly. "Besides, what else are you going to do there?"

I said no and hung up. The phone rang again after a bit, and it was Joseph. Before he could say another word to me, I repeated no abruptly, and added, "I don't think it would be best right now. I'm not ready to get involved."

There was silence on the line, and then he said in a sober tone, "Christi, you and I know we share so many common values and understandings. We can have a wonderful relationship if you just let me in a bit..."

"What for? All you guys are alike," I answered in a matter-of-fact tone.

"Damn it! I am not the other guys. Just trust someone for a change, would you? You can trust me," he said, as he calmed his voice.

"Oh no, you're not going to get in that easily," I responded.

"I wish I could reach over this phone and shake off that damn shield of yours. It's your loss then," he said. He hung up.

Lost for words, I felt a sense of confusion and loss hit me at the same time. I paced the hotel room as I sorted out my feelings about this person. He had been straightforward with me whether I liked it or not. Unlike the others, he didn't play games or deceive me about his interest.

"You can trust me. Just trust someone for a change," I heard over and over in my brain. That comment twisted around in my head as I paced the room, wanting to believe him. I grabbed the phone and dialed his number. As it rang, my hands gripped the phone, and I took a deep breath.

"You're right. I need to trust someone," I said quietly, overcoming my fear.

I did need to trust someone, so here I was on Blood Mountain.

The time on Blood Mountain passed quickly, and we talked constantly. We did not notice that the mist turned to rain and the daylight had begun to dim. We started to hike back down the mountain on slippery rocks and in wet clothes. I felt a warmth against the rain and the cold air. I was slowly thawing from the pain in my past.

Joseph reached his hand out to me, and we walked down together. A connection existed between our thoughts.

"What do you think about marriage?" I asked, wanting to know more about his perspective and to know more about the traditions in his simple life.

He stopped, looked at me and said, "Would you marry me?"

He caught me by surprise with this question. I stood stunned for a moment.

"Would you marry me?" I repeated his question.

"Yes!" he answered. Then he asked me again, "Would you marry me?"

"Sure," I said.

"My missing piece is having you to share my life." He kissed me to seal his promise. He held my hand tightly, and we continued to hike down along the trail.

After the weekend, we drove away in different directions. We promised to meet again to exchange our vows. As I drove back, there was the usual skepticism that this magic moment would vanish after I got back. I was still doubtful and not holding my breath. We had not confirmed a date. We pretended well. I called his bluff, and he called mine.

When I arrived back at my hotel, I found a message: "Saturday, May 18, is the day. Love, Joseph." Shocked, exhilarated, and skeptical all at once, I did not believe our marriage would come true, but I played this marriage game. For a week I waited and watched for the end of the game. He did not stop.

He called later to say, "Meet me half way in Pigeon Forge, Tennessee, at the courthouse." At the time, Joseph was in Ohio and I was still in Spartanburg in training. We were to meet on Friday to get a license before the elopement. He handled all the details. Would we both show up? Would this really happen?

I arrived first. Looking at my watch, I realized there were only 15 minutes before the courthouse closed, and there was no Joseph. My natural doubts arose, and I prepared myself for disappointment. I sat on the bench in front of the courthouse, watched cars and people go by and hoped to get a glance of Joseph before I had to leave. Just then a blue car peeled into the side parking lot of the courthouse. My heart raced as I ran to meet Joseph. He grabbed his jacket from the back and ran toward me.

"I'm sorry you had to wait. My meeting went on longer than I planned," he said, catching his breath.

We rushed toward the courthouse with great eagerness, racing against the clock. We barely made it inside before it closed. We went in and asked the clerk for a registration form for a marriage license. We both signed soberly, and I realized it was for keeps now. The courthouse closed its doors behind us, leaving both of us walking aimlessly down the steps toward the front lawn. We sat on the bench with our own thoughts of this beginning. We would learn to love each other and know each other in time, I felt assured.

"What's with the worried face?" he asked.

"Because there is so much you don't know about me," I answered.

"All I know is that you have a lot of love to give, even though you go out of your way to hide it with your toughness." He smiled. "And you have a kind heart. That's what matters most to me."

I wondered if he could really understand me.

"We'll get to know each other in time. I know there are two good souls sitting right here! Whatever secrets or problems you are going through, we'll work them out. I knew from the first day I met you that you were hurt. In time, Christi, you will know I will be your Rock of Gibraltar," he promised.

I looked into his eyes and thought about how much he couldn't imagine about me.

"Joseph, there is a lot we don't know about each other. My life has not been perfect, and I do not expect yours to be either. Agreed?" I wanted to be up front without telling him my sordid life story.

"Agreed," he said. "I know this might come across as bizarre, but you are the soul mate I've been looking for. I cannot explain it. I sense it in my heart."

While Joseph seemed so excited about our plans, I felt numb. My heart grew heavy with not knowing how I should feel.

"Thank you for feeling that way," I answered.

I never asked Joseph to love me, and he never said that he did. We both took our own risks in this journey together. We knew love would be there in time. Was this to be forever? Were we risking too much? Too soon? Too fast? Would we make it through with all the unknowns and the challenges?

I didn't know. It always seemed that whenever I tried to escape my past, a path kept leading me back to face it.

CHAPTER 25
The Healing Begins

Jason and I gained so much during our stay in Vietnam and grew to love the new family in our lives. We continued our morning ritual of walking to the center of town for coffee. They revealed to me that in this society only men usually get together for café. I was the only female in the groups of men, except for my mom. I sensed a toughness and respect toward my mom in this world dominated by men.

I admired my first role model. I had lacked one in all my years of growing up. Michael observed the great adventure, yet he also became an integral part of it all. I took in as much as my body and soul needed with our rediscovery.

On Christmas morning in Vietnam, Mom surprised all of us with her understanding of our customs. The house was full of neighbors, and they helped her prepare a great feast. They moved two large tables into the living room. Mom placed fresh flowers in the center of the tables, and the kitchen was filled with enough food to feed the whole village. My mother radiated with joy, having her family back again. This was her greatest gift.

She placed a beautiful three-layer cake in front of us in our

*Our first Christmas
with my Vietnamese family*

honor. A Christmas tree crowned the top layer. Someone wrote our three American names on the side of the second layer, and the bottom layer announced, "Happy Reunion Family." I watched my powerful mother carry out her tasks and transform her home to make this party a success. I took in all the love and watched Mom in her element.

The guests arrived in large numbers. My mother, sister, and I changed into our traditional Vietnamese dresses, the *ao dai*, for the occasion. My mother and sister picked out the material for me and took me to a seamstress in Dalat. I wore the dress as a reminder of my Vietnamese heritage. The sounds of approval from our guests filled the air, and we pleased everyone when we started the party.

My mother and I exchanged gifts. Mom presented us a copy of the only photograph of our father, sketched in black marble, as our remembrance of him. I handed her my album and letter in exchange for her notebook of our family history to help me remember.

"You will know who you are, and you will come back to me as my daughter," she said. I held her notebook tight against my heart.

We all toasted to our family reunion. It was our best Christmas Day ever.

Her gift helped me take my first step in finding my soul. My mother took us further into our past, and she also took us back to her as her children. Everything she did helped us get closer to our faded memories. We visited our grandmother's grave and burned incense to her spirit. Mother told us that her last words before she died were "Sang" and "Hai." She had called for us before her death.

As my mother held me, I felt the love of my family enclosing me. My mother became my second reality check, and I remembered my first reality check, which started on my happy wedding day with Joseph.

1991

On a beautiful day in May, we said "I do" to a solitary minister in a chapel of empty booths. Then we drove back to our separate, daily routines the day after the wedding. Joseph went to Ohio, and I headed back to Spartanburg.

Our announcement surprised everyone, including his family. Joseph was based in Columbus, Ohio, while I got ready to move back to Dallas—1,000 miles apart! We adjusted to our living situation. Apart for the next three months, we prepared to consolidate our lives in one place, Dallas, for the climate.

We stayed with my family when we got to Dallas. While we decided where to buy a house, I provided a normal family history for my new husband as much as I could and kept my secret to myself. I phoned Mr. Willis ahead of time.

"Mr. Willis," I greeted him. "I'll be flying into Dallas next week with my husband." There was silence, and I knew I had shocked him for the first time.

"What are you talking about?" he asked, gathering his composure. "I thought you and Beau broke off the wedding."

"Yes, we did. I didn't say I married Beau," I said, pleased to throw him off for the first time in my life. "I need you to be normal about everything. He doesn't know anything." I hoped to enjoy my new life without Mr. Willis's interference. I felt a sense of victory from the surprise, but I feared the unknown. I knew him and the enjoyment he would find in taking advantage of a new quarry of information.

Joseph was the best thing to ever happen to me, and I wanted to make every situation perfect. I pretended I had a perfect family for him to meet.

Mr. Willis played the part well by welcoming Joseph to the family. Mr. Willis's ability to woo newcomers with his great entertainment offerings, free-spending lifestyle and his great stories hypnotized Joseph. We all enjoyed ourselves as Joseph and Mr. Willis found a common interest in politics.

Still I lived in fear, watching Joseph's reaction to anything unusual. Mr. Willis offered to build our home as a wedding gift, and we started a search for an ideal lot in a suburb of Dallas.

Joseph and I adjusted to our new jobs. We had violated the first unwritten corporate law with our marriage, but the company was flexible this time, and gave Joseph my Dallas slot and transferred me to a new division within the company that required more training.

There was a new career and a new marriage for me to balance in the midst of my tangled web at home. I took it upon myself to resolve it and continued to pretend. Joseph spent more time with Mr. Willis without my supervision. I traveled a bit more for training. My senses were alert for any changes, and just as I expected, Mr. Willis slowly began attacks on our marriage, attacks disguised as funny stories with stinging intertwined messages.

"I hope you both keep working hard for Christi's expensive tastes," he would say, winking at Joseph.

He kept Joseph entertained with his intellectual discussions during the dinners out—that part had not changed. This family never ate in. Every meal was at a different restaurant. We continued our family norm while Joseph quietly observed and tried to put all of the pieces together.

One evening, Joseph closed the door to our bedroom and asked me to sit down for a minute and talk. Appearing puzzled, I sensed his question.

"Tell me why your father keeps telling me to watch out for you? I feel like he's constantly trying to warn me about you. It seems like he is trying to pull our marriage apart. Is there something you have yet to tell me?" He spoke in a calm, analytical way, as if to solve a puzzle.

"Don't pay too much attention to what he says. He's full of it. I'm sure you realize that by now from his jokes," I said and smiled to lighten the situation.

"Christi, don't avoid the issue with me. I am not a child who cannot see what is going on. This might be normal to you, but it is not. Explain to me the love-hate relationship you have with your own father. You're rude to him, actually hate him, and you're not consistent." His voice showed irritation, and I ran out of lies.

"Another thing," he added, not letting the moment go. "He deliberately lied to you about the house to stir a fight between us. Actually, he made a liar out of me in front of you."

I felt numb. He shook my shoulder to get me through my emotional block.

"Christi, I feel like I'm being pulled between the two of you. What game are you playing?" he continued to press harder.

"I'm sorry, Joseph," I said. "I didn't mean to hurt you by all this.

I was just protecting you as much as I could."

"Why are you protecting me?" he asked, puzzled.

"We'll be moving into the house soon and things will be better," I said, avoiding his question.

"Hell, there's an unspoken war going on here, and you expect me to accept it and go on! Mr. Willis dragged this house construction out for some reason. I thought we trusted each other when we got married," he said as he cornered me.

"I do trust you. You're the only one I've ever trusted in my life. Please believe me!" I pleaded. "He's just trying to pull us apart with his tricks, and I'm trying to keep us together. Joseph, you are my hope. You're the best thing that ever happened to me, and I don't want to lose that. I have to win this one." I hated the fact I had not better supervised his interactions with Mr. Willis.

"You've got me! What are you trying to win?" he asked.

"All my life, he tried to destroy me no matter what I did. I have nothing that does not belong to him. He owns me!" I felt trapped and fearful of Joseph's reaction. "Stay in there and fight with me. I need you to be on my team."

"What are you talking about? We're not in a war," he said calmly.

I stopped and realized I had been at war all my life.

"I am," I said. "I'm sorry I brought you into it." I resigned myself to what naturally would take place in my life. Another ending. Another start. Another disappointment. Another blow.

I finally risked getting it over with and moving on without Joseph. My confession began. After I finished, I was resigned to end it all. It did not matter how he reacted. I felt I knew already.

"Oh Christi!" he said in a low voice. He put his arms around me. "I'm sorry. I should have guessed. Now things make sense." He held me while I collected myself. I could not look him in the eyes. I felt ashamed as he lifted my face to his.

"I still want you and our marriage," he said.

I cried to hear the words that I had wanted to hear for so very long.

We sat on our bed, feeling connected for the first time in our marriage. We survived our first major crisis. He did not turn against me. He did not blame me.

"Let's go for a walk," he suggested as a way of getting out of the house.

We walked along the subdivision roads, taking in the night air and thinking. I sensed Joseph working things out in his head as we walked in silence. Finally he spoke.

"Why did you want to move back to Dallas and into his house?" he asked.

"Because it's the only home I've got, and I wanted to pretend that I had a normal family for you," I explained.

"We could have lived in Ohio," he said.

"Well, it's too cold for me to live there for one thing. Remember, Vietnam, my birthplace, is near the equator," I laughed, trying to lessen the heavy weight we both felt. "Honestly, I wasn't sure where our marriage would take us. I did not want to be stranded somewhere new. Dallas is the only place I have. I could not totally trust you yet. It is hard for me to count on anyone totally. At least, I know how to handle the situation with Mr. Willis. I still don't know you that well."

I stopped talking. He waited in silence and eventually I continued to open up.

"Please hear me. I trust you more than I ever trusted anyone. You had to prove that to me. I needed to know you would fight battles with me. You did not turn against me when I told you my deepest, darkest secret. Thank you," I said. "You are the second person who knows. My first experience with the truth burned me to the core, and I'm still gun-shy. I didn't want you to turn against me, too."

I took a deep breath.

"I regret bringing you into my rotten world, Joseph." I reached for his arm to stop him from walking and emphasized my sincere apology.

"Thank you. I realize now that you think nothing of what you've known all of your life," he said, slowly putting the puzzle together for me to see. "This is unhealthy as hell, but you never saw it like that. Christi, you've been sexually abused and God knows what else. Do you understand the implications of this? You have been molested by your own father!"

His directness pierced my ears with its meaning. I put my hands to my ears.

"Nobody ever used that label before. I did not know anyone cared to understand what I went through," I said. "I just knew this was my life that I had to lead."

I needed to hear an outside perspective, but I felt uneasy taking this in.

"That's because you didn't tell anyone. The person you told is a damned fool," he answered. "Have you talked to a psychologist or anyone else?"

"No! What for?" I asked.

"Christi, any adult would help you out of this corner," he said.

"Right, like I could trust any stranger," I laughed. "No, thanks. I have done fine these past eight years. Weird at times, but that's my life." Joseph looked puzzled and perplexed by my answer.

"What?" I asked as if I did something strange. I felt I had to give more information for him to understand. "You don't understand, Joseph. I had no one. I needed to eat, sleep and go to school. It is not as simple as you say. All my life has been going here and there without roots or a family to call my own. I got this far to have a life. At least you had a family." I started to walk ahead and felt the weight coming back on my shoulders. He caught up with me and continued working through the puzzle.

"Christi, it's not your fault," he emphasized.

"I was guilty. It takes two to tango, as they say." I gave him a wry grin. I swallowed my guilt. I felt I had to confess it all. "I had to pay for being stupid and naive at 17, that's all. It is not great living with that kind of punishment. I paid for my mistake for the past eight years. Isn't it enough?"

I looked at Joseph for some sort of answer or pardon for the crime I had committed in my teens.

"I am not asking for pity, just a little understanding, that's all." I felt flushed, exhausted from the release of telling my story for the first time to a sympathetic listener. He was silent. I felt uncomfortable with the silence. I needed to fill the silence with my words.

"Do you think I like being who I am?" I asked. "I fight and hate myself everyday. I can't change it! Oh, how I wish I could start my life over again, and I can't! I am stuck with me inside, and I cannot wash deep enough to get rid of it. I was stupid! I hate myself for it! I should have known better. I was stupid," I cried, wishing Joseph would say something. I felt like one of the unfinished houses that surrounded us. They looked good on the outside but contained only a cluttered shell within.

"Christi, you've been blaming yourself. Mr. Willis was 40. He did know better. He was the adult in all of this. You were just a kid," he said, helping me see the truth about the relationship.

"You were just a kid," he repeated, slowing the tempo to help me soak in every word. "You just have to understand. He was the culprit in this. He's the authority figure."

I cried as he held me against his chest. I was exhausted from the release.

"I still want us," he said.

I cried with him for the first time in our relationship. He stood there, letting me cry my heart out as I showed my true self. I sat on the paved street, too tired from the hurting inside to move. I had never been so truthful with myself or another person.

"I hurt so much, Joseph! I hurt! I hurt!" I cried out, banging on my chest to get it all out. Between the bellowed cries, I hung on to Joseph as he held me. I sat in the middle of the street, crying and screaming out my anger and pain. "I want to just be free from all the filth I hold in me. I need you to be on my side! I am tired of fighting alone in my life. I do not want to be the one who is responsible for Mr. Willis's life anymore. I am tired of feeling selfish when I think about a life that does not include him. I'm the only thing that keeps him alive."

Joseph took his shirtsleeve to wipe my tears.

"I've been carrying the responsibility to keep him alive all these years. Do you understand?" I took a deep breath to regain my bearings.

"Hell, we don't need this house," Joseph answered. "We'll move to another state or out of his house this very minute. To hell with everything else. We'll figure out something." Determined to rescue me from my misery, he held me tightly.

"No," I said, becoming sober. "We've got to stay in this house until..."

"Christi," Joseph interrupted, "you're not responsible for his life." He showed his first frustration. "If he wants to kill himself, let the bastard die."

The construction on the house lingered in the back of our minds. In the meantime, we tried to act as normal as possible. Joseph stayed busy working his new territory, and he did not want to travel anywhere overnight if possible. On his longer trips, he would leave at four or five in the morning to make sure he was back that night. He promised that no one would hurt me again. I promised to check into hotels on the nights he had to be out of town.

He stayed by my side, and I struggled to act as if my world was normal at work. It was difficult to get going in the mornings because I felt vulnerable having opened up to Joseph. Uncomfortable from this exposure to a new world, I learned to live one day at a time with my newfound honesty. I feared being on my own during the day without constantly conferring with Joseph. I needed his reassurance that he was out there, still with me, as I traveled around the Dallas metropolitan area, trying to start my new career.

He taped a note under the speedometer on the dash of my car: *"Hi! I am riding in this car with you! And my thoughts are with you. Everything will be fine! I love you!"*

He introduced me to a psychologist to help me through this tough period, but I often missed sessions. I was not ready to deal with all my secrets and confusion. My world seemed so complicated, dealing with a new career, a new life and now the new confession. I used all my strength to fight for my superficial place in the business world. I found it was full of soulless male egos, and my very soul was going through an enormous reconstruction. As I fought for my sanity, I projected a distant, hard-nosed "don't mess with me" attitude to those around me. I pressed to move into the new house by my birthday to set a deadline for the completion.

Soon after moving into the new house, news from our childhood surfaced. Jason and I located our mother and our sister in Vietnam from another now-grown orphan who had traveled to Vietnam. She had married a Vietnamese man, and they found my mother in the same village. Her parents lived in the same village as my mom. I saw my mother for the first time on the video, but I did not understand the message she spoke to us in our mother tongue. The Vietnamese couple stayed overnight at our new home while I asked them thousands of questions about my mother and sister.

The next morning, we all went to our orphanage reunion. I saw Mr. and Mrs. Ha, Mrs. Xuan and Mr. Tam, the staff and many other orphans for the first time since 1975. Jason and I found out that the orphanage had two other reunions before, but we were the only two that they could not locate. I could not remember most of the children, now grown adults. It was strange to be among them again. I realized how many memories I had put away and how disconnected I had become from the orphans and anything Vietnamese I once knew. Many of them could still speak the Vietnamese language while I could not remember one simple word.

The orphanage represented a family that I had forgotten. Jason and I were lost sheep from their flock. Our American family never encouraged us to stay in touch with the Has. I started to write to my family in Vietnam after 20 years as an American, not knowing about their lives or their well-being.

Joseph continued to help me sort out my past. We sat at the kitchen table in the bow-bay window drinking hot tea. He told me his thoughts as I sat there, warming my chilled hands around my cup of hot tea, looking across the yard and listening to his insights.

"You know, just living around him for eight months, I can clearly see what kind of a person he is. You and Jason have been too close and isolated in his small world to recognize the reality of the situation," he said, touching my hands to rouse me from my blank stare.

"His main focus was to keep a false idea of being superior to you both. To even think that Mr. Willis would tell me that his normal greeting for Jason was 'Hey, asshole.' He belittled you when he'd say, 'You're too damned short to have an opinion.' He pushed the button that would hurt you most when he said, ' I don't want to look at you any more, get out of my face.' It isn't normal for a

Reunion at
Buckner Children's Home, 1992

Cam Ranh Orphanage reunion
with headmaster Ha Nguyen, 1992

parent to call you the names he called you both. If Mr. Willis's intentions had been remotely good or parental, he wouldn't hurt you by degrading you," he argued.

"We learned to ignore those comments," I said as I realized that Joseph was an outsider who had managed to enter our world. He brought new information to me as I sorted out what were correct and incorrect behaviors in parental roles.

"It takes somebody who is horrible and mean-spirited to do what he did to you. His strength comes from the fact that no one holds him accountable. No one has challenged him for the sake of both of you."

Joseph's fist hit the table. I was so amazed that Joseph put my undefinable feelings into these terms for me.

"Christi, if we have a little girl and she is seven or 17, we are still the most powerful figures in her life. If we repeated to her that she was the only thing that kept us alive, she would fear and feel responsible for us as long as she lived. At the beginning, I thought he showed a heart when he said the only reason he lived through some hard mess was because of you—because you were the joy in his life. What he said doesn't add up, when you consider what he did to you. He is nothing but a walking, talking, self-inflicted illusion. Do you understand that's what happened to you?" he asked.

I nodded, too immersed in his logic to respond.

"On top of that, he abused you in every way. You thought we had to be there for Christmas for Mr. Willis and Jason because you take responsibility for keeping the tradition going. You have to see what has happened to you. Your life will never be complete here with him around. I won't have him investigating our lives for his perverted needs." His frustration boiled up while I absorbed new perspectives.

"I wish you'd tried to make it to some of the sessions with Dr. Spencer." He was gentle, but did not hide his disappointment in my cancelled therapy sessions. "She can help you understand for yourself. You are in denial now. That's normal, but you've got to stay with it to make it work." He walked over to his office, brought back a book, and put it in front of me: *The Courage to Heal*. "If you don't want to talk with her, read this book. She said it would help. Go at your own speed without anyone pressing you."

I stared silently at the book.

"I'm not being the bad guy, Christi. I am just trying to help. There's a sensitive, beautiful person inside who I want to know. That is the reason I married you. Now I see more of that Vietnamese girl is still inside of you. Your tough exterior is just a facade. She wants love so much! You still have bad dreams at nights," he said.

I sat there listening to his explanations and felt that he was the first person who understood.

"I promise. I will not take advantage of her. I want to know that person, Le Thi Hai, Christi. I know what I have with you, but you have never known who you are," he continued.

We moved to the couch.

"I'm tired," I finally said. "I'm very tired from all of this, Joseph. I can't talk about it anymore."

I let my husband become the microscopic lens into my soul. My body grew numb as it healed itself. I had sustained a wound that threatened to destroy my spirit and slowly kill my soul. Now my journey had really begun. Where would this journey of healing taking me? Would I find my peace somewhere in the world?

CHAPTER 26

The Departure

While in Vietnam, Jason, Michael and I toured different places with our family. The children took turns staying home from classes and traveling with us. They drew straws among themselves and joined us with Mother's approval. Doan took out a map of Vietnam, and we recounted our journeys with our new family. We explored the country from Nga Trang down to Vung Tau, south of Saigon. We promised to come back to visit and explore Hanoi in the far north of Vietnam and further south from Vung Tau to the Mekong Delta in the tip of south Vietnam.

While we traveled and saw many sights, what I enjoyed most were the many simple trips beside my mother to her small village. As we came home from the market, we walked hand in hand as mother and daughter. Mom casually carried a bag full of vegetables over her shoulder, and I carried another load. Enchanted, I dearly loved my daughter role. I better understood what I lacked in my life, the simple things.

One day I stopped and signaled to her: "How old am I?" I bent down to write on the yellow clay, "34?" pointing at myself. She understood. She shook her head to indicate "No" and wrote: "36.

1964." Then she pointed to me. I smiled with satisfaction.

"Cam on," I said and began to figure out my age in Western terms. I knew that the Vietnamese custom counted a new born baby one year old the day she was born. The time in the womb counted as the first year. I was 35 in American terms. I could not wait to tell Jason our real ages.

The end of our visit neared, and we planned our trip back for a Saigon departure. The night before we returned to Saigon and the United States, my family gathered around the kitchen table, filled with food and drinks, and said goodbye. We decided that the trip to Saigon would only consist of Mom, our step-dad, Doan, my sister, the youngest boy, and ourselves. Vinh, the youngest boy, had never been to the city, and he showed his excitement.

From happiness to sadness, we gave each other hugs and kisses and promised to visit again. We emptied our suitcases to leave behind all our American worldly possessions for the children. We packed some souvenirs to take back with us from the places we visited and had a little more room to collect any last items from Saigon. We handled all the details so my family would also enjoy their visit in the city.

The guys went to the front room with the rest of the family to share all the videos that we took during our visit while I spent more quiet time with my mom and my sister in the kitchen. I sat in my favorite room, my mom's breakfast area where all the family gathered for their meals. So many fond memories had taken place at this table for us in the past 15 days. While my sister Le wrote, my mother shared her thoughts and feelings with me by writing her last words to me before I returned to America. I sat there quietly and watched. The greatest gift I wanted from her was my family's memories and history in a notebook. She talked to me in words I could not understand, but her voice and affectionate touches that night gave me so much more. She left an imprint on my heart with her love. My sister looked up from her paper to look at my mother's tears with her own tears. I took all our tears into my heart. No translation would appropriately capture the precious moments I had with my mother and sister. I sat there open and receptive to my mother's love. My hardened heart thawed out. I realized my journey of healing continued through these connections with my past. Their warmth circled and penetrated my heart and soul that night.

I had waited so long for this moment. My mom had given me more courage to heal as I reflected back and thought of Joseph's help during the first steps of my healing process back in Dallas. I saw the many gifts my ex-husband gave me to help me become whole. I believe God sends many angels our way to help us fulfill our destinies. I felt blessed for those wonderful days with Joseph. He helped me see that I did not have to live in guilt and shame. Although we were not meant to be together for a lifetime, we gave each other gifts that will last an eternity.

1993

Just as when I was the Vietnamese orphan, Le Thi Hai, who came to United States in 1975, I didn't understand the new language and the new information Joseph gave me about the process of healing. He shared with me through books and through many hours discussing personal growth and healthy solutions. Joseph talked openly and encouraged me to face my issues one by one, as I cautiously opened my heart to him. He became my first counselor because I did not trust anyone else. No matter what credentials they held, how could anyone fix my lack of inner worth? I wasn't ready to be open about it to anyone. My first husband became my first teacher in this new process, this language of the heart and of healing.

Similar to Mrs. Willis's breakfast table where I had learned to speak English, I now learned another language, one which would enable me to process my inner self so I could live again. I struggled to comprehend. I dug deep within and awakened new thoughts and feelings. I entered into another dimension with a new level of understanding. I prepared myself to leave everything behind and start an unknown journey.

Joseph and I also planned our escape from Dallas.

"Your life will never be complete here with him around." Joseph's voice still echoed in my brain.

My need to leave became desperate when I came home from work one day and sensed someone had been in the house while we were gone. The faded smell of cologne, a familiar fragrance, scented the air. A chill ran down my spine, as I automatically recalled Mr. Willis's scent and his cigarettes. I found large footprints still imprinted on our white carpet and cigarette ashes that fell on the stove counter. Jason and he were the only other people who had the master keys during construction.

I visualized Mr. Willis in my house, leaning against the kitchen counter, his back supported by the cabinets—his cigarette in his hand as he propped it with his other arm beneath his elbow. I could see a vivid ghost of him standing there to view our large, open kitchen. He took in his creation of a new floor plan and invaded my life at the same time.

A sense of despair overtook my new courage. I called, beeped and left frantic messages for Joseph. I wanted some kind of solution to my fear and anger. Joseph was angry yet not shocked. Ironically, I felt safer to suspect a burglar than who I knew it was all too well. All indications, proved Mr. Willis was the culprit. I picked up the phone to confront him, and he denied it with no defense but a tone which proved his desire to keep a hold on me.

Joseph's words, "Your life will never be complete with him around," rang through my mind as the insights sunk in deeper.

My desire for escape intensified. I wanted to get rid of my past and the deception I now saw more clearly. I withdrew from the corporate world and the outside world to deal with my inside world. My greatest supporter, my husband, became the spirit of Mr. Ha in my life. Mr. Ha made the Vietnamese escape possible. Now Joseph made my Dallas escape possible. My prince defended and protected me. He put up a "for sale" sign in the yard, and I gave notice at my job for the end of the year. Joseph requested a transfer to Atlanta, knowing he might be out of a job. We risked everything to make the move. I looked forward to stopping the merry-go-round and getting off for a while.

The house sold in five days.

Mr. Willis retreated into the background, and he never asked us the reason for selling the house so soon. Joseph was not fooled.

Even as we celebrated the contract, he made the reality clear for me.

"Christi, I hope this tells you something about him. He does not have the dignity to call you because he does not want to face his crime. If he cares so much for you, he would at least find out when or where we are moving. He knows! He knows!" Joseph pressed the point. "What he wants you to do is the very thing you are doing—disappearing. That way he does not have to face it. He knew what he had been doing to you all along. He was the parent who took advantage of an innocent, adopted child still learning English."

We moved out of the beautiful house and packed our things. I never returned to Dallas after the Christmas of 1992. Joseph concluded his unfinished business with the Texas territory and transferred to Atlanta in March of 1993. We never heard from Mr. Willis again.

Once again we had to separate for three months. We prepared to move to a new foundation and new beginning in Atlanta. I was determined to fight for my new life and to feel good about myself. I flushed away my past life and started my new life in Atlanta with a different level of insight. I was ready to reach a new level of understanding about self and life. I nurtured my soul and finally escaped from my sophisticated, city war of eight long years.

I stayed up in the mountains of Blue Ridge, Georgia, with Joseph's mom until he joined me in Atlanta. I had learned not to put myself in another unhealthy environment as I altered my life. Joseph's mom's house was secluded in woods with a steep driveway up among the natural beauty of the mountains. She welcomed me into her home. She brought me comfort and harmony as I made new discoveries. She often shared many stories of the simple life.

"Now, Christi, Blue Ridge is just simple mountain country full of plain fine people. We're not like some of these city folks you're used to," she said, saying so much more to me than she realized as I appreciated the simplistic nature of her world.

I knew I stood out as an Asian in this small town, yet she was not intimidated by my differences when we went into town for breakfast at the Blue Ridge Restaurant. Many eyes were on us, but it didn't make a difference to my strong-willed, vocal, and respected mother-in-law.

I stayed in touch with Joseph, her youngest son whom she adored. She became the mother I missed, and I became the daughter she enjoyed since she only had sons. I loved being there to soak in all the good things in life. The people I met were different from those I dealt with in my other lifestyle. The seclusion gave me time to read more books about healing and to search for a deeper meaning into my own existence.

It was also then that I searched into the "box of alienation" from Mrs. Willis again. We had stored part of our furniture and belongings in the basement, until we could relocate to Atlanta. For the first time, I went through everything in that box. A box I ignored since 1983. I found many missing pieces of my past. Sorting through them helped me put things into perspective. I met the young and innocent me in all those notes and birthday cards to Mr. and Mrs. Willis. I wrote, "To Mommy and Daddy." My spelling books and my early attempts at English reminded me of the little Vietnamese girl inside. I even found letters written in Vietnamese when I used to write to Mr. and Mrs. Willis from the Dallas orphanage. I found more than I wanted to see. I also found all of Mr. Willis's love notes to me.

I sat on the floor with my life from this box in disarray around me and read. I wore my husband's old clothing. His thermal shirts, pants and wool socks from his youth helped me fight the cold weather. This cold was too familiar to me, regardless of how much I chose to avoid it. I realized that my cold ran deeper. Even with the heater turned on high to keep the basement warm, the cold chilled my very heart.

Christi, the tough defender, cried for the little girl in her. This box reminded me of so many things. Sweet notes and broken English crayon handwriting blended with his love notes. My sweet notes were for the same Mr. Willis who wrote his love letters. How could they be in the same box? How could the different loves be in the same language? It was my first glimpse into myself.

I had forgotten about this self because I needed to survive. I cried when I realized how needy I was for affection and love. The adult in me realized how very powerfully those love notes affected my young life. I now saw the cruelty in those words. I had once believed them, but now I saw how those words destroyed my innocence.

Something dormant in me stirred, and I sensed that the two me's, for the first time, felt each other's pain. I had so much more to work through as more and more layers of my hurt and confusion surfaced. I didn't know how to deal with my discoveries. I needed more help. The resting period was good for my wounded soul, yet it also stirred me to reach for something I could not define.

Atlanta was only two hours away from Blue Ridge. I drove down to find a place and prepared for Joseph to join me in Atlanta. Our lives were not easy as we again adjusted to another new place. While I fought to find directions, Joseph struggled through many difficult adjustments to keep everything balanced for the sake of our new marriage. Everyday he proved to me that he was my Rock of Gibraltar. He was my stable force while I struggled to keep my spirit flickering and not let it burn out to blackness.

For the three months after fleeing from my past in Dallas, I was alone to face myself. I experienced a great sickness which no medicine could cure. This sickness attacked my spirit and soul. My life reached a point of hopelessness. A lost soul, I wandered aimlessly. Everything confused me about life. I survived living in a strange land with my familiar scars. I had hidden my scars for so long. Now life exposed them, and I learned to walk down the street with them.

My background prepared me to keep fighting when I did not feel like fighting any more. My soul was too strong to give into my weakened spirit. I had been a good soldier all my life, yet I lacked knowledge to remove the bigger obstacles in my path to get to peace. I knew how to "survive," but "living" was more of a challenge.

"What do you mean I can live a different kind of life than what I've been taught? What do you mean I have the power in me to do so? How?" I desperately reached for new experiences to help me see beyond my damaged perspectives. I wanted rebirth. I wanted to breathe a new life. But I didn't know HOW!

Joseph empathized with my search while I empathized with his struggle to maintain some sanity. I was still that Vietnamese orphan, again learning a new language and a new way of life.

I attended programs and workshops and learned to begin again. Others became my parents in my new life. The new regimen required intense learning. I fought hard to trust again. Trust was something I rarely gave away. I had to change my self-image from my past lifestyle to one of healthy self-esteem. The programs gave me new information, knowledge, and directions to aid my search for a better life. Learning psycholinguistics and the power of healing gave me a new outlook in life. I came to these programs with a history of pain and suffering and reached out for anything that would make a difference in my life.

I fought to break through as many barriers and layers of hurt to uncover my greatest pain. In the total unconditional acceptance of this new environment in the programs, my newfound role models understood me more than I understood myself. I came to them as a lost soul willing and desperately seeking my way home to a more balanced life. I was passionate to get results as I fought hard with all my efforts. I wanted to heal and move beyond the wars I fought in my life. I struggled, I cried, I felt pain, I learned and I worked hard to get these messages. Slowly the old, familiar destructive tapes that played in my head gave way to newer, healthier tapes about me and my life.

I had to learn the language of healing, love , trust and self-worth to add to my new healthy life. I was a student wanting to know so much more than I could grasp. My learning was not fast enough for my need to know more about this better way of life. Strangers accepted me and became my friends during this journey of discovery. I needed to find sanctuary to feel safe and heal a layer at a time.

After one of my experiences with psycholinguistics, I wrote the following in my journal:

I started my life in a war zone and never knew peace. As I escaped from that war, I entered into many other wars in the United States. As I listened to the cassette of the story that I shared with others, I heard my own story for the first time and I

acknowledged that I did go through many terrible events in my life. Surviving for so long, I did not allow myself to see the many successes that I claim for my own.

My greatest hidden pain was released!!!

I now realize that I have been layering my many pains, but I did not recognize my greatest pain. I have been dealing with having "enough to eat," shelter and living with sexual abuse which I accepted because of my great fear of being hungry and homeless. My loneliness, fear and losses in this world have become so great that I was losing ground.

By attending Psycholinguistics, I received the greatest gift... a safe environment for that suppressed frightened little girl from Vietnam to come out for the first time. Le Thi Hai has been so scared and lonely in her little world. She became Christi who is tough and strong. Her normal operational procedure has been "surviving" and hiding from that fear instead of "living." The safest place for me was to go back to my mother's womb, and the Psycholinguistics classroom provided me that safety in order for that frightened child to emerge.

My surrogate mother touched my child and invited her to come out; Le Thi Hai received her first mother-love, hugs, and comforts. My heart cried out for the first time for my own biological mother who is still alive in Vietnam. I am now eager to meet her and to feel her arms and love around me. Thank you for helping me to realize my greatest pain is the loss of my mother's love. However, I do realize that her greatest love was also when she gave the gift of life by sending me to an orphanage during the war.

I am now here because of her. I have been lost without her for so long. I know that I desperately need to feel her presence in my life. Perhaps I will be able to feel "WHOLE" again.

I learned about feelings. I feel grateful. I feel hopeful. I feel lighter. I feel loved. I feel I count. I feel that I can feel again. But most of all... I feel elegant, exquisite and irresistible.

CHAPTER 27
Awakening

Our last two days in Saigon gave us an appreciation of the differences in the quality of life between Vietnam and the United States. Saigon had a different sense of time than where we came from. It was a different century. I registered Vietnam's condition all around me. The lingering effects of the Vietnam War were obvious. Poverty hovered over the country like a plague. While the same plague exists in every village across Vietnam, the conditions were more visible in the condensed area in the city as the children peddled their plastic goods and begged from tourists to feed their families. In Vietnam, the city life stays busy and hectic while the villages offer a quieter perspective. I found I loved the simplicity of the villages so much more than the city. Yet we roamed the city to get another view of Vietnam before we departed.

In a bookstore I searched for some books to help me better understand Vietnam's current issues. Divine Order sent me to the rack that held my answers. I learned that poverty is greater in those villages since there were fewer opportunities to attract foreign visitors and their dollars. Vietnam's population of 80,000,000 people survives on $200 per capita income. Over 7,000,000 families live on less than $20 per month. More than 4,000,000 children under the age of five are malnourished today. I could not bear to see children like my daughter in this condition. My protective motherly instinct surfaced. How grateful I was that my daughter was safe and warm in America. How could words ever convey?

I walked in my own reality and saw things that my party did not see. I watched a little boy with no arms approach two tourists. He carried a small pouch across his shoulder for those who would give him money. He swung his whole body from side to side to move the bag and signal his plea. I watched a woman take his pouch in her hands to give him some money. So many similar scenarios painted the streets of Vietnam.

Yet the city gave me insights into its inner spirit as well. The people experience much material poverty in this land, yet they hold great inner strength and value the human connections that we Americans often miss. In our own country with all our technological advantages, opportunities and luxury, we still starve for human connection. In America, we often have an inner poverty even though we live a rich lifestyle. I was seeking my inner spirit in this poverty-stricken country. Vietnam held my past while America held my present. Somehow, I knew my future would be the blending of these two nations.

I wished someone would invent a better way to say goodbye. We kissed and shook hands, hugged and cried with our new family before we boarded the plane in Saigon. My mother and her family stood outside to watch us leave. All three of us returned once more to kiss and hug them again.

"Don't be sad, we'll be back soon," we promised.

Jason and I both went to my sister and said good-bye with the same promise. I hugged and kissed my mother tightly in her Vietnamese custom, sniffing her cheek and neck, not wanting to forget her scent, and whispered, "Cam on. I love you."

Torn between wanting to stay longer and needing to return to our responsibilities in America, we paced the airport as we waited to depart. I carried an emotional overload from all that was in me. I could not begin to process as much as I held, but I managed a piece at a time. I realized how desperately I missed my daughter.

Then came the time when we waved goodbye and boarded the plane. Michael, Jason and I felt exhausted, lost in our own memories of this journey. I held my mother's notebook in my hand with the many answers that I came hoping to find. I was eager to get her words translated. My mother and sister had helped me find the missing pieces of my life. I'd had them all along. I simply misplaced them along the way.

I realized I was no longer an orphan. I was the lost and found child of my mother. She gave me hope to work through the challenges in my new life. Without spoken words, just by her loving presence, she stabilized my world and soothed the fears I carried all my life. I brought back the seed of hope for my journey of the soul—a seed to nurture and cultivate to fulfill all areas of my life. This tiny woman brought me enormous hope for a fuller life. I had been in the shadows for too long. I now stepped into the sunshine again.

The plane took off, and I waved goodbye to Vietnam. I thanked my God with a prayer first and foremost.

"Thank you for always loving me. You gave me courage to face my many dragons and become a stronger, better person. My life has been in your arms of grace and love. I am now convinced that You were always there for me. It was You who carried me through all my pain to get here. I am a lost and found child."

I thanked the other part of my soul, my mother, "Thank you for accepting me for who I am. You gave me back my childhood

I found my place with mom.

dream of having a mother, and I am your daughter, Le Thi Hai." My mother gave me a healing gift to go on with the rest of my journey. She gave me life.

1993 - 1996

With Joseph, I continued to grow and emerge and feel again. The more I worked on my life, the more layers I discovered I had to process. I appreciated and understood what Oliver Wendell Holmes said, "Man's mind, once stretched by a new idea, never regains its original dimensions."

Meanwhile, I struggled with the expectation that I must be productive. My old pattern of thinking allowed me to stand still for only so long when I found an old house in Dunwoody, Georgia, to renovate. While I fought to allow myself more time to renew inside, I physically turned an old, abused house into something better. Joseph and I made the house into our first home, and then we sold it after nine months.

Joseph and I began our two-year-old marriage aggressively in Atlanta. We carved out our careers. I took on whatever life had in store. He maintained a steady sales position while I entered the homebuilding construction business at age 28.

Declaring myself a home builder, I entered a male-dominated industry. Of course, I did not fit the conventional stereotype of a builder in the south. As a young, petite woman and as an Asian, a foreigner in their eyes, I was anything but typical.

Because of my history, I came into the business with the strength to endure any hardship, and I had gained knowledge of the industry from living with Mr. Willis. Then I learned more about the business as I went along. Proving myself to the building industry was exciting, intense and challenging.

In spite of my knowledge of the industry, I built up my building business more by sheer determination not to be discouraged. I had unique obstacles to overcome that other builders did not experience. My first business opportunity took me to Forsyth County in Georgia. It was a tough proving ground. It was also where I finally convinced a small local bank to grant my first construction loan to build my first home. I learned to speak their language to bridge the differences. I told the bank president what he wanted to hear, "If I have to peddle burgers at their local restaurant to repay your loan, I will do so." I explained that because of my immigrant culture I could not let this opportunity pass, and that I would honor the opportunity by repaying his loan.

The local southern "good ol' boys" didn't really know what to do with me as a newcomer in their arena. I discovered that when it came to dealing with county permits and inspections, there were rules for all other builders and then there were rules for this foreign female builder. I knew I had to perform at a different and usually higher standard than my male counterparts.

The most important inspection in building is the framing and mechanical inspections that include electrical, HVAC and plumbing inspections. This is a major inspection stage that allows the rest of the building process to move forward to complete the interior of the home.

In the industry, you must pass certain inspections, and each builder is given time to correct any exceptions and then call for another inspection on those items. After that first inspection, I would get turned down for whatever reasons in any of these areas and I would be presented with a list from the inspector that prevented me from going further with the building process.

My recall inspections would often create another different inspection with another list of things in addition to checking off those items that were corrected. This was a personal challenge for me as a builder especially when I knew other builders' in the same subdivision inspections took less than five minutes to deal with the local inspectors. They were given a pat on the back and off they would go.

Obviously my first home took longer than the other builders' to complete. I would spend extra time to personally sweep my site squeaky clean from any construction debris and check and double check my subcontractor jobs. To prevent future complications and setbacks, I paid premium for better than good contractors to do these areas before I would schedule the next inspection. I learned to accept the reality of my situation, and I learned to rely on others' skills to be successful.

I had come with the corporate culture's ideas of how to run a business properly but soon threw those rules out of the window. I became a good student and learned how to deal with subcontractors and to change their perception of taking orders from a petite female builder. Not only did I add to my bilingual vocabulary of English and Southern English, I also mastered the art of the subcontractors' lingo to communicate my requests more effectively. My initial experience prepared me to be smarter, more detail-oriented and more tenacious after the first home. Through sheer willpower, I adapted and stretched to meet the circumstances. As I adapted to their games, I became bold.

The industry's intensity matched my war veteran background. Every day going to work on my construction site was like being on the front line of chaos. This industry was about taking risks and living with unpredictability. Not only did I have to deal with the unpredictable nature of the real estate market for my revenue, I had to learn to manage the unpredictable behaviors and personalities of bankers, inspectors, homeowners, subcontractors and also deal with constantly changing mother nature... weather conditions! I watched the weather channel the way investors watch the stock market.

I exercised and stretched my bold personality and learned to take risks in my business to reach my goals. Because I loved the intensity of the business that not only challenged my wit but also my grit, the men gave me a site nickname: the "Dragon Lady."

In 1997, Atlanta had the wettest season from February to April. I had begun a new subdivision in Dunwoody with two homes. I dug two basements with foundation footings and walls up and had to sit there over several months waiting for mother nature to give us more dry days. But the southern red clay took longer to dry out during cold and wet weather. The spare sunny days were never long enough before the next storm that turned these basements' soil into Florida muddy swamps.

Finally, we had a sunny day and I decided to go for it and risk pouring a concrete foundation on these homes. Because many builders had the same plan, the concrete company was booked for that day. I put my name in early with two concrete teams, one on each home.

On that day, another storm was predicted to come in to Atlanta by 3:00 in the afternoon. I received a phone call from Slick, the manager from the concrete plant. Slick discouraged me from pouring concrete that day. All other builders had cancelled their orders. I was the only builder on his book who had not.

"No," I told him. "I'm going to go for it."

I will never forget that day, as I rolled the dice and prayed that luck would be on my side. Slick warned me. He read me the riot act, saying that I would have to "eat" all nine trucks of concrete when that storm came. But I stayed firm with my decision on that freezing cold day. I was bundled up for the weather but on that particular day, I didn't need the extra warmth of my layers. I was hot from running on adrenaline.

Slick was helpful enough to send the concrete for one home at a time but I demanded to get all nine to line up on my site. With persistence, I stood my ground against his recommendation. I walked from one cul-de-sac to the other with two concrete crews in their water-proof boots and bibs with rakes in hand. I had to radio back and forth to the concrete plant to get the concrete trucks on site while they had to deal with traffic, accidents and slow downs on their way to my homes.

I knew there was no turning back as the first truck arrived, no return policy as I raced against the clock and the gray clouds moving into the Atlanta skies. The weather turned dark and the wind picked up and light rain began as the men poured and raked, then smoothed and sanded the concrete as fast as they could. The adrenaline of these men moved the mission for the day. They had a down and dirty attitude to get the job done. The intensity of that male energy was a powerful force, and I could sense victory.

I instructed one of the men to find the nearest building supplier and buy all the plastic covers available to salvage the floors when the storm hit. We got the plastic, and the momentum of the men built as we raced against mother nature—and won! I stood above the basement tops in the cold, feeling the light rain as the last roll of plastic covered the last home's floor. The men and I laughed out loud even as the rain began to pour. We had made it, and it was thrilling to achieve against such odds. That was the most memorable day in my building career.

While other builders gauged their success by the number of homes built and home sold, I gauged my success by the numbers of odds and the decisions I had to make to complete each home. From there, it led me to become an "in town" homebuilder in Buckhead.

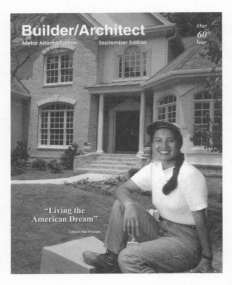

I applied my training from life to my business and my business trained me to prepare for my future transformation. My will, hard work, and my desire to succeed were recognized in *Builder/Architect Magazine*, which described my life as "Living the American Dream" as I succeeded in my quest.

More importantly, I also became a builder of another kind. I grew to understand that building the structure of a solid home is very similar to building a life with many obstacles to overcome. I had learned the logic behind the building process of a home and now transferred that into my own life. As I did so, I questioned the solidity of my own life. I faced life with more questions than answers.

CHAPTER 28
Home

I closed my eyes on the way home from the airport to decompress from the long journey from the other side of the world. This time machine brought me back to the same place we had left 17 days earlier, but I was no longer the same person.

Coming home, I was delighted to return to all my creature comforts and conveniences. Michael made hot tea while I soaked my body in the Jacuzzi tub, one of the many treats I missed. My skin had taken a beating in the tropical climate in Vietnam.

"I have to get back and check on my place. I'll be back later," Michael said as he came to kiss me on my forehead to say goodbye. It was a gift to be alone after experiencing no privacy with my large family.

"Mommy, mommy!" Lauren's voice screamed over the phone. I smiled with tears in my eyes to hear my baby's voice on the other side of the phone. "I miss you so much, Mommy. I want you to live with me and Daddy. Why aren't you here?" She started to cry. She pierced through my heart and my soul with her sweet, innocent questions.

"Oh, I missed you so much, sweetheart!" I said, holding back the

*A welcome home sight
from a journey into my heart*

tears. "Grandma sent you pretty gifts from Vietnam." I changed the mood and fought back the guilt. Eager to see her again, I made plans to be together over the weekend. Hanging up the phone, I cried.

Adjustments can be long and difficult under normal conditions. My adjustments were particularly difficult when I returned to America. I could not pick up where I left off. My inner self had changed before my eyes. My heart still beat, yet my soul lay dormant. I didn't know what to do. I experienced a formless state for the next four weeks as I processed my profound insights. How could I explain it all to others? No words can convey my experience. You cannot see the unseen that has taken my heart and soul to the next level.

I came back from my long trip home to know my life was in God's hands.

Life pushed me to step beyond the cliffs to better understand my search. I willingly stepped off, but I still could not see what was below me. And yet I was getting closer to my answer.

1996 – 1998

While Joseph and I both succeeded professionally in those years, our marriage slowly drifted apart. I proved my worth to the world and gained my confidence as a person, not a victim. I also proved more capable than I gave myself credit for. The world had taught me to think small so I would fit in my cage, but my own strength released itself beyond my expectations. For six years, I faced the real world as an adult, as an entrepreneur with my strong male yang energy while the ultimate challenge was becoming a mother using my feminine yin energy.

I was also building a family with little warning or planning. Each day as I walked from one site to another to build the homes, my baby was growing in my belly. Those nine months were filled with the pressure to deal with the world while my hormones amplified my inner struggles. My insecurity about becoming a mom and concerns for the safety of my baby intensified.

Although I craved more protection from my husband, his career took him out of the country so that he was rarely there to comfort me and remove my fears. I now realized my mother's struggles to keep her family safe during the chaos and challenges of war without her husband. I had also created my own chaos and war-like environment. I felt unsure in my new role. Both our careers had more directions than the making of a family, and I was numb throughout this magical process. Unfortunately, I kept so busy that I never slowed down long enough to enjoy the miracle in my life.

But the miracle would come no matter how numb I was. On the night before I gave birth, I tossed and turned and was awakened by the pain for my first contraction at 4 a.m. on that Friday morning. I gave up on "trying" to sleep and went and took a shower to start my day in my home office. By six o'clock, the contractions had increased. I woke up Joseph to take me to the hospital where the midwife would meet us.

The contractions came more frequently and the pain became sharper, pinching every nerve in my back. I had to walk and soak in a bathtub to ease the pain until noon. I had chosen natural child birth, and my painful labor lasted for the next four hours. With doctor, midwife and nurses standing by for this magical moment, I was still numb with fear. I could only feel exhaustion from my efforts of pushing my daughter into this world. By 4:07 that afternoon Lauren was born.

When I saw my daughter's pink, wide-eyed face, the numbness vanished. As the midwife placed this tiny precious baby at my side, Lauren nestled into my arms and took my milk and hung on to my breast instinctively for the next hour. I was exhausted from my long birth process but the instant she was in my arms I realized no pain could compare with this gift of joy. I was amazed by the feeling of connectedness with her, a feeling beyond my understanding. She was a part of me, innately programmed to my own being. We both fell asleep, complete and connected.

Joseph and I were closer on that day but it did not last long. My future with him looked more doubtful than ever when I took my new born daughter home on Mother's Day. She was now my reality, and I felt disconnected from my own husband. How could he understand my internal demons, all the fears that motherhood brought up in me? What if I couldn't take care of her? I thought of my own mother leaving me at the orphanage so that I wouldn't starve to death. What a choice for a mother to have to make.

My child was now in the world, and she had awakened more questions in me. She was so defenseless. Life could easily take her power from her. I saw all my inadequacies as an adult to protect her. What did I even know about being a mother? "Nothing," I told myself. All my inexperience would influence her life in this world. Every day I strived to put my many missing pieces together in order to be a whole person again, now that I had her in my life. She became my inspiration to be a better person while I kept our world safe.

As I adjusted to my role as builder and mom, I took Lauren with me on sites. She often made her playground on the pile of sand in front of the homes as I prepared to brick them. Usually, I would stop to play sandbox with her between my walk-through and inspection. Sometimes she and I would ride in the bobcat together and I would pretend to drive it with her in my lap or we might play with the garden hose. I was beginning to understand there was more to life than work. Those innocent moments were short lived, however.

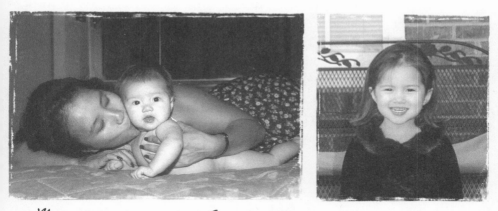

My daughter in America has peace and the stability of a bright future

While I was experiencing joy from my little daughter, I also encountered men like Mr. Willis. I found so much greed in the business world. I wanted to be so much more than the dollars I created or the number of houses I closed. I wanted something else. I did not know how to verbalize my desires for my life.

My search for myself, for wholeness, unfolded in many challenges during this time. Conflicts and issues came up continually. Even though I had created a family, I didn't feel like I was part of it. As a woman, I was unfulfilled and I became emotionally distant from my husband though I kept silent about my feelings. While many young couples enjoy the beginning of a family, my marriage was falling apart in front of me but I didn't have the clarity to deal with the issues at home.

Meanwhile, as a builder with all my differences, I faced bigotry and hatred. Small incidents and challenges are part of life. But an important lesson came to me when I had to confront the ugly face of racism.

We live in a free country, and yet the most educated and affluent areas still breed these kinds of divisions. It was in the heart of our city, an All-American suburban of an affluent area of Dunwoody,

Georgia that I awoke from my innocence. My hope for a peaceful future for my daughter was also tested.

I had begun a new subdivision. One of the people who owned property adjacent to the subdivision was a man his late forties. Though he didn't know me, this man hated me because I represented an idea he held about the Vietnam War. Each day when I came to work, I had to put up with his verbal harassment and his expression of dislike for progress. He constantly tried to interfere with our work. He would stand in his back yard and shout out obscene comments and foul language, telling me to leave the area and even the country as I conducted my business on the site with my subcontractors.

I ignored his comments for several weeks, but one day, he came on site inside my under-construction home, and I had to encounter him face to face while I was trying to meet with two men about the fireplace specifications. Maintaining my professionalism, I asked him to leave the property. Since the house was still under construction with bricks and materials all around, I explained that he had to leave for safety reasons.

Then he lunged at me with his towering 6-foot 4-inch frame and a mean-spirited, demonic look on his face. The two men who were there instinctively jumped between me and this angry stranger. As I stood there with two large black men as my defenders, I took a deep breath and asked him again to leave my property. I pointed out the "no trespassing" and warned him I would call the police. He stood his ground and continued to verbally assault me while my subcontractors continued to physically protect me.

But I was in the battle zone to be strong. I had no room to show my emotions. I immediately walked out of the house and called 911. This stranger with his verbal abuse and refusal to leave tried to paint me as the enemy. If words could kill, then this man tortured me with his obscene words and his attempts to erase my existence.

As I waited for the police to arrive, I knew I had to do something to protect myself and my property against his harmful intentions. All my personal issues of safety and trust rose up. As a businesswoman trying to protect my assets, I had to look into legally carrying a gun on site for my personal protection. I also filed a report for a temporary restraining order to protect unforeseen property damages, and I adjusted my work day to leave the site before the sun went down. All this turmoil created an increasing need to feel protected. But it seemed as if my husband would not or could not do anything to protect me.

During this time, my subcontractors and the local policemen became my protectors. The policeman who came to defend me that day began to drive around the subdivision on a daily basis. His presence with his police car and his badge were my guard, my armor through the duration as I continued to work to finish the last home in this subdivision. My men even offered to silence this man for me as their way of showing me their loyalty. During the difficult times, I was able to see the goodness in other people that gave me hope for humanity.

I never understood my attacker. Evidence ultimately showed this stranger had not even been in the Vietnam War. Nevertheless, my prayers and strength carried me through this ordeal. I had faced many similar kinds of abuse in my past. Putting on my armor of Sir Thomas More, I stood up for my rights. A total stranger played out the old pattern, but I no longer tolerated my status as an outsider, a victim or gave in to the abuse. My dignity and my right to pursue my happiness and safety would no longer be determined by other forces but only by my own rights as a child of God.

This time, however, I was not only defending myself. I was a mother lioness, defending her young. It was not common knowledge at the time but the last home I was building was a home for my family. I purposely selected a site across the street from my daughter's future elementary school so that she could walk to and from school. I was determined to create an ideal world for my daughter, so very different from my own childhood experiences.

Determined to protect my baby, I planned to give her the gift of home and stability that I never knew. I created a house that would provide everything a person could want and named the floor plan "The Lauren."

For a year, I worked on this home for my daughter while I defended myself from the outside threats. Those threats influenced my building choices for this particular home. The four car garage, two story brick home with circular stairways with impressive façade of wealth stood prominently in the center of the private subdivision. It contained security wiring that would support a camcorder security system around the home. I put in a door bell system that would ring through the telephone specifically so that my daughter could screen all visitors through the speaker system before coming to the door. While other homes have wooden fences, I built an 18-inch-thick brick wall around this home. It came to be a fortress. I was not trying to impress others as much as I needed a sense of having a China wall around us.

As they say, the kitchen is the heart of a home and it was an important step in the building process. My husband and I would discuss the kitchen designs and appliance selections. He never questioned my decisions up to this point. But since I know little about the rituals in the kitchen, which were important to him, he took charge of these decisions. He made his selections and I made the cutouts to complete the home.

I fought hard to ensure that my daughter would know only one home and that she would be safe as she walked to and from school safe from harm. I decided I would not alter my plan for my family because of a stranger's hatred.

Empowered, I stood up for myself in the arena of my choice—in court.

"Your Honor, God created me the way that I am. I will always have the black hair, slanted eyes, even a history of the Vietnam War that differentiates me from others. But this man has no right to hate me or treat me with disrespect. I am a child of God. How dare he attack me in this way," I declared.

The judge agreed and put a permanent restraining order on the man, but I wondered how many similar stories could we tell? How many future generations must live with our lingering hatred for each other? What legacy, what teaching are we leaving behind for our children?

While the restraining order ensured my daughter's safety from this hateful man, I realized that I did not know how to build a safe house for myself. No matter how luxurious or how beautiful I had made our house, it became less and less important to me personally.

It had been my last attempt to save my marriage and hold our family together, but instead of a being my fortress, it felt more like a prison.

Eventually, my husband reached the limit of his understanding in dealing with the issues I faced. Like the two bean sprouts that grew in a glass dome, one reached its fullness while the other needed to expand beyond the glass dome to breathe. I slowly withered in this "perfect" world. My search continued for something for which I had no label or definition. I knew my safety, belonging and love was not his issue but my own personal journey. I must find all that within myself but where would I begin?

I knew my search – an ending and a beginning – was near while I put all the energy I had left to complete this home for my daughter. I made my intention known by wrapping it in a giant red ribbon and a sign to give it to my daughter and her father as my Christmas gift to them before the marriage fell apart.

The only language of love I had to express my struggles as a mom and a wife

My search evolved into another dimension. Directed and driven into the unknown, I journeyed deeper. My yearning stirred up my impatient and suffocating soul, and finally I exploded. No longer were material things what I depended on. It was not the number of accomplishments, titles or recognitions I needed to prove myself to others. My image was no longer so important to maintain. I had reached the end of this part of the journey.

Joseph and I began living separately within our marriage. Even our child could not hold us together. The disconnectedness existed in the small things that grew larger than life for us. Was it my own creation? Was it shortsighted for us not to see other options within our dome? Could we not see beyond our differences?

My marriage to Joseph ended after seven years. That marriage now is also a part of my past. Within this history, our daughter is a gift from that connection. She is my greatest teacher. Lauren is my most important connection to become who I am. God granted me pardon, love and grace in my life. He blessed me with a life full of experiences and I was able to make a choice for my life beyond the understanding or even the approval of others.

During the divorce, my daughter's welfare was my most difficult dilemma. We were both right, and we were both wrong. I made a tough decision, but I made it for her. I took the visitation role to give her a family and a home. I traded in everything to assure her stability. Our choices altered our lives forever. With no crystal ball to predict, no guarantees that a better situation would come out of this, we both accepted the responsibility of the outcome. We both had to own our piece of the madness. Directly and indirectly, a child's history would be altered by the effects of our decisions.

I left everything, including the house I had built six months earlier, to my ex-husband and my daughter so I could find my purpose. I took only my clothes and my career, as I learned to give myself permission and time to heal and to learn about my life and self again.

CHAPTER 29
The Beginning

I was healed in so many ways by my visit with my mom. When I returned I was ready to face new challenges and to find my purpose in life. As I grew spiritually, I yearned for more meaning and dignity in my daily routines than the merry-go-round I had so often created. In spirit, heart and soul, I was wealthy even while my bank account stayed empty. I waited to see God's will for me. I no longer used energy to plan and do. I used energy to love and receive love. I was quiet and waited. Instead of always doing, I spent more time "being."

Though I was not free from life's daily struggles, I rested from a career, from making business deals, from worrying about what other people would say or think. I spent more time writing in my journal. I educated myself with personal development courses in order to have a healthier life and to find more of my true self that I had somehow lost along the way. I realized I'd spent so much of my life surviving in the earthly realm, investing so much of my energy on outer appearances that I had neglected the more important inner gains from all those years. I grew as a powerful person with more insights and understanding of the spiritual being I was inside. And

I yearned to have purpose and meaning beyond just survival, to live for a bigger reason than mere existence.

1998 - 2002

Pastor Ha Xuan Nguyen, the headmaster of the Cam Ranh City Orphanage and the only trustworthy earthly father I had ever known, moved with his wife from Texas to California for health reasons. The last time I saw him was in 1996 when I took my daughter to visit him and his wife to get their blessings. He reminded me that I was his lost sheep. His sunken face and frail body was evidence of his poor health.

I stored memories of Mr. Ha playing and making baby sounds to my six-month-old daughter on the tile floor that kept the home cool in the California climate. He loved to spend time with his "grandkids" as he called all the children of his now-grown orphans. This precious time with him was a chance for me to share my own history and heritage with my daughter.

During that visit he handed me all the original orphanage photos. He told me bits and pieces of information that stirred my own memories of our journey and our beginnings. Mr. Ha admitted to me that his own memory was fading from the long ago journey.

In 1998 Pastor Ha died from a kidney transplant's complications. The photos he gave me sat on my bookshelves until I knew my purpose. How did he know to give me those precious photos?

My marriage ended quietly on paper as I gave up all my worldly possessions from the marriage. I didn't see the value in going to battle in court for material things. I just wanted to claim all the incomplete pieces of my life. I had no energy to engage in the battles that it would take to claim the material possessions. I knew I would manage somehow. As I adjusted to my new single life as a part-time mom, the separation from my daughter gave me new insights into my own mother's soul. My life mirrored hers from a different kind of war. The crash and burn period of my life hit hard and devastated my heart and ego.

After my divorce, I was lost. I had no one to turn to and no family to claim me while I figured out all the pieces of my unraveling life. I desperately had to find my brother again but could not locate him for a while. My brother and I had lived separate lives from the days in the orphanage when they separated the boys from the girls. We never knew any different.

The isolation took its toll. I no longer felt independent and self reliant. I questioned my empty world without any connections to other people. With no family to phone or visit, my refuge was the nearest church. I knocked on the door of the minister for help. That's when I met Don, my first spiritual brother.

"I crashed and burned today," I told him. "Where do I go from here?"

"We can start with an eight-week commitment, and all you have to do is show up weekly. God will do the rest," Don promised me.

My eight weeks turned into a year and half of a different kind of nourishment than I'd been getting. He spoon-fed me soul food for a new life. Even when Don had to travel, I was in good hands with the other minister. Ken became my second spiritual brother. The church office people became my family. I looked forward to our visits as my only connection to life. It was the only regular thing I had to keep me going. I was grateful that I came to this open door when I needed Him the most. With my newfound surrogate family to lean on, I lived in God's grace as I survived through the many challenges of my daily routines.

The first two years after my divorce were like shedding old skin. I was now living inside my new skin as it grew in. I closed my building business and moved into the last home I had built in Buckhead. Since I could not sell it, I shouldered the financial burden myself so I wouldn't have to file a business bankruptcy. With no income and no desire for money or material things, I stopped building. Instead, I worked two jobs to pay my bills. I understood my search was for something more and I was willing to recreate my life no matter what I had to do. I refused to look outside myself for my self worth. It was in this time of less that I gained more in life.

Daily, I felt every pore of my new self penetrated with new feelings, emotions and challenges. I didn't just live day-by-day; I lived moment by moment to breathe in this new life. The new oxygen of a new realm was hard to take in at first. But I began to restructure my life and apply my discipline to it again. My passion to redirect my life took on even greater zeal.

First, I had to slow down yet be disciplined. I went back to my work out routine to find my discipline again but I needed to make ends meet at the same time. So I called every sports club in Atlanta and asked for a job to open the club in the morning for them. The people at the other end of the line didn't know what to say since I was over qualified for the position and specifically requested the most undesirable shift. But image was no longer important to me, and I was grateful to have my life back on my terms.

I found a job that started every morning at 4:30 a.m. I got up at 3:30, went in to work and served up smiles and greetings to the health-club members. Each day I worked out to get my discipline back and didn't worry about the minimal wages. I never missed a day. I met people and developed friends who enriched my life during that five-month stage. I knew that anything you do more than 14 weeks become a habit, good or bad but after five months, it becomes a lifestyle. I created some form of structure in this fluid stage of my transformation. I also filled my time with personal development courses so that I would have insights as I struggled to transform and renew myself.

Life was difficult in many ways as I began to live my life from the inside out rather than from the outside in. Joseph and I had some additional legal battles, even six months after our divorce, and they continued for the next four years. Our differences overshadowed the happy days and even our love for our daughter. He did not understand me. He did not understand my Eastern values. I mourned the death of our history. It was painful to be a mom during this period of our lives. I cried tears of hurt and shame for the losses we could never recover. My once good prince became the boy that I outgrew. He was dead to me, but he did not die the death of Sir Thomas More. Although we became two strangers, I was grateful that my daughter had a loving father in her life.

I had lost a marriage, yet I found something more important when I began my spiritual search. I finally found an inner safe home to rest from an already long journey. I finally found a solid refuge to come home to, a place to lick my wounds while I dealt with the changes in my life.

One benefit of not having any family traditions has been that I get to create and invent my own traditions. On my birthday in 1999, I staked my commitment to God with a formal ceremony for my daughter and me. We both came home to God as His children. God is my spiritual anchor. I found a home on earth to claim and to rest my weary soul. I dedicated my life to Christ while my daughter went through her christening. I asked for His love, forgiveness and protection for us. Mrs. Ha flew in to walk me home along with 70 guests. It was the most exquisite experience I have had in my life.

The other step in my journey home to God was my trip home to Vietnam.

It was after that crucial visit that I was able to turn my journals into a book. I looked at the photos that Pastor Ha had given me. The visions of my orphanage home surfaced in my mind and became clearer each day. So many children needed help. So many veterans of the war needed healing. Who was better than I, a former orphan and a veteran of many battles, to help them?

Every piece of my whole life came together and helped me see my next step as I learned to live from my heart. I began to find myself in the midst of my stretching, growing to new dimensions. My heart felt painfully alive. I came home to myself in order to feel and breathe my first breath of life. With my heart open, I found that God can do the impossible. I listened to God's whisper for my purpose.

In May 2000 I came to a place where I found my heart's secret. It is beating with my own purpose and a passion that fuels my work with a greater meaning. I took a step of faith, and I established a non-profit organization to promote peace, goodwill and humanitarian efforts between the United States and Vietnam.

Achild.org was born with a vision. The vision of our peace project is to obtain the original seven plus acres of my orphanage home in Cam Ranh City and rebuild a modern facility to assist the children in Vietnam; also to create and represent the healing and reconciliation among Vietnam veterans and orphans of the war.

We, as nations, must be willing to move beyond the lingering

*Mother & daughter
on a spiritual journey together*

*My promise...
Coming home to God*

*Mrs. Ha Nguyen's
support*

hurts of the Vietnam War and to move beyond our individual inner wars to reach peace. As Americans, we lost 60,000 human beings in that war. We Vietnamese lost 600,000 in that war. When will war end? I wonder how many inner and outer wars are out there that need to be healed? How many more generations will sow hatred and division? When will we learn? Why can't we leave our children the gift of healing, reconciliation and peace instead of lingering differences?

My hope is to create friendship among each other with no divisions by sharing this vision. I am just one person who can make a difference to others and to our world. I began my production of this book to share my story for this purpose. New opportunities opened for me and propelled me along a new career path as a speaker. As I began to speak my truth, I was invited to speak to veterans, churches, colleges and clubs to tell this story. My life took on a new form that fueled my passion for life again. I knew I was trained for this mission. I am directed to align my talents and personality, to learn new skills, and to manifest new possibilities.

I am no different than anyone who is searching for more meaning in life. The prompting from my heart's voice leads me to share my song of healing and peace in this book. God gave me a chance to live and reach this point. I lived on grace and hope. There are so many worthy causes and visions that started with a seed. I hold one seed with my own journey and story. I offer this opportunity to those who see the importance of healing and peace while helping the poverty-stricken children on the other side of the world. They are like you and me. My journey can be like any one of yours or any of these children's. I chose to share it, learn from it and draw from it. Is your path leading you here to be a part of this vision with us or to begin your own personal path for a meaningful life?

There are no endings, only beginnings. The secret is simple: you have the choice to fill your life with purpose, meaning and passion.

I am still evolving and searching for my human and Divine truth in the midst of earthly realms. My way of seeking has no course but to "be" through living consciously toward peace. As my spirituality grows, I have learned to draw on that strength and wisdom with my faith. My search for my inner self profoundly affects every dimension of my life.

My book is only one of my many choices. I chose to share and accomplish a process of healing with this book. This healing is not only mine; it is all of ours. I have dedicated this book to the vision of peace. I am using my own life to make a difference and to offer my story of grace and hope. I have discovered that my life has been filled with Divine intervention. Every step prepared me to be here to plant the seed for others and for future generations.

It is in Divine order that our life takes its course and gets us where we need to be. Do we trust that guidance or do we question our own understanding? When do we know we are on the right course? Does the human part or the Divine create our individual course? Where are we going anyway?

I believe we all are in the pursuit of healing, hope and peace. I believe we must first move beyond the wars we carry within, heal and discover our true selves and add that part of ourselves toward a universal puzzle. We need to find our unique place to find the gift we hold for the world. So, I declare…a name of my own.

On my birthday in April 2002, I performed an act of self-expression. I anchored my true identity by legally "redesigning" my name. I went to Fulton County Superior Court in the State of Georgia to officially declare my new legal name as LeChristine Hai.

When I was born, my parents named me Le Thi Hai. In Vietnam the family name or surname comes first and the first name is last. So Hai is my first name in Vietnam. When I came to America, I was given a new name by my adoptive parents. They called me Christi Lyn and gave me their family name. Then when I was married, I took my husband's family name. But after completing my memoir, I was ready to let go of my past, and to set forth into the future with a name of my own and my own making.

So I chose LeChristine Hai—honoring both my Eastern and Western heritages. Le is my Vietnamese family name, so I honor my father and his ancestors. Christine is my American name, so I, also honor my life in America; Hai is my first name in Vietnam and my last name in America.

As I walked down a narrow hallway toward the Judge's

chamber with my six-year-old daughter, Lauren Christine, beside me, holding my hand, she tugged at me to bend down.

"I am a grown up to be here, right, Mommy?" she whispered.

"Yes," I smiled at her.

I felt all grown up, too, as I got ready to take on my new name. At the big, dark, wooden conference table in the Judge's chamber, we sat quietly and waited for the Judge's official signature to seal my declaration. Five minutes later I marched out of the court on that spring day as LeChristine Hai. It was a simple but profound ceremony. A new me was brought to completion at this important juncture of my life.

After the ceremony, I turned to my daughter and asked, "Lauren, what is Mommy's name?" She replied loudly, "LeChristine Hai." She began to skip and then stopped to add, "Like my middle name, your Vietnamese's family name and your real first name are from Vietnam, Mommy." My child understood the meaning behind the symbol of a name.

I am proud to claim this name for my own after living with so many other names as an orphan. But my journey is not complete. I am still learning, growing and processing the lessons of my life. As I continue to discover the beauty and power within my own soul as a student of life, I am blessed to use it to encourage and empower others.

This message of healing, reconciliation, hope and courage is my personal gift from a life that bridged the East with the West. My reason for sharing my heart and soul in this book, *In the Arms of Grace*, is to share the lessons that I have learned and continue to learn and to share my deepest belief with others that the meaning of LIFE is... Love Intensely Forgive Eternally.™

The beginning...

Hello, James August (Gus) Swanson...

Looking for More?

This book and future books to come are my personal means to reach out to humanity with an open heart.

In the Arms of Grace is my personal story to begin a series of books to come.

Please look for future books titled:
In the Arms of Love
In the Arms of Compassion
In the Arms of Forgiveness
In the Arms of Family
In the Arms of Joy
In the Arms of ....

LOOKING FOR A SPEAKER FOR YOUR NEXT MEETING?

Please contact **LeChristine Hai** to arrange a speaking engagement or lecture:

LeChristine Hai
toll free   1-866-5-ORPHAN
email   lechristine@lechristinehai.com
web   www.lechristinehai.com

EPILOGUE

Life is here and now...

U Christine —

LeChristine Hai's Healing Message
to America:

Speaking at the
Memorial Day celebration
Georgia, May 26, 2000
at the 25th Anniversary
of the ending of the Vietnam War

"I speak to all Americans: Good morning! It is a privilege for me to be here among you today, to honor and celebrate the men and women who served our country.

My Vietnamese name is Le Thi Hai, but I am known by my American name as LeChristine. I was born in 1966 in Vietnam, and I lived there for the first 10 years of my life as an orphan. My orphanage home was built with the help of American GIs in wartime, who were there in Cam Ranh City in 1969.

There was a navy base stationed there. Along with missionary outreach from churches in the United States, you helped support our livelihood. By 1975, the whole 100 orphans and staff escaped, literally 15 minutes before the Communist seized Saigon.

My headmaster, Pastor Ha Xuan Nguyen—may he rest in peace—traded in every penny he had for an old, unwanted, ragged boat that was left. He had to build two platforms inside this tiny, 30-foot long boat, to pack all his children in. We were like sardines as we fled for our freedom!

Many of you at one point or another wondered: "Whatever happened to those orphans who came in 1975?"

Well, I am a living proof of JUST ONE of those many orphans who came in 1975. I am here because of you! You fought for my FREEDOM to be here. So I am here on the 25th Anniversary since the war to share with you that I am: your daughter, your friend, your neighbor. I am also a mother of our next generation of Americans. This is my daughter. She is 4 years old. She was born in Roswell, Georgia, and she is a proud Native Georgian.

She is an Amerasian—a blend of both worlds. I am an American citizen like my daughter because you fought for our freedom to live here in peace. Any parents would want that for their children. You all were the parents who wanted the same for me when I had no parents.

Recently, I am privileged to be a Rotarian. The objective as a Rotarian is to "serve above self." Thus, I now have an opportunity to give back to my club, my community and to the part of the world that gave me my heritage.

But FOREMOST, no matter what history we have, or what country we came from, or the color of our skin, WE ALL ARE CHILDREN OF GOD and we all are potential productive beings to serve our society, our humanity, our country and our GOD. The PERSONAL message I would like for you to take in your heart from meeting me and my daughter for today and forevermore is this:

Though war is a tragedy and terrible things do happen during war, our part today is to highlight the brighter spots and remind you that within this war, you made a difference for thousands and thousands of orphans out there!

I want to leave an imprint in your hearts, to remind you and all of us and to honor you for these wonderful gifts you gave us:
—YOU FOUGHT FOR OUR FREEDOM!
—YOU FOUGHT TO GIVE US HOPE!
—YOU FOUGHT TO GIVE US A FUTURE!
—YOU FOUGHT FOR OUR CHILDREN, OUR
    NEXT GENERATION!
—YOU FOUGHT TO GIVE US LIFE!

I knew my part was to give back to the men and women who gave their youth and lives in the Vietnam War when I met our Rotary District Governor and also a veteran, Al Lipphardt. We spoke briefly of my vision to build an orphanage in Vietnam and of his past history as a soldier. Tears were in his eyes. I have seen so many tears from so many veterans through the past 25 years as a Vietnamese orphan living in America. Today, I want to, from the deepest place in my heart, if nothing else, wipe one less tear from the faces of these soldiers who fought for my freedom.

I also, personally, want to let you know that your duty as soldiers was not in vain. So, to ALL Americans who gave their time, their hearts, their youth and lives to the cause of war... THANK YOU!

Many of you are still survivors of your tragic past. While the world may never fully understand all your personal pain and your private memories of the Vietnam War, I am one of many orphans that would like to personally thank you for passing through my life.

In my eyes as a young orphan, you gave me affection and HOPE. You silhouetted my young life with your smiles in green uniforms and the bubble gum that created my fond memories and brought some sense of normality in my childhood in the midst of war. Some said we're enemies, yet I only saw you as my Giant Friends!

So, to all my American GIs in Peacetime… hear my voice of your past and of your future. It is time to heal our hearts today! It is time to remember the many lives you've touched like mine and celebrate LIFE! It is time to bridge the gap from War to Peace, and it begins with soldiers of war meeting orphans of war, to know our parts as God intended for us to live in Peace as One.

I have brought a life-size picture that will help remind all of us of the HOPE we once shared. I was the same age as my daughter in that picture, being held in the arms of a US soldier in Vietnam in 1969. I wondered whatever happened to that soldier in my picture? If you recognize him, please let me know.

We want to say thank you for our freedom! And I am confident that I speak for thousands of orphans out there. *Cam On…* is my "thank you" in Vietnamese. GOD BLESS YOU! GOD BLESS AMERICA… My Home, Free Home!"

Written & spoken by LeChristine Hai

A Pictorial Journey
Through Vietnam

My motherland...

*Through my eyes
as her native & her visitor*

The real beauty of Vietnam is in the faces of the people

There are 100 other orphans from the same Cam Ranh City Christian Orphanage with their own stories and perspectives. I encourage them all to share their journeys and touch lives with the lessons they hold.

Most importantly, I pray that we all can come together to remember our headmaster, Pastor Ha Xuan Nguyen, and honor his family and staff for their efforts.

To all Vietnam veterans, churches, organizations and individuals that knew of us, please let us hear from you today.

orphans@achild.org

Life is about making a difference...

Please help achild.org by supporting our mission with donations. Now is the time for general operating fund donations, we are also seeking the following donations: products, services, time, and expertise to support the orphans in Vietnam with specific projects.

It takes just a little of our finance, time, talents and prayers but make such a world of difference!

Achild.org is committed to see poverty-stricken children in Vietnam have hope for a better future and touch the wounded Vietnam Veteran in our efforts to facilitate world peace and understanding.

achild.org is a non profit 501(c)3 organization. If you would like to learn more about us and contribute toward our Vision, please explore our website: www.achild.org. For more information or to become involved, email us at: orphans@achild.org

Please fill out the following form, detach and mail your donation today!

I VALUE PEACE! I WOULD LIKE TO DONATE:

○ $5000   ○ $1000   ○ $500   ○ $250   ○ $100   ○ $25

○ Other Amount $_____

_____ Please call on me for my time when you need help.

_____ Please call on me for my talents/area of expertise when you need help. I can help in _____.

_____ Yes, I promise to pray daily for achild.org efforts.

_____ Yes, I would like to be active in your organization.

_____ I would like to request a speaking engagement with LeChristine Hai.

_____ I would like to share my thoughts, feelings and feedback after reading.

_____ Please put me on your mailing list for any future publications.

NAME _____

ADDRESS _____

CITY _____ STATE _____ ZIP _____

PHONE _____

EMAIL _____

○ **YES** I AM A VETERAN!

For your Convenience Amex, Visa, M/C, Discover Accepted–

CREDIT CARD NUMBER _____

EXPIRATION DATE _____

SIGNATURE _____

Amount of "tax deductible" contribution: _____

Thank you for making achild.org part of your Charitable Generosity!

PLEASE MAIL THIS FORM TO:
(Your receipt will be mailed to you for your tax records)

achild.org   Toll Free:
P.O. Box 420276   1-866-5-ORPHAN
Atlanta, GA 30342   (1-866-567-7426)
U.S.A.   www.achild.org

In the Arms... of Grace

One Saved Child's Journey

LeChristine Hai

Foreword by Former U.S. Senator Max Cleland

QUICK ORDER FORM

MAIL:
UniVoice International, LLC.
P.O. Box 420276
Atlanta, GA 30342

FAX:
404-252-0047

EMAIL:
orderbook@lechristinehai.com

PHONE:
1-866-5-ORPHAN

	PRICE		QTY.	TOTAL
In The Arms of Grace	$24.95	x	_____	_____
In The Arms of Grace— *Author's Signed* *Limited Edition (500)*	$100.00	x	_____	_____

LeChristine Hai will personally sign and number each copy of this limited collector's edition. A very unique and beautiful design is created for this first edition of five hundred as a piece of art to treasure with it's own ribbon marker. The proceeds will support achild.org's mission to establish a facility for orphans on the very spot her own orphanage once stood.

Subtotal:	_____
Shipping & Handling:	$ 5.95
Sales Tax: (Georgia Only 7%)	_____
ORDER TOTAL:	_____

Please make checks payable to: UniVoice International, LLC.

NAME _____

ADDRESS _____

CITY _____ STATE _____ ZIP _____

PHONE _____

EMAIL _____

For your Convenience AmEx, Visa, M/C, Discover Accepted

CREDIT CARD NUMBER _____

EXPIRATION DATE _____

SIGNATURE _____

VERNON GONZALES · CLIFFORD N GREEN
JOHN P MALLOY · THOMAS W UNDERWOOD
CHARLES A ROBERTSON · DONALD B REES · ROBERT S RICHMOND
FREDDIE D MIZE · JOHN P WANTO · RONALD W WILLIAM
DONALD L GRANT · NOEL A HARRIS Jr · MICHAEL R HATFIELD
GORDON E ZIMMERLE · JAMES H ADAMS · RONNIE E ASH
WILLIAM PIRKLE · JOHN S RICK · TOMMY H SWAIN
CARRIS M FRANCIS · BERMAN GANOE Jr · GUADALUPE GONZALEZ
JOHN C HOSKEN · LARRY J JORDAN · DONALD W McKEE
ERNEST J BROWN · ARCHIE L WHALER · RONALD L WHITE
DENNIS J HAYES · KENNETH H HELTMANN · FLOYD B COATES
ROGER A LAKIN · SANFORD G PACK · THOMAS PADILLA
JOHN P DIDIER Jr · JOSEPH WAKEFIELD Jr · HENRY J ALLEN
RICHARD G EZINGA · JOE A ESCANDON
NORMAN H STRENGTH · JOHN R WYNN · MARVIN SHELL
ARNOLD GARZA GARZA · BILLY J HARTSFIELD · JOHN L HOUSE
CECIL S McCLAIN · GARY D POEK · RALPH R QUICK Jr
DONALD W COOK · PAUL J FRANCIS · KENNETH J GARSKI
THOMAS F LACOSTE · EARL L POOLE · SIDNEY L ROHLER
JOSEPH P SOOLE · BOBBY GENE SWANSON Jr · DANIEL R TROYE
DWIGHT J ADE · BARTOLO AMADOR BARELA Jr
JAMES M FURGERSON · GORDON M GUNHUS
PAUL E HARVEY · JIMMY J HICKS · JAMES R HOLMES
DAVID M KING · DONN M LORBER · WILLIAM A BROWN
MICHAEL J RANDOLPH · WARNER STARKS · PAUL R STEPP Jr
DAVID W BARRUS · BRUCE W BRACE · FLOYD S FRANKLIN
GLEASON C HELTON · RUSSELL C HIBLER · NICHOLAS M MOLNAR
EZEKIAL MARTINEZ · JAMES JACOBS · HARRY E BAKER Jr
ROBERT E FENNELL · DAVID H HARLOW · HARRY E HAYES
KIMBALL H SHELDON · THOMAS J SHRINER · JACK R SMITH
ROBERT E WILLS · BOBBY LEE BARKER · BENJAMIN V CHILDRESS Jr
THOMAS R BOWEN · CLEAVELAND E BRIDGMAN · JAMES C CARLIN
CARTER W DOWD · DAVID G DRAGOSAVAC
CRAIG P FIELDING · ROBERT G FLOYD · DANIEL L FLYNN
SYRIAC HEBERT Jr · DON R HEIMARK · ROBERT A HILL
WILLIAM P KASTENBECK · MICHAEL R PATTERSON · JAY W KING
DAVID H LASSEN · ROBERT M LIDDELL · CLARENCE LOGAN
JAMES C MILLER · ELDON W MOORE · LARRY L MULLINS
JAMES M McMILLAN Jr · LEN E NIXON · GEORGE F PATTERSON
GERALD R POLLARD Jr · GERALD W PURDON · MELVIN D QUINN
TERRY W RATCLIFF · BILLY JOE SCHAFFER · TERRY LEE SCHELL
VINTURE SCIARRETTI · JOHN E SMITH · PHILIP J STEMPER
LAWRENCE E SUTTON · MILTON T SWAIN · GEORGE M UNDERDOWN
CASEY O WALLER · DAVID WELCH · CLIFTON P WHEELHOUSE Jr
JOHN E YOUNG · DONALD G ARMSTRONG · MICHAEL E BORGES
DALE E CHRISTENSEN · JOHN H DILMORE · RICHARD ELLIOTT
CARL F KUECHTENICHT · SPENCER A GOETHE · LARRY GRAVES
KENNETH F HAWLEY · MELVYN H KALB · STEPHEN M KENOFFEL
ORVILLE L KITCHEN Jr · RONALD V KOLB · HAROLD J McDONALD
DANIEL E MYERS · JOHN H YONS · DENNIS N PIPKIN · JOHN E RARRICK
SEVERIANO RIOS · HENRY N ROCKOWER · WILLIAM L VASPORY
MICHAEL E THOMAS · STEVE W TRAIN · WILLIAM L VASPORY
ROBERT S ALEXANDER · EDWARD J BAKER · DWIGHT H BALL
WILLARD L CLEMONS · EVERETTE E COTER · RAINER L COLE
NICHOLAS L CARDIFIS · GERALD L GRIFFIN Jr
JAMES E LEE · WILLIAM A MILLER · RONALD N PARSONS
JAMES E LEE · RICHARD E WILKERSON · JOHN W WILSON
WILLIAM T SMITH · STEPHEN E BUSBY · CLYDE E COFFMAN
FREDRICK W GAUTHEN Jr · THOMAS F FRASER
MARCUS R DAVIS · JOHN F DUFFY · DAVID P ROY
LEONARD E NYBERG · SAMUEL L ROBERSON · JEFFREY L YOUNG
GARY M WEEKLEY · DANIEL K WELIN · PAUL M CAHIL
CLARENCE J CARSON Jr · ELIJAH E DAVIS · LANCE A DE ROO
ALAN H LOWE · CALVIN J LAYTON
JOHN W ROHR · ANDREW M SIMKO
FRANCISCO J BORRECO-RUIZ
GORDON M GAYLORD
ROBERT F STEWARD

GERALD T BUTLER
JAMES E LOCKETT · KENT W LONG
RICHARD H WARD · ROBE
RALPH N BRIGHT · RO
MARK FARKIN · DANNY W
ERIC G OHM · DOUGLAS F WORTMAN
KERRY L VANCE · EUGEN
THOMAS Y ADACHI · KENNETH A
DONALD G FISHER Jr
RONNIE LEE HENSLEY · ROBERT
DONALD C LAMB Jr · DO
THOMAS MILLSAP III · JAMES M McDO
RICHARD M SPEER · JOHN C TO
CHARLES COOK · MIC
KENNETH R JONES · GEO
BENJAMIN A NICKS III · JOSEPH E
DOUGLAS W MURPHEY Jr · ALLEN T WHITE
STEVEN M CRONRATH · JAM
OSCAR T FRANCIS · DONALD E CARPENT
PAUL J GUELIG · GERALD V
WILLIAM P McCONNAGHY · JO
NORMAN D ADKINS · RODNEY K
JAMES T CONWAY · WILLIAM F DAC
DAVID A BARBARINO · PAUL W HANDERH
JOHN R MATTOX · MICHAEL J MAYBERRY
JOSEPH E NUNN · ROBE
ARMAND E RISTINEN · BILLY JOE
ERNEST L THORSON · DONNIE
DARRELD E FISHER · D WID J
GERARD F O'CONNOR · ROBERT E ROGER
MICHAEL D BROWN · GERALD
ROBERT W GARDNE
ROBERT T KOEHLER · LARRY
JAMES H PALMER · MICHAEL R PICKLES
JAMES A RUSS · GARY A
ROBERT D WALSH · JOHN L WARD
KEITH N W AU · ROBERT E
JOSEPH C JISZECK · CHARLES M
FERNANDO RIOS-MALDONADO · PAUL E
MICHAEL J VANGELISTI · WILLIE A
PAUL D BRANNON · WENDELL C BRO
RONALD E HAZEN · DENNIS V
TED R MILLER · JAM
MIGUEL A HERNANDEZ-DIAZ · JOHN C SEE
ANCEL J TERRY · LINWOOD A WAL
JACK C EVERTS · VERN
DONALD BARRETT · DANIEL FE
JOHN R HUNTER · LA
DONALD R LEDUE · DONALD RAY MAR
ROBERT D PALMORE · LARE
ROBERT J SHANNON · CHARL
FRANK M VALENTINE
ROBERT L COLLETT Jr
MARTIN S HUSKA · EDWARD JACKS
SAMUEL S LANCE · CH
WILLIAM S SIGMON Jr · JOSEPH
JOHN P BECKER · RICHARD D BREWE
WILLIAM W DAVIS · VASSAR W
RODNEY L GRIFFIN · EDWARD C HAGGER
GRADY E LESTER Jr · LANE FA
MILTON PEREZ-RIVERA · JERRY N P
JOHN C SHERMAN · GEO
RAYMOND N TAYLOR · MICHAEL B VAN
CARL R CHURCHILL · LAWRE
GLENN G DUNCAN · R
JOHN L KOTORA · ARTHUR E LAC
THOMAS T SMITH · EDWARD W
THOMAS O AHLBERG · JAMES E
STEPHEN B EMERY · LEON GA
FLOYD W LAMB Jr · ARMANDO CERVERA
THEODORE E ROBERTS · ALBERT C
WAYNE L TORSIELLO · MICHAELA VAN
PHILLIP C ADAMS · HORACE AND
GARY W BROWN · LARRY D BUFFINGTON
CHARLES G DOUGAN · STEPHE
ROBERT E HERNDON